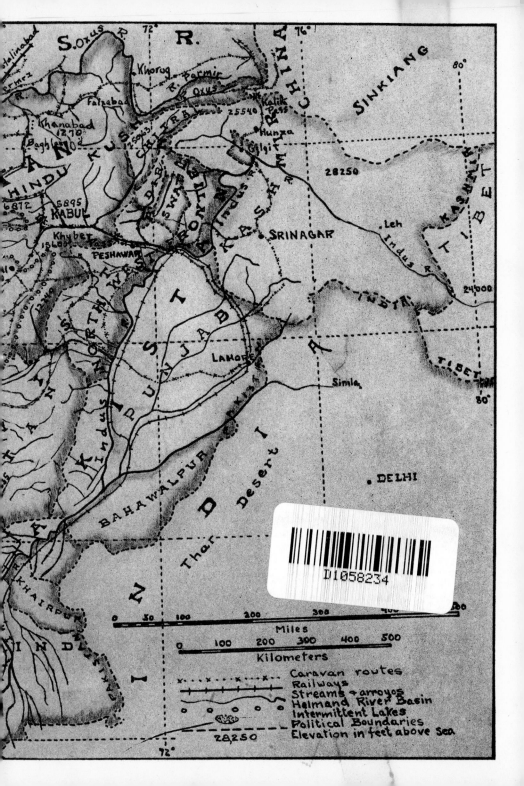

3800 S. Minnesota Avenue
Fair Oaks, California

_____

_____

_____

_____

Aiming to assist in promoting friendship and mutual understanding with peoples of the Middle and Far East, and especially with those of a strategic, landlocked remote Asian kingdom — Texas in size — a buffer between Red Russia and a free world, the author is pleased to present AFGHANISTAN VENTURE to your campus library for the reading interest and enjoyment of the students.

In the spirit of Rotary International and with greetings from the Rotary Club of Fair Oaks, California,

Sincerely,

Paul S. Jones (SIGNATURE)

PAUL S. JONES

Afghanistan Venture

Discovering the Afghan people — the life, contacts and adventures of an American Civil Engineer during his two year sojourn in the Kingdom of Afghanistan.

by

PAUL S. JONES

AFGHANISTAN

THE NAYLOR COMPANY

Publishers of the Southwest - - - San Antonio, Texas

Afghanistan Venture

Discovering the Afghan people — the life, contacts and adventures of an American Civil Engineer during his two year sojourn in the Kingdom of Afghanistan.

by

PAUL S. JONES

AFGHANISTAN

THE NAYLOR COMPANY

Publishers of the Southwest - - - San Antonio, Texas

This book is dedicated to the memory
of my son,

CAPTAIN NORMAN R. JONES,

Pilot, United States Army Air Force —
World War II in Europe, and China;
and Civil Air Transport, China —
who did not return, but
"Proved his selflessness in assisting
his crew (Chinese Nationalists), even
at the expense of paying the supreme
sacrifice. No man can do more."

Contents

Acknowledgments

GRATEFUL APPRECIATION is extended by the author. . . .

To Morrison-Knudsen Afghanistan, Inc., and American personnel, whose boldness in promoting and constructing engineering works of great magnitude in a land-locked, remote Asian Kingdom, has rendered these rich, but rugged experiences available to him.

To Afghan national and provincial government authorities, whose direct cooperation and moral support in doing the job well, were to him invaluable. Among these were:

Abdul Ghani Khan, Governor-General of the Province of Kandahar; the Provincial Commandant in charge of military forces; Refiq Khan, District Governor of Girishk;

Sayet Wuhdut Shah Khan, Chief Engineer for the Royal Afghan Commission on M-K-A Projects;

Aslam Khan, Acting Director, Agricultural Exploitation Department; Jan Mohammed, Director of Building Construction; Abdullah Rahim, Colonization; Abdur Rahim, Agriculturist.

To top military commanders in Kabul who trusted him in taking pictures of Afghan armed might in review — to Kabul police who rendered him every courtesy.

To miscellaneous Afghan M-K-A personnel of especial help to him, particularly:

Abdul Jabbar, — interpreter and law student.

Alam Terikee, — interpreter and advisor.

Esah, — construction boss.

Ghulam Dastigar, Sayed, and Karadeen, — surveyors.

Ghulam Sakhai, — office clerk and timekeeper.

Mohammed Nadir, — supervisor of general construction.

Piute, — "trouble shooter" and automobile mechanics' foreman.

Sheer Ahmad, — hydrographer, fighter, interpid adventurer.

To Jacinto ("Jack") Sabiniano and Reinaldo ("Ray") Entienza, — field engineers; Tim Fijardo and Don Riva, — accountants — all from the Philippines — faithful, dependable, energetic, of cheerful mien.

To Wallace ("Wally") Segurta from Milan, Italy; machinists' foreman, whose endeavors were urgrudgingly extended beyond the call of duty.

To Aktur Mohammed, chief of the Karoti, — who set the pattern for mutual understanding in the settlement of wandering tribesmen on irrigated lands — and likewise to chieftains of the Durrani, the Baluchi, the Waziri, the Isazais, the Chakhansur people, — whose trust in American impartiality was inspiring — to Sooltan, and other landed patriarchs like him in the Arghandab River Valley, whose utmost faith in the Americans' ability to provide irrigation water in steady and permanent abundance, was to this writer stimulating.

To Dr. Aurang Shah, physician and surgeon, of Sacramento, California; born and reared near the Khyber Pass and thereby endowed with that same centuries-old spirit of independence which his countrymen have so courageously and invincibly defended from the Hindu Kush Mts. to the Arabian Sea, on both sides of the borders of Afghanistan to the Indus River — that land of free Pakhtun clansmen united in common brotherhood — to Dr. Shah the author is much indebted for discerning enlightenment.

To Shirley Rumph, whose typing and other assistance were so ably and conscientiously performed, and whose unflagging interest throughout the preparation of the manuscript was ever heartening.

To Carl A. Behrens, my friend and former associate in

x

the United States Army Engineer Department at Sacramento, for his professional skill in perfecting the maps.

To a wife, daughter Natalie, and high school lad Wayne in the absence of his two older brothers in the United States Army and Naval Air Force . . . for ardently keeping the home fires burning.

To friends everywhere for well wishes and frequent inquiries.

Orientation

THE "STAR OF ASIA" — remote, mysterious, ancient, — land-bound by those fabulous countries of the Middle and Far East — such is the Kingdom of Afghanistan.

In its northern parts rise slopes bedecked with a scattering of pines, and snow-crested ranges rising to the modest height of California's Mt. Whitney and on upwards to 16,000 feet. But beyond and above these are even mightier masses, crowned with glistening glaciers, eternally profiled against a blue sky and fleecy white clouds at elevations up to 25,000 feet. And these are the Hindu Kush, — branch of the Himalayas, backbone of the Asiatic continent.

On the southern slopes of these mountains are numerous streams fed by the melting snows. These give rise to the Helmand River, or Rud, which along its southwesterly course of some 500 miles to the Afghan-Iranian border, drains a tremendous region of barren, rocky mountains, desert valleys and slopes. It is a land similar to our Arizona. Here, during a brief rainy season of late winter and early spring, scattered light precipitation accompanied in places by downpours of cloudburst proportions very often send torrential floods down the network of dry washes, or arroyos as we term them in Arizona, into the Helmand River. What water is not used for irrigation purposes finds its way into the Hamun-i-Helmand, a delta region of lakes, marshes, and overflow lands comparable to our Tulare Lake basin in the San Joaquin Valley of California. This unreclaimed area, which has no drainage outlet and is at 1,500 to 2,000 feet elevation, extends on both sides of the boundary between Afghanistan and Iran.

It is in this Helmand Valley that reclamation works have already been completed and plans have been made for their

xiii

extension, which if followed out, will eventually create in this desert land an Afghan version of our Tennessee Valley Project.

But more of this anon.

First, may we ourselves get oriented in time and distance as regards this faraway realm. To do this let us travel in our imaginations by jet plane if you will, 6,800 miles straight north from Great Falls, Montana, or from nearby Lethridge, Alberta, to Kandahar, Afghanistan — 16 hours flying time or less. We cross western Canada to the shores of the Arctic Ocean and on to the North Pole, thence due south to the mouth of Russia's ice-bound River Ob. We might as well make a few notes in passing. We are over Novy Port. Here, in spite of blinding blizzards, air bases are under construction. Off to the right near Vorkuta is the terminus of a double track railway also under construction; it will lead direct to Moscow, 1,200 miles to the southwest, seat of the Politburo.

Here in the ice-bound uplands of this bleak and forbidding land are the slave labor camps, we are reliably informed, at work in the development of new oil fields, coal mines, and uranium deposits.

We cross over a newly projected railway line stretching from the Urals across the Ob River Valley to Igarka on the Yenisei River, rising metropolis north of the Arctic Circle.

Then to our right not far away is Sverdlovsk, on the east slope of the Urals. It is an industrial and railroad center.

Down there is the Siberian railway; we're crossing it between the towns of Kurgan to the west, Petropavlovsk to the east. Look it up on your map — better, the globe.

Now we cross the Steppe country, and are over Turkistan. We see Tashkent to the left. You might as well know it, folks: Here originate radio broadcasts of communist propaganda as evil as that of Moscow — subtle, lying, hateful, vicious, cowardly, treacherous — directed at and insulting to free men, free institutions, free governments everywhere and directed especially against the United States!

There's Samarkand of fabulous fame just off to our right, the city once conquered, plundered and its people massacred through the treachery of the ruthlessly cruel, hard-riding Mongols led by Genghis Khan. This was in the 12th Century A.D.

Stalinabad is just to the east, and now the Oxus River and straight ahead loom the lofty Hindu Kush. But wait — we are over Afghanistan! — the Oxus River is its northern frontier. And of further interest: It was near here that the forces of Alexander the Great and his army crossed this river and pressed northward toward Samarkand. They reached a place now called Dzhizak about halfway between Tashkent and Samarkand. They had crossed northward over the Hindu Kush at a pass some 12,000 feet in elevation near the head of the Panshir River. This occurred during the years 330 to 328 B.C., we are told by historians. Later, also, they returned southward over this same route and followed the Kabul River Valley down through the Khyber Pass into India.

History also records that the caravan, or lorry road or trail, over which we are now crossing, was that traveled by Marco Polo en route from Rome to Mongolia and Cathay. He evidently passed between what are now the Afghan cities of Mazar-i-Sharif, Khanabad, and Faizabad following the plains country between the Oxus River and the base of the Hindu Kush.

Now we emerge from a high mountain pass over the imposing Hindu Kush and soon are over Kabul (pronounced "Cobble"), which nestles in the warm sheltered valley of the Kabul River, tributary of the Indus. And here is the capital of a kingdom the size of Texas, —Afghanistan.

Then we'll continue, as it were in our flight, for 300 miles southwesterly through a wide and lengthy desert corridor, flanked on either side by rugged, barren mountains.

xv

We are over a region awesomely referred to by the British in India as the mystical land "beyond the Khyber Pass," or "beyond the North-West Frontier."

Near the ancient city of Ghazni, its picturesque walls a reminder of Biblical times, and another point of Mongol conquest, we cross over a divide. Again we are reminded of the armies of Alexander the Great, for over the very course we are flying these forces moved northeastward from Kandahar to Ghazni to Kabul.

Now we are ready to make a landing at the garden city of Kandahar. We are much impressed at sight of its massive and ancient walls, its canal of flowing life-giving water to surrounding orchards, vineyards and verdant fields. It vies with Herat for being, next to Kabul, the second city of importance in Afghanistan.

And so this, patient people, is the end of our fantastical jet plane journey for purposes of orientation as regards background, locations, distances and times. We are at about the latitude of Phoenix, Arizona, and 180 degrees difference in longitude therefrom.

Now, my friends, we are ready for the real journey from our homes to Kandahar.

Whereas the distance from San Francisco via Great Falls, Montana, and the North Pole would have totaled 7,700 miles, the one we will actually take by a more circuitous route will add up to 11,500 miles, 3,800 miles farther. It will be across the Atlantic, British Isles, Europe, touching in Africa, and over the Middle East.

Specifically, travel with me by plane in this narrative from San Francisco to New York City via Los Angeles, Albuquerque and Kansas City, landing at La Guardia Field and leaving from the International Airport; thence out over the broad Atlantic past Newfoundland to Prestwick Field near Glasgow, and to Amsterdam, Rome, Cairo, Damascus, Basra in Iraq, and Karachi in West Pakistan. After that, journey with me in a strange-appearing railway train for twenty-four hours up the Indus River Valley and across rugged Baluchistan to Quetta — still in Baluchistan — and from there by automobile to Kandahar. We leave San Francisco at 4 p.m. on a Tuesday and arrive at Kandahar 7 p.m. the next Monday, with a layover of thirty-three hours in Holland.

For about 1,075 miles Afghanistan borders the land of the Soviets. The Oxus River constitutes the boundary for two-thirds of this distance.

On the west the oil-poor, politically unsettled Kingdom of Iran extends for 475 miles.

West Pakistan, which includes Baluchistan and the North-West Frontier in name only, bounds Afghanistan on the southeast for 1,250 miles, and here Pakhtun clansmen formerly created disturbing conditions for the British and India, and continue hostile activites to this day against England's political successors, the Pakistani, — in fact have declared their independence from them.

Then there is the Afghan corridor 230 miles long by 10 to 40 miles broad which reaches out along the crest of the Hindu Kush to touch Sinkiang Province in China, and in this position geographically and effectively separates Chitral and Kashmir from Siberia.

In this faraway, remote Asian kingdom, the present narrator chose to spend two years as a civil engineer on the construction and development of an irrigation project being directed by the Afghan Government under contract with a great American construction firm. In a modest way, the writer on this job is proud to have helped to initiate and advance, in accordance with good American tradition, a forward looking and ambitious program in the interests of the common people.

So in the pages of this book a humble attempt has been made to set forth an interesting and true account of his contacts with the Afghan people. That this attempt was ever made at all is due to the inspiration resulting from the unfeigned interest in the matter by loyal friends with whom he had worked on the United States Government's Central Valley Project at Stockton, California, — and especially to four lovely young women associates there: Norma Martin, Eleanor Berglund, Marie MacLaughlin, and Urla Mae Underwood.

Scores of other friends, both in Afghanistan and the States, by persistent suggestions also have made the project seem worthwhile. A son, Bruce, on flight patrol duty with the Naval Air Force over Far Eastern waters, frequently inquires, "What progress, Dad?" Elizabeth, a favorite niece and high school teacher in San Francisco, exclaims, "Lock him up and hide the key until it's finished!" . . . . "You write that before painting the house!" admonishes a sister, Fern, in San José. Thus the pressure grew until this amateur started something he knows little about: writing a book.

Fortunately I had been faithful each day — regardless of any other diversion, irrespective of fatigue from the intense heat or from long days on foot, on horse, or just rough going by car to distant places — in recording in diary form the happenings of each twenty-four hours. No day seemed complete until this was done.

To folks at home and friends in the States, Juma was the day to write them. These letters depicted life in Afghanistan just as a coterie of American construction men and engineers was finding it. Some of those letters are introduced herein, verbatim. Diary notes have been repeated much as recorded at the site of events.

Many pictures were taken of scenes on the construction; of views in cities and in remote places; of people, their activities and surroundings. A selected few of these in color, or black and white, are reproduced herein. Color films were difficult to obtain due to import restrictions in Pakistan, and to our field locations in remote places. When exposed, films were sent to Eastman laboratories in the United States for processing, after which the laboratory mailed them directly to my home. These exposed 35 mm. color films were transported to the States by employees returning home. One dared not mail them for fear of confiscation in Pakistan or elsewhere. Black and whites were developed and printed by my friend, Iqbal, the official photographer of the Company, an Afghan, who also had a laboratory of his own in Kandahar.

So, set forth in these pages are the results, in prose and pictures, of an attempt to present in interesting and easily readable form a factual account of just what did happen during those two years among the Afghans.

What of their daily activities; their ways of doing things so differently from ours; religion and education; marriage; home life; health; food; methods of travel; agriculture and industry; defense preparedness; courtesy and hospitality?

What about those silent witnesses of bygone ages, those remants of an historical past — the ruins of ancient fortresses, the weathered and battered walls of ancient civilizations?

As for those battlefields where ancient as well as modern forces clashed, the Afghan is vaguely aware that something of mighty importance happened there.

And how do these strange people take to modern construction under way in the immediate vicinity of their fields and villages? These huge dams rising on their rivers to impound millions of acre-feet of precious water; this immense, arduous and bold enterprise has exceeded the scope of their own imagination and that of their ancestors far beyond the time of recorded history. So how do they react to all this?

River diversion works, canals and laterals to make available to their lands this wealth of water — do these people display an animated interest? The Dasht-i-Margo, this desert of death, springs to life from centuries of lethargy as these vital streams transform its wastes as if by fairy wand into fields of waving wheat.

What about these canals of times long past being changed into adequate channels of year-round water supply — canals so ancient as to be almost hidden by masses of silt excavated by the laborious effort of countless generations of turbaned men? Yes, the American foreigners brought this about. Will there be any more water shortages?

And those personal adventures and contacts — experiences both humorous and sobering, — some safe from danger, others invitations to tragedy . . . and a multitude of events and things typical of a rugged exsitence in a far away kingdom with monotony ruled out.

And the women? Throughout the pages of this book, the reader may detect a subdued but key theme. Foreigners may thus become acquainted with the hopeless (not exactly) plight, as we in the West would view the situation, of one-half of Afghan society. This resistance to progress is viewed with some concern by high officials of the Afghan Government. Only fearless, aggressive leadership can bring about corrective measures. It well could be that His Majesty, King Mohammed Zahir Shah, is in a position to initiate such action. He has been well educated in France and is said to be keenly aware of the uplifting influence of womanhood in other than Moslem nations. He knows of the progress made by Turkey's exalting women to a more important status in home, social and economic life. The King is highly esteemed throughout his nation.

So, Reader, may it be your desire to come with me to this oriental realm of enchanting mystery.

Enter into the spirit of its trackless deserts and rugged mountains bathed in lemon-yellow sunshine, — eternally unchanging, yet clothed in moods of warning or promise, disappointment or hope — temperaments rightly in keeping with the hovering mirages.

Follow the winding rivers, explore the irrigated valleys!

Enter into the friendliness of the people, understand their deep, though often unexpressed yearning towards progress. Meet them as equals, respect their ideas, their customs, their religion.

Acquaint yourself with the tedious efforts of the dark brown farmer with his ox team and wooden plow. He works hard for the meager living he affords his family.

Accept the hospitality of the village chiefs and their people; mingle freely with the construction laborers; make friends with the soldiers and their courteous officers.

Consult with specialists in Agriculture.

Meet men of education and prominence, men of the Government. Confer with Provincial Governor-Generals, District Governors. View Afghan military might, — experience the thrill that you are being granted this privilege because you are an American.

Contemplate this huge construction job nearing early completion!

Prepare to turn back the pages of time 2,000 years and more to understand the present.

And glimpse the women of Afghanistan — meet the Belles of Shamalon!

"Truth can make men free."
Dwight D. Eisenhower

I

Decision

CHAPTER I

Decision

IT WAS AT THE Damascus airfield in Syria. Although only January, the sun covered the surrounding desert with blinding, glittering brilliance. Could it be we were in Asia — in ancient Palestine — having "brunch" in an Arab dining room? The attractive blonde across the table had boarded the plane last evening in Rome.

"What . . . Afghanistan . . . wild savage people . . . they will kill you!" In limited English, it was not so much what she said. Her air of fearsome amazement was, however, alarming, as in confidence I had just told her that my partner in travel, Neale Poole, and I were destined for Afghanistan.

"Yes, we are traveling inland from Karachi by railway train some 500 miles — beyond that by camel caravan another 400, possibly," I added vaguely.

The interest of the young lady from Holland sharpened appreciably.

"You've been there doubtless?" I queried.

"Oh, no, I've been employed at Weesp," she said, naming a town or place in Holland quite unfamiliar to me. "It is the Queen's Palace . . . like your White House in America. You do not know about it?" blushing the while disconcertedly because of my Amercan ignorance on this subject.

"I travel to Djakarta. Four days more I arrive . . . to stay three years. My parents are reluctant that I go. So. . . ."

"Quite right that they should be," I interrupted. "Road blocks — machine guns in ambush — much unrest in Indonesia. But as for us, we will remain in Afghanistan but two years."

Having somewhat allayed our new friend's anxiety for our safety, and at the same time expressed concern for her welfare, she was then quite composed. So I said to her, turning to an Arab waiter, "Won't you have another cup of java?"

But wait, we are ahead of our narrative.

Again having settled down comfortably in the huge Dutch airliner for the take-off, I fell to reminiscing. Perhaps that Dutch miss was right after all about heading right into a frightful situation, I reasoned with some misgiving.

Hadn't my spouse admonished, "You're being selected only because the construction company can't find another civil engineer who wants to go to such a place! And you doggedly are determined to venture into darkest Africa?"

"Dark Africa? Who mentioned the Dark Continent? That can wait until later. I'm talking about the Middle and Far East." So that did it, that is, arrival at a decision to go — not to Fairbanks, Alaska, where a two-year job awaited me on airfield construction with the United States Army Engineers — not to Okinawa — not even to a desert in southern California to help out a little on guided missiles . . . but to Afghanistan!

4

"Yes," had been my answer by telephone to the company's personnel agent, Al Kincaid, in San Francisco, from my home, for nineteen years, near Fair Oaks, California.

Al had put it this way: "Say, mister, you don't look at all like a man the age you say you are. I watched you walk out of my office the other day. We need a man of your caliber on our big irrigation project in Afghanistan. Will you come down to talk over the situation with our Chief Engineer?"

En route to San Francisco on Highway 40, flanked by the lush green fields of Yolo and Solano counties, over the rolling and velvety verdant oak-studded hills of Marin in our trusted maroon-toned Ford sedan, there was time for reflection. Suddenly the radio blared forth: "This is radio station KTRB, Modesto, California." A minister of the gospel was expounding on a passage of scripture. Crisply he read a text and explained, "You go into a far country — a strange land — inhabited by a different people. Let God within you point the way!" Could this be a providential admonition, I wondered, surprised at its application to my present state of possible indecision. And on this I pondered meditatively as the car rolled smoothly along past Hamilton Field and San Rafael and joined the city-bound traffic over the Golden Gate Bridge.

And then followed three weeks of active preparations: medical and physical examinations at one of the most up-to-date medical establishments in San Francisco. Nothing about one's person did each of the several stations there fail to examine most painstakingly with the use of special scientific equipment. Besides these tests, previous examinations with army medical personnel seemed less complete and thorough.

An extra pair of reading glasses was acquired. This was a forethought of wisdom, I was to learn months afterwards at Chah-i-anjir in Dasht-i-Margo, the Well of the Fig Tree

5

in the Desert of Death. Also an expensive pair of sun glasses was added to my equipment.

Teeth were examined and necessary repairs accomplished.

And there were short intervals between vaccinations or inoculations for typhoid, typhus, cholera, smallpox, and, the last, for yellow fever at the United States Customshouse. This last, one took at his own risk . . . sign on the dotted line, please. And finally one was feeling so low as to imagine being attacked simultaneously by each of the five diseases.

Then one visited the office of Don Cox, Sacramento County sheriff, for clearance as to any misdemeanors with which he might possibly be charged. A document was handed out cautiously admitting that on this date a "search of the files fails to disclose any prior record on this subject," meaning me — that fingerprints had been taken for purpose of visa, and that the document is to be shown to police of foreign countries at ports of entry upon request.

The Social Security people in the Federal Building off Market Street at the Civic Center promptly assigned me a number for identification on payroll deductions.

And then there was the birth certificate secured with the help of older brothers and sister in furnishing notarized documents.

The passport and visas were to come from Washington. In this connection pictures of oneself of the lowest order of quality were required, so it seemed.

Some engineering books recently off the press were procured from a leading technical book store on Market Street. Should occasion so demand in the isolated places to which destined, those texts would be most convenient for ready reference.

Not to lose contact with the civilization I had known, a Hallicrafter S-72L radio set was procured from an agency on Market Street. Tried out in my Fair Oaks home at midnight, a "down-under" station — Melbourne, Australia — was heard distinctly, and with only the whip for an aerial. I was satisfied. As an afterthought I checked with Al Kincaid.

"Al," I asked, "is there electricity over there to operate a radio set?"

"Not where you're going, Jones," was the positive response, not without a hint of mystery.

Clothes and various assortments of supposedly needed articles were packed in small locker trunks and delivered to the company's warehouse in San Francisco for shipment. These containers were then packed in one large wooden case bound with steel bands and sealed for shipment by boat, rail and truck.

All this while there proceeded other preparations at home of a different nature. For some years before, aside from my regular work as a civil engineer with the Corps of Army Engineers on their Sacramento and San Joaquin Rivers flood control and river improvement projects, and later with the United States Bureau of Reclamation on the Central Valley Project, I had been developing a home and acreage at the base of the Sierra Nevada foothills along the American River. My two boys at home, in high school and junior college, must carry on alone now — Wayne and Deane. Peradventure this independent responsibility of no little weight would make men of them. I assumed it would. So we three carefully reviewed the present and possible future situations. Plans were made accordingly.

During my last days at home, heavy rains in the mountains and valley sent down the American River an unprecedented flood, inundating lowlands and threatening residential areas around the city of Sacramento. People were rendered homeless. As for us a stock fence in path of the high water was swept away. "Well, it's up to you boys now," said

AFGHANISTAN VENTURE

I. "Put up a temporary electric fence to shut the cattle off the lowland. Then replace the main fence with steel posts and four strands of barbed wire. You'll have to do this when home from school on weekends, as you find time!" I further admonished, the while carefully selecting sixty-six pounds, no more, of gear to carry with me on the airplane.

"You're bound for an overseas assignment also?" said I to the rather ruddy-faced man seated next to me in the company reception lobby. I was waiting to complete certain papers with the very pleasant young woman behind the counter.

"No, I represent the Royal Dutch Airlines — Hugo K. Mayr. Why don't you ask the company to send you on one of our planes?"

"Well," I replied, "you see I'm new here. I wouldn't ask for this favor just now. But I've heard there are none better — the planes and accommodations — the service, I mean."

Promptly the KLM man disappeared in direction of the company's transportation department just down the hallway.

The young lady smiled and beckoned. "Would you care to look over this pamphlet while waiting, Mr. Jones?" said she. "It contains information and instructions to our employees bound for Afghanistan."

"It looks to be very helpful. Thank you, Miss Bendelli," I said appreciatively, and proceeded first to check the items covered by the section on "Processing Procedure."

Yes, I had my passport — ten passport photos — letter of good conduct from the sheriff — personal history resumé — visa applications — baggage list — and my medical papers were already with Miss Bendelli. I had made actual progress.

As to "General Conditions in Afghanistan," this is what the pamphlet stated:

"Afghanistan is a Kingdom with an approximate popu-

8

lation of twelve (12) million, and an area about the size of Texas. In climate and topographic features, Afghanistan bears a strong resemblance to Arizona and New Mexico. The southern two-thirds of the country has an arid climate with a rainfall of about six (6) to eight (8) inches in a year and temperatures of 110 down to 20. The northern part is mountainous with temperatures of 95 to zero. There is no excessive rainfall. Snow varies from a few inches to several feet. Altitude varies from 2,000 feet in the southern part to 6,000 feet with various summits and mountain peaks near Kabul, the capital, exceeding 12,000 feet.

"Every effort will be made to furnish our employees American standard camp accommodations, including waterproof quarters, comfortable furnishings and American food prepared under the direction of or by American cooks. A reasonable amount of recreational facilities will be provided, together with subscriptions to current magazines. A commissary will be provided wherein it will be possible to procure a limited supply of work clothing, toilet necessities and other items. A competent American physician and surgeon is at the job site for the protection of the health and welfare of our employees.

"You have familiarized yourself, undoubtedly, with the general geographical and political conditions of the country of Afghanistan. If one has not traveled in the Middle East, he is cautioned that the standards of living, sanitation and travel are not those to which he is accustomed in the United States. The governments of these countries are attempting to improve the conditions of their people but the changes, by American standards, have not been great. Employees of Morrison-Knudsen Afghanistan, Inc. will, by necessity, be in direct contact with these people and subject to much lower standards of living and sanitation than those prevailing in the United States.

"Anyone who has any hesitancy in accepting these conditions of living, sanitation and travel should not consider employment on this project."

Having put in some twenty years of service as a reserve officer, Corps of Engineers, United States Army and, in addition, experienced active duty in both World Wars I and II, the following on "Military Release" was interesting:

"Reserve Officers will be required to furnish proof of permission to leave the country, from the Commanding Officer of their reserve area. Young men within the draft age group must also furnish such proof from their draft board. Any periodic reports by mail to be made by members of either of the two classifications above will be the individual's personal responsibility."

Concerning availability of money en route:

"It is recommended that you carry $100.00 in American Express Traveler's Cheques of $10.00 and $20.00 denominations. These cheques may be exchanged anywhere for the currency of the country. You should not, however, leave the United States with more than twenty-five ($25) in cash, preferably in one dollar bills."

"Observance of Afghan Laws" was briefly to the point:

"The employee will respect and obey all Afghan laws, rules and regulations and will not interfere with the Afghan political or religious affairs either directly or indirectly, nor engage in commercial trade or enterprise."

Now here was a statement to scrutinize and think about deeply. Herein lay the essence of success — for the project — for one's own self. It was a paragraph entitled, "Working with Native Labor," and read as follows:

"Working and living conditions are regulated by the geographical location and laws of the country in which the job is located and by the temperament, customs and ability

10

of the people who live in it. A great number of Afghans are employed by this firm, and every American will be required to work with them. He will instruct the Afghans in various crafts, direct their work in large groups, and assist in keeping the time of those working under him. This applies to every American on the job — Supervisor, Journeyman and Foreman alike. This is one of the most important requirements on the job and must be fully understood and agreed to. The successful completion of this job and your personal success depends largely on your ability to direct groups of Afghans effectively. You have been selected for this reason, as much as for your qualifications as a Supervisor or Craftsman.

"When you are are working with the Afghans, remember these few simple instructions: Never curse or strike an Afghan under any circumstances;

Keep your temper and you keep yourself and everybody else out of trouble;

Report any Afghans that refuse to work to a responsible authority;

Do not talk religion or politics with Afghans."

Then there were several miscellaneous items:

"Due to a recent ruling by the Pakistan Government, firearms of all types and ammunition are not permitted to be shipped through Pakistan. Therefore under no circumstances should firearms and ammunition be packed in your baggage, either hand-carried or shipped.

"At the time of your departure, you should have the following papers in your possession: passport; one letter of good health; international certificate of inoculation and vaccination; copy of contract; plane ticket; good conduct letters.

"Present all of the above papers to the Officer Manager upon your arrival in Afghanistan."

AFGHANISTAN VENTURE

Satisfied as to having been fully informed on all matters covered by the pamphlet, and having read and studied the terms of the Employment Contract, I stepped up to the desk and signed the latter.

Said Miss Bendelli: "Your plane leaves the San Franciso Airport for New York City tomorrow, Tuesday, January 23rd, at 4:15 p.m. Goodbye, and may you have the best of luck!"

"All experience is an arch to build upon."

— Henry Brooks Adams
(1838-1918)

Note on pronunciation of Persian words as used in this book:

(a) similar to "a" as in "ah;" also as in "dare."
(i) similar to "ee" as in "bee."
(u) similar to "oo" as in "coo."
(q) similar to "k" as in "Kodak."
(r) rolled, as in Spanish *perro.*

Stress is generally on last syllable.

II

Flight to Holland
and Karachi

CHAPTER II

Flight to Holland and Karachi

LEAVING THE San Francisco Airport at 4:15 p.m. yesterday we were soon over Santa Clara Valley and Mt. Hamilton and the Coast Range Mountains. These presented a beautiful sight in the late afternoon — a mosaic of green fields and orchards and plowed lands in the valleys, soft rolling green range lands in the mountains, with patches of timber.

At dusk we were circling the Los Angeles Airfield for a landing.

And then there was Palm Springs, Albuquerque and at 1:40 a.m., January 24th, Kansas City. I was really tired after this strain of several weeks of preparation and had slept soundly in the reclining chair. At 2 a.m. we left in the bright moonlight, and this condition prevailed until approaching the east coast at daybreak, when the sky became

15

black and stormy. Our hostess appeared excited and alarmed as we circled La Guardia Field and came down to the ground with visibility zero — heavy fog and rain. This was at 7:20 a.m., right on time, ten hours and ten minutes out of Los Angeles.

We apparently cut through the outskirts of New York City on the way to the International Airport — block after block of huge six-story brick apartments — single ones in places seeming to occupy one-half a block in area — and this congestion with the rain and fog indeed presented a dreary outlook to one accustomed to the wide open spaces of our West.

As of this moment we are traveling northeasterly along the New England coast toward Newfoundland. The fog bank below is breaking. Revealed is a scattering of tiny islands, in a calm blue ocean. There is still a ceiling of clouds overhead. Being passed out is a leaflet showing cabin plan and serving as an introduction to fellow passengers and crew. The Captain is Frans Peetoom; Stewardess, Liane Latour.

Today there are only twelve passengers aboard. The seating arrangement will accommodate forty. Several are bound for Paris, Frankfurt, Prestwick, Hamburg and Munich. The crew are most courteous and friendly. The name of the four-motored plane is "The Flying Dutchman Gouda" — speed now 325 m.p.h. — altitude 19,000 feet, and the flight is non-stop to Prestwick in approximately ten hours out of New York City.

As darkness falls at 4:50 p.m., the ocean is again hidden by fog a clear blue sky is above and the cabin lights are turned off. One dozes and suddenly arouses to view the ocean in the bright moonlight far below with just a scattering of small white clouds — and then sleeps soundly again.

And then: "Mr. Jones, are you at all cold?"

16

"No, this light blanket is just right," said I, yawning, thinking it was morning.

"It's 28 degrees below zero outside," added our smiling hostess turning on the lights. "We are about to serve dinner."

And then there were helpings of several kinds of fish and champagne, soup and rolls and crackers, roast meat, stewed apricots and ice cream; fresh fruit: pears, bananas and oranges, coffee . . . and one feels most appreciative and kindly toward our KLM friends.

In two more hours we will land in Scotland; a few stars are visible — the horizon is discernible.

Right on time — 2:45 a.m., Thursday, January 25th, and ten hours out of New York — we are landing at Prestwick Field.

Starting toward the dining room, I hesitated, suddenly remembering I had no Scotch money — the nearest to it being $12.50 worth of Dutch guilders purchased back at the International Airport this morning — no, yesterday morning (my watch read 10 p.m.).

"Oh, this is on the airline," said Miss Latour, noting my self-consciousness, and leading the way into the restaurant. I looked about for a counter and stools. Doughnuts and coffee would suffice this early in the morning, but a waiter in most formal evening garb led me to a table with a white covering. Then I noticed other waiters in similar attire, and it dawned on me that hot dog stands and the U.S.A. were now far behind across the Atlantic.

And a large friendly man, in his fifties maybe, sat down with me to have tea. He seemed to have important agricultural interests in New York State and in Holland. This was his thirty-sixth round-trip across, he said. He was raised in Amsterdam, and always travels KLM. There is much rivalry between the airlines, he continued. French fliers have a certain degree of unreliability. If a motor hesitates — so

17

what? They neglect things mechanically they should promptly correct. Airline fares, my Netherlands friend said, were now low enough that Europeans could afford to vacation for a couple or three weeks in the States, and the same with Americans in Europe — that now it's the wealthiest people that travel on the luxurious ocean liners.

This gentleman was an interesting conversationalist.

Additional passengers were gathering. My Dutch friend and I walked out to the plane with a Scotch lady whose quite young baby was being carried in a small basket by two airline attendants. Well experienced in traveling, she appeared.

And now, folks, it is 7 a.m. — only thirty-one hours out of San Francisco and we are flying southeasterly over Scotland and nothern England, altitude, 10,000 feet; speed, 230 m.p.h., and we're due in Amsterdam at 8:45 a.m. The earth below is covered with dense clouds or fog, while above the sky is clear, and sunrise should be soon. . . .

Now we are over the North Sea — at this moment crossing the lane flown by Pilot Norman and his B-17 Flying Fortress crew, and by many other courageous fliers, from Norwich Airfield in England on missions to enemy-held territory, and to the Battle of the Bulge. . . .

The plane is descending through heavy fog banks now to about 1,000 feet elevation. Here is a fine view of the Dutch countryside. One can well imagine being over the Sacramento-San Joaquin Delta countryside of California — at Walnut Grove and Rio Vista. There is a network of long straight canals flanked on both sides by concrete-paved highways on top of levees. Homes are of brick, large and substantial, for the most part on canal banks, with individual properties extending in narrow strips away from the canals — just like along the lower Sacramento River. They remind one of the model farms and homes depicted at a state fair — the premises in perfect order, the fields laid out in perfect geometrical figures. . . .

The Amsterdam Airfield is a long way out from the city and from the downtown office of KLM. The bus takes us through what must be a charming countryside in spring. . . .

The Scotch lady is there with the baby, and as the vehicle comes to a stop in front of KLM, I am one with three Dutchmen who simultaneously step forward to carry the basket with baby off the bus. While this might not be correct in San Francisco, it seemed exactly the right procedure in Holland. Promptly a KLM attendant from outside entered to take over. "This is our business," said he, in an authoritative manner.

On way in from the airport, the lady had told me she was en route to a place called Basra in Iraq and would leave on the 5 p.m. plane tomorrow afternoon.

"I'll be aboard it, also, bound for Karachi, Pakistan," said I, "and Afghanistan."

*   *   *

The KLM provided me with a book of coupons covering taxi fare to and from the Noelen Hotel in Amsterdam, lodging, dinner, supper, breakfast and dinner again.

Some Dutch money was spent in sightseeing. A guide at the hotel offered his services. Said he, "First we will walk for two or three hours and then take a taxi to cover a wider area." This man had served in the Royal Canadian Air Force, but apparently was raised around Amsterdam.

"This Noelen Hotel," said Mr. Lugtenaar, "is where Rembrandt, the noted Dutch artist once lived."

We walked through the University grounds. Here was a group of buildings with long corridors pretty closely surrounded by downtown business and public buildings and the attendant bustle of a big city.

AFGHANISTAN VENTURE

We walked through the downtown shopping area, saw many old buildings dating back to the days of the Mayflower — old churches and the Ghetto. My guide explained how the people live and work. It is the strangest-looking city it has been my privilege to visit, with a population of 800,000 — a maze of interconnecting canals of all sizes — winding streets ranging from wide boulevards to narrow, twisting alleys, where abound first-class shops and business places, reminding one of Maiden Lane in San Francisco.

By this time it was between 5 and 6 o'clock. People on bicycles homeward bound poured down the streets by the thousands, with a scattering of automobiles traveling at dangerously high speeds, crowded buses and tramcars jammed full — all losing no time.

Seemingly all the people of the city live in five-story brick apartment buildings. Lugtenaar said that apartments for a family of three or four rent for 10 guilders per week ($2.50 U.S.) — that all Dutch people keep well-occupied. In the evenings after supper they relax for a time; then the man studies, or has his own work to do.

After this we rode all around in a taxi for an hour or so and saw many other places in the industrial sections and along the shipping front.

For all this service, I paid Lugtenaar 13 guilders and the taxi driver 10 guilders — total, 23 guilders, or $5.75 U.S.

After that I had supper. All the waiters wore formal attire — tuxedos. Two very good musicians on piano and violin entertained with soft, melodious music of a classical nature, with now and then a familiar U.S. air, like "Good Night, Irene." (They played this twice; had me, an American, in mind, I assumed.) I could not read the bill of fare, but the steward kindly explained it, so I just said, "I'll take that."

After this, I started out by myself — to see the town,

should one say? Not far from the Noelen Hotel and in a narrow but well-lighted street just off a business district I saw one man slug another. A fight ensued. Men came running from many sides. As a crowd was collecting, police whistles sounded shrilly. The street was almost as quickly vacated.

Then I window-shopped for a long time, and the streets were filled with people until quite late. I would compare prices for goods in window displays — furniture, clothing — with what similar things would sell for in Sacramento; and always the Dutch articles were selling for much below our U. S. prices.

I walked along the harbor front. Many ships were at anchor. The streets and piers were well-lighted. Many seafaring men were relaxing in saloons and cafes. Along the streets, pianos dinned out accompaniments for rather raucous vocalists, and juke boxes added to the confusion of melodies.

Knowing the hour to be getting late, I decided to take a short-cut back, and turned down a narrow street to get over to what appeared to be a main boulevard. Two men ahead attracted my attention, one standing in front of a cafe or saloon, another opposite across the street. They looked in my direction and made suspicious hand signals to each other. Nonchalantly, I altered my course diagonally across the street so as to keep as far from each as possible, and neither changed his position. (I was wearing a leather jacket, fleece-lined with high wool collar and warm and comfortable — tempting booty.)

Streets were becoming deserted and in the intricate system of canals, alleys and streets, coupled with inability to speak Dutch, the improbability of finding one's way back alone now seemed apparent. It then dawned on me to inquire of hotel clerks. Around a hotel, undoubtedly, some one could speak English. So I found I was about two miles from where I thought I was. One hotel clerk even came out into the street to direct me, saying, "It's is not too difficult," and I thanked him profusely.

And then on Friday I went on a long excursion by motor boat over the city and around the harbor. The Captain explained in Dutch the many points of interest. Shipping facilities are vast — to Java, Sumatra, Borneo, the British Isles, West Indies, Central and South America, and other parts of Europe. The "Hendrik" Floating Dock accommodates big steamers laid up for repairs.

A couple of Dutchmen asked was I from Texas. I said from both Texas and California. I remarked about the immensity of the Amsterdam Harbor. "Nothing in comparison to that at Rotterdam," one of them assured me. He said he lived in Rotterdam and was connected with shipping interests.

Amsterdam is immaculately clean. Except for a few wooden shoes, the Dutch people dress like we do, and look and act like we do, with this exception: Walking along the streets should you out of curiosity casually size up a young woman, she will return your gaze looking you squarely in the eye and take your measure from head to foot and this could be embarrassing! . . . and this is not done in San Francisco.

*　　　*　　　*

We have just left the airfield at Rome. It is now 10:30 p.m., Holland time. What a disappointment that this flight is by night.

We left Amsterdam at 5 p.m. and reached Rome at 9 p.m. Except for eating dinner, I slept most of the time, as the landscape was hidden in darkness. The plane traveled presumably over Germany, Switzerland and northern Italy.

Approaching Rome, the lighting system of the city was

plainly visible in different colors, indicating the pattern of the boulevards and parks, like the design on a piece of Italian lacework.

Two ancient public buildings I readily recognized — no other buildings were evident. These two were brilliantly illuminated. Appearing suddenly out of the darkness below, they struck me as remarkable and startling, for they perfectly resembled scenes depicted in my school geography book of long ago — the one, the Colosseum, built by Vespasian and Titus about A.D. 80; the other, the Forum, ancient place of popular assembly.

The passengers went into the cafe at the airfield and waited an hour and a half. The field was covered with metal work in flexible sections. The ground seemed soggy. Here I again met the Scotch lady and three-months-old baby, smiling and wide awake in her little basket. Over cups of tea the mother told me of her home in Basra, Iraq — a seven-room home, new, furnished and very comfortable. Basra, she said, is near the mouth of the Tigris and Euphrates rivers at the head of the Persian Gulf.

Now folks, it is exactly midnight. No land or sea markings of any kind can one discern — just a few fleecy clouds below and stars overhead. Warmer. We are crossing the Mediterranean.

*　　　*　　　*

At 3:20 this morning our plane lets down at the Cairo, Egypt, airfield. After a light breakfast, we sit around a comfortable fire at one end of the dining room. The waiters are dressed in long white gowns, with a wide, red belt in the middle, and wear red fezzes. This field is in the open desert, barren of all vegetation. Flower gardens about the airport buildings, however, give a welcome touch of colors.

We take off at 8:30 a.m. The sun is bright and warm, for which one is glad. The plane travels northerly along the westerly bank of the Nile, as near as I can tell from my map. One can look southerly up the river, a winding stream, for perhaps thirty miles. The valley is level and covered with green fields and orchards in variegated patterns. It is hard to discern places of abode, but once I saw what appeared to be a small town of adobe houses with dome-shaped roofs.

To our left could be the town of Damietta and the plane heads northeasterly out over the Mediterranean. The sea is a beautiful blue this morning with fleecy white clouds at intervals far below. A big ship is making its way southward toward the entrance to the Suez Canal.

Now we are passing over the Lebanon coastline near Tyre, and that city back to our right was Haifa in Israel. There appears to be a narrow stretch of irrigated lands along the coast — orchards and green fields again.

Then we go inland over a hilly country, partly green, with a few winding roads leading over the hills to little towns of thirty to forty adobe houses, flat-topped and massed close together, with no evidence of cultivation anywhere near.

Then there is a higher mountain — barren — with a skiff of snow, Mt. Lebanon, and now the descent into a valley probably twenty miles wide by thirty or forty long. It is cultivated and has green orchards — likely, olive — and green fields, but no evidence of habitation except in towns every few miles where 500 or more houses, all flat-topped and of adobe, are jumbled together. Some are square and built around a courtyard. We circle one of these and land. It is Damascus in Syria. The airfield is on the desert overlooking the valley, where are long rows of poplar trees.

All passengers alight, handing passports to our attractive hostess from Holland. I walk towards the dining hall with a Neale Poole, whom I had met out of Rome — from Los

Angeles. His folks live in one of the Carolinas, and he is also bound for Afghanistan. Mr. Poole and I seat ourselves at a table with the Scotch lady (only she turns out to be English; her husband is Scotch, she said) and the smiling little Virginia in the basket supported on two chairs, and a blonde Dutch girl, about twenty-one or twenty-three. So we eat cookies, drink tea and enjoy some Lebanon oranges. The Holland girl does not talk English fluently. She is en route to Djakarta on the island of Java, terminus of the Royal Dutch Airlines. Her folks live near Amesterdam, and do not like her traveling so well; she is the youngest of several children. However, her parents want her to do what will make her happy, said she.

I said, "Mr. Poole and I are bound for Karachi." This causing no comment, I added, "From there we go 600 miles inland to Afghanistan," and with this our young Dutch friend was seized with consternation, and gesticulated with both hands in emphatic disapproval.

The English lady said her husband operated a steamship line out of Basra in Iraq. "The ships are named 'Afghanistan,' 'Turkestan,' 'Pakistan,' 'Baluchistan,' etc.," said she.

We looked over some goods an Arab had on display next to the dining room. The Damascus linens impressed me as most beautiful; colors and designs were exquisite. The English lady helped me select a set to send home and was for driving a good bargain with the Arab merchant.

After that I took a walk about the airport gardens, mostly shrubbery in the nature of desert plants being tried out, and met a Dutchman bound for Calcutta. We conversed for a few minutes, he in Dutch and I in English. Then I went into the airport waiting room and sat down on a bench. Right away two Arabs appeared, one with a small basin of water over an oil or alcohol burner, which was placed on the floor, the other with a towel. The first man lathered my face and gave me a good shave. The second led me to a tap of running water and I bathed my face, after which he poured into my hands some strongly perfumed "after shave." This I proceeded to use vigorously, much to the amusement of both Arabs.

*   *   *

At this moment we are flying southeasterly over the Syrian desert at 243 m.p.h. and 11,500 feet altitude. Rolling dunes. No vegetation. Below is an oasis of possibly ten acres, and a silvery water surface glitters among date palm trees.

We have covered 360 miles of this barren waste in one and one-half hours and are now approaching the Euphrates and Tigris River valleys, about 125 miles southwest of Bagdad. There appears to be no habitation but now the desert is merging into swamp lands and off to the right is a long narrow lake reaching to the horizon and paralleling a single river channel, for back there, at the town of Al Qurna, the Tigris and Euphrates have joined to form Shatt al Arab, the one channel leading to the Persian Gulf.

Coming in for a landing at Basra, one looks down on the flat-topped adobe houses, each surrounding a court, and the narrow, winding streets, and wonders why there is such a compact arrangement of dwellings when all about is open country. Date palm plantations extend on both sides of the river far toward the south. They evidently occupy the higher ground along the river from Basra to salt water at the head of the Persian Gulf some sixty miles away. A number of freighters are in port.

Upon leaving the plane, Iraq authorities asked each passenger if he had just come from Israel. Had the answer been "Yes," he would have been required to remain aboard the plane.

26

FLIGHT TO HOLLAND AND KARACHI

In the waiting room we were served tea.

Poole and I met the Scotch husband of the English lady, a very friendly man, and he was indeed happy to see his baby daughter for the first time and his attractive wife, who had been in Scotland for seven months. They wanted us to come out to see their home, but this was impossible as the plane would leave in one-half hour.

"Well, stop to see us when through here again. Just inquire for the Strick Steamship Company," they said.

Leaving Basra I took a parting look at this valley where supposedly the Garden of Eden had once existed. What a perfect set-up for an all-inclusive reclamation project — river improvement and harbor development, levees to prevent overflow, drainage to remove excess surface and ground water, impounding works for water storage, diversion weirs, canal and lateral systems, vast agricultural development. Could not wealth from their oil production help provide a modern Garden of Eden for the people of Iraq?

And then at 4:30 p.m. we were aloft and approaching Abadan and the head of the Persian Gulf, and, after that, crossing over the deserts of Iran and Pakistan — 1,100 miles to Karachi. As the late afternoon was hazy with dusk approaching, a distinct view of the landscape was difficult. At 8:50 p.m., Karachi.

Some one hundred or more people — Europeans — were waiting at the airfield to go somewhere. A Mr. Fuller helped us get through the customs and immigration office and took us to barracks formerly occupied by the U. S. Air Force.

At the customs a Pakistani lady asked would I give her a coin — just anything — so I handed her a guilder.

"Throw fear to the wind."
— Aristophanes
(446 — 380 B.C.)

III

Rail to Quetta --
On to Kandahar

CHAPTER III

Rail to Quetta -- On to Kandahar

WELL FOLKS, I have just gotten comfortably settled in a railway train out of Karachi, Pakistan, which city we left at 12:40 p.m.

This morning at breakfast we met Mr. Fred Koerner, a top engineer for the Company. He had just come from Afghanistan and was taking a plane to another project on the island of Ceylon.

I changed two American dollars into six Pakistan rupees for possible use en route. Mr. Fuller, local representative for the Company, drove us into Karachi, a distance of perhaps ten miles, to take the train.

Going into the city over a paved highway, Fuller was driving a new Chevrolet sedan with right-hand drive. One drives on the left side of the road here. I saw several kinds of transportation: turbaned men on donkeys with a large basket on either side; one donkey very small, pulling a two-wheeled cart loaded high; camels drawing rubber-tired

31

trailers, some at a patient slow walk, others on a trot; men
with pedicars carrying one or two passengers; bicycles and
motorcycles; modern buses; a few automobiles; water buf-
falos pulling trailers; oxen pulling trailers.

I saw just a little of the city — not downtown — a few
homes with low walls about, shrubbery, grass and flowers
and the brilliant bougainvilla indicating somewhat of a
frostless climate. There were yellow stone homes, as well
as ones of adobe. At one place were acres of miniature tent-
shaped dwellings very close together, and not far away were
large herds of water buffalo cows and Brahma cows. Never
before had I seen people living like this — refugees from a
troubled world.

As we approached the railway station, a motley crowd
was waiting to see the train pull out, people in all manner
of attire. Red-coated porters took our baggage. One man
balanced my suitcase flatwise on top of his head, while
another placed my zipper bag and another like it on top. He
balanced these some 100 pounds on top of his head, and I
followed him past many cars of the long train to our compartment, which we entered by a side door. I noticed some
passengers being seated on wooden benches in what looked
like cattle cars in the United States. Fuller had seen to it
that Baker, Poole and I had been provided with the necessary papers, and these were intrusted with me to carry.
"Don't lose these," said he.

An express agent, Mr. Wilson, came into the car to greet
us, saying, "You men look quite too decent for this trip,"
and Fuller added "Yes, I advised them to change to khaki."

Of course we knew that would have been the better way
to dress, but we also realized that the most practical way to
carry our good suits brought from home was to wear them.

The Pakistan army captain assigned to this compartment with us did not show up. "Well, cheerio, men," said

Wilson. "I'll see you again in two years!" I took a moment
to think over this last remark.

This compartment is the width of the car and twelve
feet long, with two lower and two upper bunks and two
chairs, and private lavatory through the door at the end.
All of our gear is in here with us (including Baker's golf
clubs!) Poole and Baker are stretched out reading and I am
writing by a window. Fuller has provided us with our own
food, coffee and water for the trip. We have just had lunch
consisting of ham sandwiches, apples and coffee.

Since leaving Karachi, we have been traveling through
a country almost identical to the deserts of southern California, Arizona or Nevada — with cactus and low thorny
bushes that look like mesquite — and entirely uninhabited,
seemingly, except near railway stations, although there are
at long intervals a few tents or brush shelters and flocks of
goats, and white stone section houses.

We are passing Braudabad, just a depot and large water
tank — a low stone building surrounded with a wide brush
fence, and groups of men sitting cross-legged on the ground.
I saw one young man with two wives unveiled, one with a
baby in arms, and all were well-dressed; a herd of goats, a
flower garden, a circular stone wall with a well inside and
a man pulling up a bucket of water with a windlass; boys
selling food on trays swarming with flies; an old man with a
bucket of water and cup to serve the passengers; an old
woman — she looked to be a hundred — asking for alms . . .
and the train pulls on through the desert.

I have my USAF Aeronautical Chart of this area spread
out on the floor and am watching it critically. Soon we
should be along the Indus River.

More goat herds, and a patch of dry cultivated ground.
This land would produce like the Salt River Valley if under irrigation. The train stops at Jhimpir. A man sticks his

head through the window, or tries to, and asks some unintelligible questions; another with food inside a screened cage balanced on his head; a boy with hard boiled eggs; a few date palms. I hope you can follow me, folks; now we cross another wide sandy arroyo just like in Arizona.

We have come out into the wide Indus River Valley, a flat desert place except for those few trees that look like mesquite, and some irrigated lands near the wide dry river bed. It is practically uninhabited. I see a man driving a white goat followed by a camel, and farther on, two men riding a camel; and then one donkey heavily laden, followed by a half dozen people. Close to the track a stack of tall grain is being threshed, but the few people here are quitting for the day.

The sun is setting like a giant yellow ball hovering over the desert horizon, and a lone camel bearing two men is heading through the brush in that direction.

This is not the Indus River Valley I had always pictured from my school geography — with teeming millions of people — no!

It's too dark in this car to write more. So that's all for tonight, folks.

*　　*　　*

Had a fairly restful night on the upper bunk. That canvas bed roll, supplied to each man by Fuller, contained two blankets, a pillow and sheets.

Shortly after dark last night at one station, there was a violent and insistent knocking at our outside door. This we ignored. Our concern was to keep both windows and door securely bolted. Afterwards Baker suggested it might have been the train conductor. At no station had we ventured getting off the train to mingle with the people on the depot platform; a wise precaution, we thought.

34

During the night we had continued northerly along the west side of the Indus River in the Province of Sind.

The train stopped at many small towns, like Sehwan, Dadu and Larkana. Aroused, I would peer out at the people as they talked with shrill voices and hurried excitedly getting on or off the train. Many carried heavy rolls of baggage on their heads.

It is now early forenoon and we are leaving the Indus River valley at Shikapur. The railway leads northwesterly through the provinces of Kalat and Baluchistan. For several hours there is the far-spread desert with numerous dry washes indicating much run-off in times of heavy rain. No signs of life but lone flocks of sheep for long distances. Over there a half-mile stands a shepherd, motionless. He wears red loose garments and nearby the animals nibble on short bunches of some desert plant. It looks windy and cold out there. We are getting away from the warm coastal climate and approaching higher levels.

The train has stopped at lonely looking villages such as Jacobabad, Bellpat and Sibi ("apples"), and now cautiously follows a succession of short curves through a jumble of gigantic blocks of rock. These look like remains of outcroppings ruthlessly strewn about by terrific earth movements of long ago. Through or under these obstructions the track follows a series of tunnels.

Now we reach the summit of historic Bolan Pass. Through this corridor ventured British expeditionary forces from India en route to do battle with the Afghan tribesmen during the war of 1838-42. They were under the command of General Nott.

After this we descend to a plateau country flanked on both sides by mountains with peaks 10,000 to 11,000 feet in elevation, some are snow-capped. It's getting colder outside and

AFGHANISTAN VENTURE

I put on my fleece-lined leather jacket and turn up the huge collar.

Caravans of camels are passing in both directions along the roadway paralleling the railroad grade.

And now we are entering Quetta, a city of much importance in Baluchistan, a trading center and gateway to Afghanistan. The railway continues to Chaman on the Afghan border sixty miles away. The long train comes to a stop. Here is much activity. A motley crowd of civilians and Pakistan soldiers is much in evidence.

Immediately there is a loud hammering on the door of our compartment, accompanied by shouts of "Em-kay-ay! "Em-kay-ay!" Without hesitation this time, we unbolt the door to let in a Pakistani who introduced himself as "James," and behind him filed several porters who began grabbing up baggage and bed rolls. We followed them out to a waiting Chevrolet sedan and James got us past railway and government officials. Then, after a short stop in the market place, we were off on this, the last lap of our journey, to the border of Afghanistan at Chaman.

Across from the railway station in Quetta is a military compound, and soldiers were conspicuous everywhere. Here it was, I was told, that not so long ago as this train pulled into the station, machine guns raked the cars. Hindu attacked Moslem; Moslem attacked Hindu, until 900 men, women and children were cruelly slain on the train and in and around the railway depot.

This is also a resort city. Those who can afford it come to these higher altitudes of 5,000 to 7,000 feet in the surrounding plains to escape the summer heat at lower elevations. There is a scattering of English people here. Quetta is the best-looking city we have seen in Pakistan — cleaner, and the people look better clothed and fed.

On the road to Chaman we passed the military post of

Pishin. Pakistani soldiers in Scottish kilts played soccer on the athletic field — and basketball — fine-looking young men.

Passes bristle with formidable fortifications — tank traps facing north. En route were several villages with bazaars on either side of the road. At each town a long pole extended between posts on either side of the road barring traffic. A man would run out with a book in which to get the driver to sign up. Others would then remove the pole to let us pass. A small but curious crowd would gather to look us over. All appeared friendly.

We crossed two mountain ranges, the first through a pass upwards of 7,000 feet high. There were also two valleys, that of the Karanya Lora and the Pishin Lora; in both was some evidence of irrigated agriculture. On each side were peaks from 8,000 to 11,500 feet in altitude. James was a fast but safe and efficient driver.

At the border town of Chaman (meaning "lawn" or "meadow") we were met by a Mr. Kelly of M-K-A, who took our papers and handed them to Pakistani border officials. Then we went into his office where, around a big table, we were served (not tea but) coffee, and got warm before an open fireplace.

Here we changed to another car driven by an Afghan who helped us through the customs. While waiting in the car along the street for our papers to be processed by Pakistani officials, I had a good chance to size up this town. I noticed barbed wire entanglements alongside the road, the side towards Afghanistan; two lorries loaded to about three times their capacities with cases of merchandise; a camel packed high with firewood was made to kneel in front of a dwelling, unloaded and let through a gate into a compound; a young couple walked past, the woman or girl being completely covered with a blue silky robe with fancy sandals to match; two Brahma oxen hauling a huge wooden cart; a boy, or two boys, showed off with a new motorcycle; two fifteen-year-olds, nice looking but for dirty necks and need of hair cuts, stood by our car and with black twinkling eyes asked unintelligible questions. I wondered if their amusement did not center on my soft, wide-brimmed, high-crowned gray felt hat, or were they intrigued by the fleece-lined, fleece-covered collar of my leather jacket? Finally an older boy came out of the customs office and apparently admonished the boys to be more polite to strangers — but at this they giggled beyond control. Then one of them backed off, rolled his jacket of goat hide around his head, and with fierce look, imitated an infuriated goat charging at me, a sheep. At this I laughed understandingly.

Then Ghulam, our driver and sponsor, appeared from the customs office with our papers. As we proceeded down the road, said Ghulam, "At that gate back there we left Pakistan. We are now in no-man's land. Ahead of us at that next gate is the Afghan border."

"What are those barbed wire obstructions for?" I queried. Said Ghulam, "Sometimes there is a little trouble and there is musketry fire across the border."

Just then we passed through the second gate and drew up at the Afghan customs house. Ghulam went in with our papers.

At that moment a young soldier came out of the adobe building, laid aside his rifle and cap and stood very erect facing the west — and the glory of the setting sun. A wide expanse of desert was bathed in light unbelievably golden. Slowly this wondrous lemon yellow ball of fire was seemingly being submerged and extinguished by the hazy mystical blue of the far distant desert horizon. A moment later the rugged precipitous mountains, slightly toward the north, were receiving their crown and share of the evening's golden brilliance.

Awed and impressed — moved — I turned and stood as it were, by the side of this soldier lad throughout his devotions, he in reverence to Allah, I to God . . . one and the same — the Great Architect and Ruler of the Universe.

Deep humility, reverence and sincerity were plainly expressed in his brown face and black eyes, as we suddenly exchanged momentary glances of understanding.

And this was the manner of my entrance into Afghanistan — this 29th day of January, 1951.

Soon we were passing through another gate where a pole had been let down, and flanking each side was a short row of bazaars. Dark people in strange clothing crowded close to get a good look at these foreigners. Such was Spin Baldak.

And then it was seventy-five miles to Kandahar over a straight concrete paved highway constructed by the Company — straight across the desert and between tall mountains, sharp and peaked, rising abruptly from the desert plains — and the road led across many dry arroyos such as those around Palm Springs and Indio.

Once Ghulam (Go-lam) slowed down for a single roadside bazaar. Here turbaned men sat cross-legged on the ground by lantern light, silently smoking water pipes. Suddenly two gazelle bounded across the glare of our headlights; we passed two camel caravans; a young camel on the loose carelessly ambled from the wayside blackness across the road, narrowly escaping injury.

"Ghulam, what are those bright lights ahead?" I queried.

"That is the Em-Kay-Ay Camp at Manzel Bagh," said he.

And that's all for now, folks.

39

AFGHANISTAN VENTURE

"The heavens declare the glory of God;
and the firmament showeth his handi-
work. — There is no speech nor
language where their voice is not heard. . . .
In my Father's house are many mansions."

— Holy Bible

IV
First Weeks in Afghanistan

Manzel Bagh
Headquarters of Morrison-Knudsen
  Afghanistan, Inc.
Office — Warehouses — Shop —
  Living Quarters — Men
On to Well of the Fig Tree
In Conference
The Gazelle Hunt
Swamp in the Desert — Wild Fowl
  Paradise
Ford Blows Up
Afoot with the Camels — Friends in
  the Desert
Meet the Kharoti
Girishk on Juma
Mike, Luke, Mark — Little Johnny
Street Crowds — Bazaars — Wares
The Fortress Impregnable — Key to
  Ancient Conquest
Government Building — New Buick
Province of Kandahar
Moslem Open Air Service — The

CHAPTER IV

First Weeks in Afghanistan

WELL, THIS MANZEL BAGH (home garden) is the headquarters of Morrison- Knudsen Afghanistan, Inc., for all its operations in Afghanistan. It is just a couple of miles outside the city of Kandahar. Here are the administrative offices; management, engineering, accounting, purchasing, storage, machine shops, garage, mess and recreational facilities, medical and hospital.

A compound of possibly sixty acres is surrounded by an adobe wall some fifteen feet high. This is ancient but in a state of good repair — and somewhat artistic, with a continuous series of archways in effect, only they are closed and recessed.

The big warehouses are of adobe, except that the roofs are of galvanized iron; and most other buildings are of adobe except the offices.

A neat new building of masonry houses the offices.

43

Dormitories are long rows of adobe barracks divided into double rooms.

Kitchen and dining hall are neatly housed in a white building, and nearby, refrigeration is available.

Families live in one- or two-bedroom cottages, surrounded by lawns and flower and vegetable gardens.

Within the compound are Company vegetable and flower plots and many shade trees. There is the hospital and recreation hall, and radio department, all housed in a large, imposing, two-story white adobe building — and this is known as the King's Palace, because before the advent of the Company, Manzel Bagh was actually occupied a portion of the year by the King.

It was in this palace that Baker, Poole and I spent our first night in Afghanistan — quite a luxuriously-furnished apartment, it seemed to us. Baker had with him a full set of golf equipment, and at breakfast the next morning made inquiries about facilities for playing this game. After this incident he was eyed oddly by others in the dining hall.

About eighty at one time could be fed in the mess hall at ten large tables, only on this particular day there was less than half this many men.

One table was occupied by Italians. They are mechanics. They conversed in Italian and were given food to which they were accustomed in faraway Italy.

Likewise the Filipino boys sat by themselves. They do office engineering and drafting, and some also work in the accounting department. They speak Tagalog when by themselves, good English otherwise. They were enjoying food prepared in the same way as at home, particularly rice and meats.

We men from the United States also were eating apart from the others, for the same reasons as were the Filipinos and Italians.

"Whitey" Leaders, genial steward, beamed over this motley breakfast assemblage and directed the kitchen and serving personnel — Afghans dressed in white jackets and caps.

"After breakfast, come over to the office," said handsome Bill Hastings, in charge of payrolls, turning to Poole, Baker and me.

Soon General Manager T. Y. Johnston ("Ted"), in his office was saying to me, "Jones, you got here sooner than we expected, but we're sure glad to see you. We are on the spot. This thing has mushroomed faster than we expected, but we'll come out all right. Your reputation has preceded you. The experience you have had will be most helpful to us."

Somewhat embarrassed, I returned, "You overrate me. But I will put into this assignment my very best efforts."

In all I stayed two nights and a day at these Manzel Bagh headquarters, meeting the chief engineer, his field engineer, the chief construction superintendent and many others. I was told that on the following day, the 31st, I would be taken 100 miles west to our camp at Chah-i-anjir.

So on Wednesday morning early we were rolling westward down the Arghandab and Helmand river valleys to the Boghra Project, where a main canal and laterals were under construction. Our route led through the outskirts, that is outside of the ancient walls surrounding the city of Kandahar.

Approaching the city, the way was blocked by camel and burro trains. In a field across from the woolen mills, several hundred people were waiting beside large piles of wool or goat hair. There were a number of large, nice homes with flower gardens and white walls about. Many well-dressed people were riding in fancy carts, each pulled by a horse. A company of soldiers marched out of the military compound; others got up and saluted as we passed.

In our car was Hal Craig, chief field engineer, and Jacinto Sabiniano recently from the Philippines. We passed orchards and small fields surrounded by low adobe walls. This road leads to Girishk, Farah and Herat. Further along we saw only sheep herds miles apart, camel caravans at long intervals, a wayside bazaar with men sitting solemnly on their heels, motionless.

Arriving at Chah-i-anjir we found several top Company men had preceded us. In the recreation hall they were discussing what to say to several high Afghan officials due in here after lunch. The conference was to concern the immediate development of some 16,000 acres near here and the settlement on it of nomadic tribesmen. This was to be the first unit of the entire project, consisting, I was told, of about 165,000 acres. So this was what the chief engineer in San Francisco meant when he had told me we've got to put the first unit of the Boghra Project, 16,000 acres, under a lateral distribution system at once. He had said to me, "You will work along with the Afghan Agricultural Commission on this development."

So about 3 p.m. I had my first introduction to Noor Mohammed, chief of the Agricultural Commission, whom various ones insisted on addressing as "His Excellency." With him was Jan Mohammed, director of building construction. They had with them an interpreter and, together with our own representing the Company, a very enlightening conversation ensued. . . . But more about these matters at another time.

Yesterday we left our camp — "Well of the Fig Tree" to you, folks; "Chah-i-anjir" to us — about sunrise to follow down the Boghra Canal some fifty kilometers to look over construction in progress. I say "we." There were Hal Craig,

Ed Carter and I. It had become very cold during the night —
down to 12° F — too cold even for the Afghans to do much
work. Hal said to Ed, "Have you the knives?" and Ed had
replied, "Just my own — that's enough."

We passed a few mud huts and at long intervals droves
of fat-tailed sheep tended by extremely dark men with cloth
bands around their heads and faces and wearing long whit-
ish gray cloaks with wide flat sleeves reaching to their knees.
Dogs as big and strong as the huskies of the Canadian
Northwest Territories, and looking like them or wolves,
would bound out from the herd to bark at us. A group of
five men would be sitting on their haunches upright around
a little fire — motionless and silent — nomads of the desert;
and all about them was the herd seeking shelter from the
cold in the bed of the dry canal.

Far out on the desert, the concrete poured yesterday for
a bridge crossing the canal appeared to be frozen, as it had
not been entirely protected from low temperatures. And
then:

Hal: "Are they over that way?"

Ed: "No."

I couldn't make out this conversation. It was getting
well past mid-forenoon and warming up fast in the bright
sunshine. We drove on.

Ed to construction foreman: "Did you see any?"

Construction foreman, making slight hand gesture indicating a fan-shaped stretch of desert at least fifty miles long
and half as wide: "Over there!"

My curiosity was increasing by the moment, but I remained silent.

Hal: "You shoot, Ed! I'll do the driving."

Ed: "Turn left on that ridge ahead."

As the Chevrolet moves swiftly across the desert, we scan the horizon to the left, front and right.

Taking a chance on what they were after — bandits or wild game, I wasn't sure which — I shouted, "There's two over there!" and Hal turned sharply to the right speeding toward two objects a mile away that appeared to move. They proved to be low clumps of brush!

We circle and turn down shallow depressions — over a low ridge. Not a moving object in sight.

Some thirty-five miles farther, Ed: "They are likely bedded down. It's so cold."

Another half hour of rapid driving. Ed: "Turn down the wasteway!"

Suddenly, Hal: "There they go!"

I counted sixteen camels of all sizes in the direction pointed — big ones, little ones, just grazing on what little there was to eat, scattered out. They didn't notice the approach of the swiftly moving car. "Those are camels!" I said.

Hal: "No! Beyond the camels! See them running!"

Ed: "Bear off to the right! Head them down the swale!"

Hal speeds up to fifty or more and we are on the left flank of a file of seven fleet-running gazelle, their movements as graceful as antelopes.

Hal: "That second buck looks the best. Get him."

Ed: "OK, separate him out!"

Hal speeds closer to the swiftly moving file. The second buck and a doe turn off. Two shots from Ed's rifle and the buck turns end for end four times!

Ed and I hold him up, cut the throat and bleed him. Hal draws him. Live weight, sixty pounds . . . and into Hal's refrigerator at Manzel Bagh this buck will go!

Further along there was another file of nine. Then there were two pairs by themselves. This made twenty in all, and they were running swiftly. But one was all we wanted just then.

Well, enough for that — a gazelle hunt in Afghanistan!

* * *

Already I'm getting oriented over this prospective 165,-000-acre irrigation project, traveling by the most available means. For example, immediately after an early breakfast this morning, I set forth to determine what is finally becoming of a large stream of water being discharged into the desert from a section of unfinished main canal. A large lake had formed — a veritable paradise for innumerable waterfowl. Ducks and geese rose in clouds from this swampland. Beyond that, supposedly, the water finds its way deviously toward the Helmand River, finally being lost in the shifting sands.

I kept well back from the shoreline of the shallow water, fearing boggy ground.

Camel caravans could be seen on the far horizon beyond the lake. Nearer by, a large flock of fat tailed sheep evidently were finding wild growing sustenance on the moist land. The shepherd watched me from a distance of one-fourth mile. His only movement was a slow turning of head like a desert owl, as his gaze followed my progress.

The going was difficult — the topsoil looked dangerously moist and treacherous. In spite of this, I noted how smoothly the motor of this battered old Ford pickup tackled the job. Suddenly without warning, the engine fairly exploded with a loud report, sending steam and hot water over windshield and cab.

Now what to do? The nomad walked over, his bearded face expressionless; but I imagined him amusedly interested.

49

Pointing to ancient Fort Nad-i-ali some eight or ten miles away, I indicated I would leave the car and join an approaching caravan headed in that direction. This fort loomed up in the distance as though surrounded by a large lake, due to a mirage effect.

I took from the car a brand new shovel gotten this morning from the warehouse, because I didn't want to lose it, and for protection should I pass near a nomad camp, where dogs charge forth like ferocious wolves. I walked for two miles before intercepting and overtaking the caravan. Glancing back at first, I noticed that the shepherd had followed me for a ways and then stopped still, watching me fixedly.

I soon overtook one of the camel drivers who seemed to be having trouble with his footgear, and passed him. He said nothing. Neither did I. Later this man overtook me and we walked side by side as we caught up with the camels and other five drivers who were walking.

"Ma-da-bashi!" said I, using some Persian expression I had just acquired meaning "may you never get tired."

At this their sober expressions changed to smiles and they plied me with many questions. These I could not comprehend. One was quite interested in my fleece-lined jacket, and I showed him how it was lined with heavy wool and zipped up the front. Where was I going? To Fort Nad-i-ali and Chah-i-anjir.

Each camel was loaded with possibly 400 pounds of wood, carefully balanced, by means of a sort of saddle, to the hump. There were twelve camels. I noticed that one walked sideways because his load needed adjusting. I pointed this out to the man who appeared to be his owner, and helped him get the load better balanced. He smiled and seemed pleased at this.

50

One man carried a rather wicked looking weapon — a hardwood 2-inch stick to which was attached an 18-inch bayonet at one end and a pointed steel shoe at the other — for sticking into the ground so that it could be handy for use at night, I concluded.

All these men wore sharp beards, white turbans and *pustins* or shepherds' cloaks that looked to be made of felt about a half-inch thick, with eight-inch sleeves closed at ends and reaching below knees. Their legs were bare and also their feet, except for some skins or furs tied on for shoes.

I trudged along with them for about two hours. Hardly a man spoke. The camels walked along patiently and noiselessly, their broad padded feet leaving scarcely any impression on the desert sand.

Every now and then I would stop to use the shovel by way of inspecting the topsoil, as this land was part of the project. I asked one man what he thought of my new shovel, but he only smiled and said nothing.

Gradually we were approaching a large camp of some 125 families near the government agricultural experiment station at Fort Nad-i-ali. The Afghan Agricultural Commission expects to settle these Kharoti on land in this vicinity to be irrigated soon. They are from the foothills of Pakhtunistan and are a very industrious clan. From this distance I could already see people coming out to greet the camel outfit, and there was a much longer one following not far behind.

The camels stopped in pairs side by side. Immediately I was surrounded as would be a man from Mars. They wanted me to stop for *chay* (tea) — how soon could they move on to the land? — dogs barked, children came running, unveiled women looked out of tent entrances and smiled modestly. Camels and goats were everywhere. Besides the tents, there were small adobe huts partly in the ground, with roofs of woven willow mats and brush piled along the leeward side to break the north wind.

To me these Kharoti appeared as primitive as our American Indians of a former day.

*　　*　　*

Well, folks, I must tell you now about our trip to Girishk last Juma, the Afghan Sunday, and our work holiday.

There were Walt Flannery, my temporary roommate; Wright Holstein, farm superintendent from Fresno; and a number of Afghans who work on Walt's drilling operations crew. Walt has assigned each Afghan a nickname — like "Luke," "Mike," "Mark," etc., and I noticed each seemed proud to be called by these nicknames. Walt is from New York City and has charge of diamond drill operations all over the Company's Afghan projects. One of his latest jobs was investigation of a mountain near Kabul said to be rich, exceedingly so, in chrome ore. Walt confirms this.

Well, we entered the town along the main street in a flashy yellow Ford pick-up and were at once the object of curious attention.

All about crowded people in turbans and loose varicolored garments — *pustins* in all shades of gray from long usage. Some were barefooted, some with sandals skilfully made from the tread of old automobile tires.

And there were camels and burros, some loaded and going places, others just idly resting.

A policeman at the main intersection waved us forward as he parted the pedestrians, and we finally parked.

There are three or four blocks along the main street occupied by bazaars of all descriptions, and two streams of water run swiftly in channels on either side. At an imposing elevation above the town on a precipitous bluff stands the remains of an ancient fortress of massive adobe walls. The streets are lined with mulberry trees, bare-limbed yet in the cold of winter.

First we spent some time looking in the bazaars. In all, the proprietors sat very solemnly on their haunches, surrounded to the floor by their tent-like clothing. It was cold but sunshiny, and we discovered they had small pots of burning charcoal under them for warmth.

"Luke," otherwise on the payroll identified as Reza Mahmud, and one of Flannery's crew, walked along with me. Occasionally he would slap me on the back in a friendly fashion after I had made some remark he may have, or have not, understood.

Little "Johnny," whose real name is Ghulam Dastigar — he is but about fifteen years old — had a brother who owned a bazaar. So he was fitted up with a new outfit from turban to shoes.

We saw for sale large baskets of raisins, beans, rock salt, tea, rice, flour and brightly-colored cotton fabrics. Suddenly Walt spotted two leopard skins for which the man wanted 200 *afghanis* apiece. *(Afghani* equals six cents U.S. officially, or three cents on open market.) So "Mark" (otherwise Eesah) carried these skins proudly along for Walt.

We climbed up the face of the bluff, following the steep path, into the old fort, which has an enclosed area of five acres within its imposing walls. There are two gates, one at the foot of the bluff and one leading in from the desert on top of the bluff. The walls are probably twenty-five feet thick and fifty feet high. At the corners and at intervals along the walls are towers or turrets. I walked to the top of a corner one and out along the parapet, five-foot wall in which are port openings at regular intervals slanting outward and downward. Here the ancient bow and arrow warriors, or more modern riflemen, could cover the attacking forces on the ground or repel any forces that attempted to scale the walls between the towers. One could see far out over the desert and the Helmand River Valley to other ancient fortresses and could well believe that messages by fire at night and reflected sun's rays in day, passed between the garrisons of these fortifications . . . westerly toward Farah; up the Helmand River toward Sangin; and down it toward Qala Bist. We could readily follow the course of the river in the distance from these towers.

Inside the compound were the living quarters of these ancient warriors and yard space for their animals and equipment. In places the structure is partly in ruins, yet by its general appearance from a distance, it must appear like it did a long time ago. It allegedly dates back to the days of Alexander the Great . . . but who knows for certain? . . . Many centuries, anyway. The generation living here now — the local people, that is — appear incapable of building any structure such as this, with its massive strength and pleasing proportions. And so it would seem these people are remnants of a more advanced race.

Then Holstein and I walked down into the town again, past the Government building, and went inside. Well, folks, don't get the idea of anything grand. It is just an adobe structure with offices and rooms of the plainest kind — openings for windows with no glass, no screens. Out in front under canvas a new Buick was parked, of beautiful maroon. It belonged to the district governor, no doubt.

You see, the Province of Kandahar, of which the City of Kandahar is the capital, is divided into areas or districts, each with a local governor. The provincial head is the governor-general. The Province of Kandahar is some 200 miles wide by 325 miles long and confronts Pakistan along a 375-mile border. It is comparable in size to our state of North Dakota.

We asked Johnny would the people inside that large

open space object if we entered. No, it would be all right. All over the open area men sat on their haunches, and also in the corridor of a building partly open to the outside . . . a mosque. A voice coming from within was reading or chanting and the people sat with bowed heads.

Across the street we saw a couple of women, or girls, veiled from head to foot, watching from sitting positions in a doorway. They followed our movements curiously.

We walked past a public bath house. Camels stood nearby with loads of brush brought from long distances out on the desert. A boy with a wooden pronged fork poked the brush through an opening in an adobe wall to keep the fire burning under the vessel containing the water.

A man with a bucket made of skins dipped water from the swift-running stream on one side of the street and threw it halfway across to keep down the dust.

We went towards the outskirts of the town and here saw many individual homes of adobe with areas of perhaps a half to two acres surrounded by six- to eight-feet high adobe walls — some with growing wheat, or a little pasture or fruit trees.

Back again in the bazaars, we saw many kinds of things from eatables to cloth. There were bakeries. The bread is of whole wheat ground up and made into a paste with water and baked in oval slabs about one-half inch thick.

The lad, Johnny, stayed pretty close to us. Said I, "Johnny, who are those two men with the high black boots?" Their cheekbones were high, eyes slightly slanting — like Mongols.

"They are Russians," said Johnny, "or Turkmen."

There were blacksmith shops, shoe shops, tailor shops — several hundred, in stalls about twenty by twenty feet. The back part of each shop was curtained off and presumably this was where the proprietor lived with his family.

On a street corner in front of an eating place a man was feeding his little girl. Occasionally she helped herself from a common bowl filled with curd.

Nearby, four little sisters, five to ten, wearing pantalets, sat on the ground in front of a bazaar. Occasionally they would cover their faces with thin pink veils thrown loosely over their shoulders.

As we walked along a small crowd followed. My leather jacket, heavy field shoes and leather leggings were objects of curious attention. Various ones wanted to know how the zipper functioned, and smiled appreciatively when shown.

I would feel the material of their *pustins* (pooseen), the long white cloaks with the long flat sleeves sewed up at the ends. The material appeared to be felt, a non-woven fabric of wool matted together apparently by pressure. It was warm and comfortable for this cold weather.

Walt took down from a rack a pair of trousers *(azar)*. Holding them up they measured three feet across at the waist. At this the crowd chuckled with subdued glee. The outside seam of the legs extended straight down from the waist. The inside seam slanted outwards, leaving an opening of about ten inches at the bottom which could be closed tight about the ankle by a draw cord, as could be the waist. This arrangement produces the desirable baggy effect.

With these baggy trousers is usually worn the *pehran*, something like an American night shirt, reaching down outside to the knees, or lower. Over the *pehran* is often worn an ordinary western vest, called a *sad-ree*. Or, instead of a *sad-ree*, a pleasing combination is a finely tailored coat, like we might wear.

The turban is worn about the head — a long narrow cloth of various colors, wound around and around a sort of small canvas skull cap of brilliant design that fits on top

56

of the head. The end of the turban is tucked under, or hangs loosely over face or back of neck.

While Walt picked out for himself a cap, turban, *azar* and *pehran,* quite a lot of interested people had collected to watch. There was further subdued merriment, especially when "Mark" would proudly display the leopard skins for Walt's benefit.

Several animals — goats, sheep and cattle — were being butchered in alleys just off the main streets.

On a side street we heard shrill shouting. The police paid no attention, nor did few others but us. An Afghan Jewish merchant and a customer were wrangling over a pair of shoes — pulling, pushing, wrestling — in an angry manner for control of the footgear.

*   *   *

Sunday evening, folks — but we had our Sunday on Juma, two days ago. This evening we had a moving picture film in the camp recreation hall. . . . "Kill the Umpire," starring Victor McLaughlin. Usually a film gets here about once a week and is passed around to the several camps — Kajakai Dam, Arghandab Dam, Chah-i-anjir, Manzel Bagh.

Did I tell you? There are three dams under construction. One on the Helmand River about seventy-five miles upstream from Girishk, one on the Arghandab River about thirty miles above Kandahar, and one near Kabul, the capital.

I guess I told you the job I am on is a 165,000-acre development under irrigation along the Helmand River and on the Dasht-i-Margo, and it literally is just that, a "desert of death" for anyone who does not observe the laws of nature prescribed for all life within its scope.

The diversion weir near Girishk is completed and water may be diverted into the Boghra Canal out of the Helmand

Rud to its full capacity of 2,300 cubic feet per second, or enough water to irrigate nicely 15,000 acres in 24 hours, if all arrangements are in readiness for its distribution along the canal to the laterals, field ditches and fields of growing crops.

The Boghra Canal and structures are around eighty per cent complete and construction of the laterals and Shamalon Canal is getting underway. This last parallels the Helmand River and will make possible an all-the-year-round supply of water to many existing canals, and in addition to new lands not now cultivated.

Several days ago I had my first experience with reinforced concrete construction by Afghan labor. It was at a chute structure some sixty-five kilometers from camp on the East Marja Desert, and very early on a cold morning. Some fifty men were waiting to begin work with heavy construction equipment being readied for operation.

Here was a motley crew dressed in turbans of several hues and shades, long loose shirts and baggy pantaloons. Some were barefoot, some in sandals or shoes made of furs or just from worn-out automobile casings. Some were in tatters. Shortly they had the Ingersall-Rand air compressor in operation. The big concrete mixer was being fed with just the right proportions of sand, gravel, cement and water; the dump trucks were rolling; the crane was moving cautiously into position; and soon concrete was rolling continuously into the forms. One Afghan started in a businesslike manner to take samples of the concrete for testing in our concrete laboratory. He would pour a sample into a steel cylinder open at both ends and resting vertically on a board, moving a steel rod up and down the while to consolidate the mass. Then he would level off the top.

The foreman, Charley Dale from San Bernardino, California, winked. I said that nothing like this had I ever seen before. Charley said he hadn't either prior to coming to Afghanistan. But they were doing all right. . . .

Yesterday and today Ed Carter and I did some hunting. He used the shotgun while I circled about in the pickup to round up or stir up the ducks and make them fly over the spot where Ed was trying to keep out of sight. We got enough for the table — mallards, fat and large. There were clouds of teal, but of such swift wing that they were difficult targets. There is a reddish duck here I've not seen before, also a duck with white front and white tail.

Last evening three men arrived who said they are Austrians teaching school in Kabul, and now on a three-months vacation. They are looking over this part of Afghanistan, they said. One had short cropped hair, and the other two would click their heels and address him as *"Tochtor."* Charlie Jones said they looked like ex-gestapos to him, so promptly drove them over to Girishk Hotel for a place to stay.

Yesterday I drove down the Helmand Valley a ways as a beginning of a reconnaissance to be made of the location of the Shamalon Canal. This will be some seventy miles long. It will provide water constantly for existing canals that now have irrigation water only part of the year. This is only when the water in the Helmand is high enough that it can be readily diverted into these canals. Small brush and stone dams of a temporary nature are maintained for this purpose.

Near Bacheron I stopped to look over the situation, and a young man came out of one of the dwellings. He seemed to know me and without a word went straight to the pickup and seated himself. Well, he stayed with me all afternoon. He wore no shoes but was able to keep right along with me as we hiked for many miles over rough fields and wastelands. We tried to follow a trail that I knew led in straight lines right down the valley. But although caravans could follow it, a car could not because the brush bridges over the irrigation ditches had caved in, were too narrow, or two abruptly high, or just too weak for an automobile.

So because of these obstacles to travel in the valley, we went up on the bluffs at the edge of the desert overlooking the valley and here parked the car. From this point we walked across the valley lands to the Helmand River near a place called Bolan (tall). This was to be my first introduction to the valley agricultural people.

Fields of wheat were growing greener with approach of warm spring weather. Around the dwellings were groups of men wearing turbans and shepherds' cloaks and sharp-pointed whiskers — or just the loose, long shirt-pantaloon attire — sitting on their haunches in the sun with not a care. Others were cleaning out irrigation ditches for early use.

There was a scattering of women (zanha) in the fields, and they had sacks and seemed to be cutting grass or greens. As we passed they would run for cover or get down out of sight, and then peer out, just like timid, frightened animals or birds.

Other men would leave their huts and come out to look me over in a friendly fashion. One group operated by foot a wooden pole on a pivot in its middle. At the other end was a rounded stone that ground up tobacco in the hollow of a half-buried log.

Dogs would bark viciously from tops of mud walls or hut tops, or come charging toward us across fields. Rocks or big clods hurled at them would halt them temporarily. They would run to sniff of the thrown rock or clod and if the scent was unfavorable, continue the charge. These dogs were big husky fellows with white curly hair tipped with grayish black around their mouths, eyes and ears — very alert, strong and intelligent-looking.

There were small orchards behind eight-foot walls surmounted by camels thorn to obstruct trespassers. Trees looking like apricots or plums were in bloom.

In pasture or wastelands close to the river were herds of cattle, small animals with a slight hump just back of shoulders, with one or two men herding them on foot.

I conversed with my friendly guide about the names of things we saw growing — like *rashqah* (alfalfa), *shaftel* (clover), *gan-doom* (wheat), *chirgmurght* (chicken), *sab-zee* (vegetables). People would quietly ask him a brief question, glancing at me, and his answer seemed to satisfy them. Late in the afternoon we had to pass near a hut to clear a wall surrounding a field, and in doing so took a young woman by surprise. She started to run, in apparent fright, but just one word in a low tone from my companion — whatever it meant — promptly stopped her, and she turned, half-smiled and disappeared behind a grape arbor.

This area is irrigated from the Bolan canal. It includes some 10,000 acres, and the afternoon had been well-spent in familiarizing one's self with existing conditions. Back at Bacheron, as my young friend, Fer-ooz; got out of the pickup he was greeted by his father, who embraced and kissed his son and spoke pleasantly to me.

"Ma-ta-shak-ker, bes-yar! Bes-yar! — Thanks very much," said I, most appreciatively.

Well, we decided to continue this reconnaissance survey on horse. This is because points along the preliminary line as surveyed last summer and fall are otherwise inaccessible except by that method of travel, or on foot. So today, the 24th of February, we started out — Jacinto Sabiniano from the Philippine Islands, and I. We have an Afghan follow with a truck along the bluffs a few miles opposite where we are riding on horses along the preliminary canal line. This truck driver and another Afghan stay with and take care of the horse at night in some village convenient to where we quit for the day. Then Jack and I drive the truck back to Chah-i-anjir and return to the line the following morning. This works out quite well.

Jack is quite familiar with this line, having worked on it last summer. So, even though people had pulled up many of the line stakes for fuel, we were able to find transit points, or hubs, driven with tops just below the surface of the silty soil, and marked by mounds of dirt off to one side.

About noon today we decided to water the horses and eat our lunch, which was contained in a tin box tied to the saddle on the little bay. We had just tied the horses to clumps of bushes, to eat the grain and dry grass nearby, and turned to go over to some fruit trees blooming behind a mud wall, when the bay pulled loose and dashed wildly toward the Helmand, the tin lunch box hitting him on the rump with a resounding whack at each leap.

"There goes our lunch," shouted Jack.

"Take it easy. I think he'll come back to the other horse as soon as he begins to tire out," I said.

Soon the bay began to circle about in ever smaller circles, and then passed directly behind my small black pony, who let him have it with both hind hoofs on the rump. This set the bay off again on a wild gallop, the tin lunch box performing as before. He ran close to Jack, who tried to grab the reins, and then ran to me and stood trembling all over. Soon we got him quieted and eating grass again.

By this time five small boys had collected and were interested observers. They refused cookies or any part of our lunch — just wanted to watch us eat. They giggled softly as Jack related to me some experiences he had had in the Philippines as a guerrilla during the Japanese occupation.

It seemed he had been a member of a small band of independent soldiers that had harassed the Japanese by surprise raids. He made motions by way of illustration. Then the boys started playing a certain kind of game with clubs they carried with them around the sheep. They drew a small circle in the sand and stood off to throw their clubs at it. The one whose club was closest to the circle, ran to pick it up and brandished it at the others who scrambled wildly away shouting *"Yallah! Yallah!"* (hurry! hurry!)

After that we started out again. But the jinx followed the bay pony; as he stepped into an innocent looking pool of water, he sank belly deep into quicksand. He struggled frantically to get out, then lay perfectly still. After half an hour we had extricated him by main force, lifting him by mane and tail.

*   *   *

"I wish to preach, not the doctrine
of ignoble ease, but the doctrine of
the strenuous life." 4/10/99

Theodore Roosevelt
(1858 - 1919)

V
A New Frontier

CHAPTER V

A New Frontier

THE OTHER DAY four of us from the Boghra Project went to a conference in the project manager's office at Manzel Bagh — 100 miles from here near Kandahar.

There were Charlie Jones from the Owyhee Reclamation Project, Oregon, construction superintendent; Frank Youngs from the University of Idaho, agronomist in charge of the agricultural experiment station at Ft. Nad-i-ali; Jan Mohammed, building director for the Afghan Agricultural Commision.

Our project manager presided. Top Afghan officials present were Mu-rid Khan, heading the Royal Afghan Commission for M-K-A, Inc., projects, and Wuh-dut Shah, chief engineer for the commission, and a graduate of Cornell University in civil engineering.

We talked about pressing early construction of the lateral systems. This would allow the agricultural commission to move right along with the colonization — the settlement of

67

these wandering people on the newly irrigated lands where they could grow foodstuffs for themselves and settle down to become substantial citizens.

We had brought along maps to show the layout of the laterals for the first small unit of 16,000 acres. Marked on it were the villages, eight in number, four kilometers apart. The idea is to have all the people living in villages, as is their custom, and cultivate the outlying lands — say twenty to thirty ja-reebs, or ten to fifteen acres per family. We really believed these set areas were far too small for the purposes intended and emphatically advised the commission it would be a mistake to follow this practice, but that's the way the government desired it anyway. Consequently we would be governed accordingly in the layout of lateral distribution works. We felt this situation would correct itself as land settlement proceeded, however, and the commission was faced with realities.

Murid, after an aside conversation with Mr. Shah, had the latter voice objection to the direction in which the streets of the villages were laid out.

Said Mr. Shah, "The people will become confused in their religious devotions unless the streets point in a southwesterly direction in due line with Mecca."

He had reference to the prayers of the people five times each day in which they are required to face toward Mecca.

The commissioners seemed satisfied with the canal construction program at Boghra, which had been underway.

In the late afternoon while waiting outside the office for the others to come to the car, a young Afghan about to take off on a bicycle, came up to the car and said, "Do you speak German?" evidently thinking I looked the same. "I teach in college at Kandahar," naming a boys' academy there, "German, history and geography. *Amrikan?*" he inquired.

"Yes, I am from the United States — California," and at this the young man's face lighted.

"Are you from Kabul?" I asked.

"Yes, a graduate of a university there — the one for law, medicine, the sciences," said he.

"But how about engineering?" I inquired.

"Oh, we depend upon you Americans to do the engineering for us," he promptly rejoined, and we shook hands smiling.

En route back to camp we passed near the provincial penitentiary. Soldiers were returning prisoners to the confines of the prison, after a day's work on the mountainside in the rock quarries, or on improvements to the city streets.

Jan Mohammed told me this city dates back to "biblical" times and to Alexander the Great, several centuries B.C.

Near the city were almond orchards in bloom.

Frank Youngs pointed to a canal high up on a mountainside. "You should go up there and follow the canal around. It is warm there and soon they will have early cucumbers," said he.

The mountains about the city rise abruptly and precipitously from the level plains to great heights and their profiles are black against the sky. In groups, or alone, they stand as if some giant had poured sand into the valleys around prehistoric mountain ranges and leveled this sand off smoothly, leaving only the peaks projecting.

Further on, high winds were raising clouds of white dust or fine sand to our left along the Arghandab River, like fog at sea. It was dusk. Jackals bounded across the road in front of the car — Afghan version of our North American coyote.

The sun was setting through two horizontal slits in the gray clouds as we passed down the steep winding turn where, in the morning, an M-K-A diesel fuel tank truck and trailer had jack-knifed backwards down the grade when the engine, then the brakes, had failed. The tanks were empty, fortunately. Soon we passed Piute with a helper returning to camp, having come out fifty miles to get the truck and trailer out of the difficulty.

And then it was pitch dark. Rounding a bend of the Boghra Canal bank near Girishk, the lights shown full upon Woodrow Knight beside his pickup truck with a broken left front spindle. This accident could have resulted in the total submersion of truck and driver in the deep ponded water alongside. "Piute will take care of you! He's not far behind!" Charlie called to Woody.

*   *   *

Well, work is progressing steadily on the first project village. The army has soldiers at work on this — apparently a battalion of infantry. I was with Jack's survey party for a time the other day while he was mapping the layout. A major came up to me and in perfect English introduced himself as Ghulam Mohammed, chatted a moment to acquaint himself of our intentions, and returned into an adobe hut, apparently battalion headquarters.

Here will be some 480 dwellings. Jan Mohammed had laid out the streets and sites for each building.

Water was being run to the townsite in a small stream to shallow basins where crews of civilians were making adobe brick from stiff mud poured in molds, left to dry and harden, and then carefully placed in the walls and partitions of two-family dwellings. I was here most of the day and had a chance to observe these Afghan soldiers, a happy, carefree-appearing lot, living in small tents on the open desert. Most wore heavy overcoats, heavy woolen slacks and jackets, and good shoes.

Without appearing too curious, I covertly observed some

twenty or more men, possibly a squad or platoon, coming
in relays to a platform on the ground near headquarters.
They would form single or double ranks with a leader out
in front. All faced slightly south of west toward Mecca. With
thumbs in ears, fingers extended, palms to the front, they
stood momentarily at attention, then stood with bowed
heads and hands clasped in front of belt line, then they
bent forwards with knees on the ground and each hand resting palm down on leg, and then they bent forward keeping
knees on the ground and resting forehead on ground between hands of outstretched arms, palms to the ground.
Then they would stand erect, and except for placing thumbs
in ears, would repeat twice this series of movements. These
devotions lasted about twenty minutes — that is, the three
series. At the end of the third series, they would stand upright with bowed head and palm of right hand over left
breast. These devotions at the battalion headquarters were
continuous throughout most of the day.

One Afghan surveyman acted as best he could as my
interpreter and went wherever I went on this day taking
notes and measurements in connection with the dwellings
under construction. We frequently talked to the soldiers.
Finally Ho-sain said to me, "In *Am-ree-ka shoo-maw* in
hermy?"

"Oh, yes," I replied, "about thirty years."

Hosain turned at once to a group of soldiers nearby and
evidently imparted this information to them, for they all
then directed their attention at me in a most respectful
manner.

Said Hosain to me, "Pretty soon I go Kabul-Herat-
Kandahar — someplace — I join Hermy, too."

By now it was time to load up and return to camp. Jack
took time out to show Ba-ron, the Afghan rear chainman,

how properly and more rapidly to do up the fifty-meter steel tape into the form of a figure eight. Observing this we were startled and shocked to suddenly hear Say-far Mohammed, the head chainman cajolingly admonish Ba-ron, "Come on. Come on! Jesus H. Christ, come on!!" — his black eyes fairly sparking the while.

Some predecessor of ours had undoubtedly taught Say-far this expression which he appeared to be repeating innocently.

*   *   *

This is a sort of new frontier over here — as one *Amrikan* views it anyway. Perhaps you'll understand, folks, in what I have to relate.

The other morning I went early to Ft. Nad-i-Ali. All around it are located our agricultural experiment station and 2,000-acre wheat farm together with the first unit, consisting of 16,000 acres, of the Boghra Project. The station has been operated about five years under the able direction of Mr. Frank Youngs, agriculturist from the University of Idaho. On the wheat farm is being raised grain for distribution in form of flour to workmen of the M-K-A, Inc. My purpose was to confer with Jan Mohammed, director of building construction for the agricultural commission.

Now first about this ancient stronghold — how old no one seems to know. It can be seen across the desert from points many miles away. The mirage effect adds to the already fantastic. Suspended on the horizon, it appears at times; then again it seems surrounded by water. The adobe walls are high and broad, fifty feet at the base and equally as high. Massive towers, or turrets, project from each corner and from the middle of each side. A broad rampart is on top of the walls and in front of this a low wall or parapet surmounted at intervals by blocks the height and width of a man. In the low wall and in the turrets are small square openings slanting downward. This arrangement in days of old not only shielded the defenders on top of the walls, but also enabled them to direct their arrows or rifle fire at hostile forces approaching from any direction, or attempting to scale the walls.

A moat completely surrounds the place, and lies between the inner walls, still intact, and the outer walls, now all but obliterated. This moat was undoubtedly excavated during construction of outer and inner walls, and of old was kept filled with water as necessity required. Such is Ft. Nad-i-Ali. Only on this particular forenoon of our visit, the fort was actually flooded on three sides. Some one during the previous night had allowed a stream of irrigation water to get out of control filling the ancient moat.

Well, we found Jan at Village No. 1. Here a large number of soldiers and civilians were erecting adobe buildings. The village occupies a square kilometer. The dwellings, all identically the same, are in long rows, 120 to the village. Each has four apartments — one for a family — and one *jeribe* (half acre) of land to each family for garden purposes. Each family will have twenty or more *jeribes* of land outside the village. That's the way people cultivate or farm land in Afghanistan — living in groups like that with their animals — walking two or three kilometers to their small farms. The land we are helping develop will have towns four kilometers center to center.

Then we went with Jan to and inside the fort, which incloses a square area of about ten acres. Inside, the Afghan government has recently erected a long low adobe building to contain offices connected with this land development and the experimental farm. Also in here are pens for plow oxen, camels, burros, goats, sheep and some hump-shouldered dairy cows. There are storerooms for wheat, provisions, some hay and seeds.

AFGHANISTAN VENTURE

Going through the south gate or archway to this ancient place, I must have appeared a strange-looking character to the several dozen loosely clad workmen waiting about to begin their day's work among the test plots of the experiment station and farm. They gaze fixedly at an American. Some are inclined to follow and discuss him as they walk along. At the entrance to the long building a dignified looking official greets us. Jan precedes us down a long graveled passageway, on each side of which are open doorways where can be seen men gathered at work around crude tables or desks. We enter an office filled with a dozen men seated at tables. In the dim light I notice several rise and bow politely and touch the palm of their right hand to left chest. Removing my headgear, I do likewise.

Said Jan apologetically, "Very dark in here to you. We don't have electric lights."

By way of encouragement, I rejoin, "Well, Jan, you will have them here and in all of your towns before too long. You know there is to be a power plant at that drop in the Boghra Canal near Girishk."

Jan is a most agreeable man with a ready smile and has had some engineering education at a German college in Kabul, I am told. He brings out several neatly finished maps. They show the subdivision layouts for the colonization plan . . . how provision is being made in each of the villages for a school, hospital, mosque, hotel, sports or playground recreational area, bazaars, business offices, etc. Five villages are shown on these maps for inclusion in this first unit of the Boghra Project. This development we discuss at some length, after which I suggest Jan go with me to inspect the work underway.

"First we have *chay*," says Jan.

We drive through the gate of the fort again and to the

74

residence and office of Noor Mohammed, president of the agricultural commission, who is absent in Kabul. The floor is covered with fine rugs. In response to my interest, Jan explains these rugs are from northern Afghanistan — the Oxus River Country along the Russian Turkistan border. Here are made the finest rugs, says he. The window and door openings to this office are without glass and screen. Flies, wind and dust have free access. But one scarcely notices these details any more.

Jan looks over a sheaf of papers a barefoot man lays before him. The writing is of a strange script. There is brief discussion in low tones and this *jamidor* (foreman) leaves.

A man servant enters with hot tea and sugar — one pot is placed on a low table in front of me, the other on Jan's desk.

Then we make a general tour of the experiment station. I am especially interested in observing the layout of the irrigation ditches distributing water to the various fields. We pass many plots of different kinds of alfalfa, clover, grasses, flower beds, cotton, fruit trees, garden truck, grapes, wheat. They have found out a lot of things about what will grow well here and produce . . . grains, fruits, vegetables, forage, cotton, melons, a great number of plants, trees and vines. The best varieties, proper time to plant, how and when to irrigate, the amount of water required to produce most satisfactory results — that is the "duty of water," as we engineers designate it . . . all of these factors are being investigated. Even varieties of trees are tried out for growth and fuel value, fuel being so scarce in this country. And in all of these operations the Afghan government is intensely interested through its agricultural commission.

Here is an experimental herd of cattle — small black animals with humped shoulders.

Scattered over the fields are scores of men handling the irrigation. Many are agricultural students from Kabul gaining a few months of practical experience.

Over there is a team of oxen pulling a wooden plow. Modern plows are unknown to the Afghan farmer — that kind with the steel share, moldboard, landside, colter, gauge wheel, beam, clevis, handles and all — so essential to modern agriculture. This plow was developed and has been in use in the United States for many generations.

There goes a man riding a bullock off somewhere — perhaps from the field to his home in the village.

Then we go out on the desert past the 2,000-acre wheat-field. Here three survey crews, miles apart, are running lines for dividing the land into square kilometers — locating and setting grades for irrigation laterals and attendant concrete structures (checks, drops, turnouts) that will bring water to these thirsty lands.

And all this work is proceding under stress. The Afghan government insists water be made available to the fields and new farmers within sixty days. . . . And I remember the admonition of Chief Engineer Bleifuss back in San Francisco to me weeks before this: "That 16,000-acre unit, the first on the Boghra Project, must be completed at once, Jones!"

So Jan and I join up with Jack Sabiniano's survey party. They are laying out location for one of the new villages — something of immediate interest to Jan.

As we walk along abreast of Jack's Afghan chainmen, I endeavor to get Jan's slant on what is being projected for the Afghan common man in connection with this irrigation project.

"Jan, what will each of these villages be like — how many people — schools?"

"Each village ees one square kilometer — four kilometers

to next village — a hundred and twenty dwellings — four families een each — one *jeribe* for each. In entire project 18,000 homes — 72,000 people farming the irrigated lands," Jan explains.

"You mean they will all walk to and from their farm units?"

"Yes, that ees the way we live," replies Jan. "In each dwelling ees space also for the animals."

"What's this, Jan?" and I point to a scar across the smooth desert. "Maybe an ancient irrigation lateral?"

"That ees old canal — here 400 years ago — took water to Ft. Nad-i-Ali — many people here then."

"Do you have any idea as to the identity of these people?"

"May be Genghis Khan people — may be Persians — we do not know," replies Jan.

"What became of these people?"

"We don't know."

"What else will be on this project?" I further query.

"We will have a central city. Here will be a big hotel — big mosque — big business," says Jan.

"Well, Jan, will there be any tall buildings — a skyline — skyscrapers you know, in the villages?" I ask jokingly.

"Tower for mullah (Mohammedan priest) may be," Jan says smiling.

"May be you shouldn't joke like that, Jan. It's sacrilegious, no?" say I, also smiling. "How about a good school system?"

"In each village we will have school through eight grades — compoolsury education for both boys and girls — you say in *Amrika* — no?"

"Fine. Yes, in *Amrika* we make all children attend school — both the girls and the boys. And you will have high school?"

77

"Oh, yes — high schools. Here weel be ooneeversitee," says Jan with enthusiasm.

"That will be wonderful — wonderful! What crops will these people raise?" I ask further.

"Oh, many theengs — wheat, cotton, corn, sugar beets, alfalfa, clover, fruit. We weel have sugar mill — and fabreek factory — and what you call (pointing to my fleece lined jacket) . . . yes, woolen mills — we will make wool fabreeks," continues Jan matter-of-factly.

"Fine. How about Hereford cattle? That is, beef cattle — and dairy cattle — how about these, Jan?"

"Yes, we weel have all those, too."

"Electricity — power for lights — to grind your wheat and corn — to run the factory machinery," I suggest further.

"We want that very soon," Jan emphasizes. "We weel have hospitals. We weel have sports area in each village."

"How long will it take to get going on these things, Jan?" I inquire with fervor.

"May be ten to fifteen years," replies Jan with assurance.

"That will be marvelous!" and I share Jan's eagerness.

Then I look at Jan with an inner feeling of incredulity — the more so because all around lies the unending desert in the bright rays of the Afghan sunshine.

Ft. Nadi-i-ali seems surrounded by water. A camel train miles away walks on thin air above the horizon. The distant mountains lie on the far shore of a great lake. The desert scarf to the west, the Dasht-i-Margo, has become fantastic shapes, flat and broad. Over there far to the south appear a grove of trees, yet I know at that location are only clumps of sage brush on low sand dunes. Mystified, I went to investigate one day.

And then I take another look at Mohammed — Jan, I mean — and am puzzled as to whether he is dreaming of a

78

future as impossibly fantastic as is appearing all around us in this land of strange mirages.

And then it dawns on me his ideas aren't so out of place. Farm units, villages, schools, hospitals, recreation centers, industry, improved agriculture, electric power, stockraising — a wealth of productive unihabited land —enough for all Afghans who want it on a basis similar to the American irrigation reclamation project plan — and water to irrigate it from the Helmand, a veritable Colorado River with its many tributaries, right here in the heart of Afghanistan, and fed by the melting snows of the lofty Hindu Kush.

No, in Jan's plans for his country there is really no element of fantasy. His plans are becoming a gradual reality at this writing.

Over there is the Boghra Canal already delivering water to the thirsty desert from the imposingly long diversion weir in the Helmand River near Girishk. Its waters mirror the clear blue of the desert skies for 100 kilometers.

Here already are networks of laterals completed or being constructed; the sub-structure of a sizable electric power plant in the Boghra Canal near Girishk; an experimental station serving as a guide in present and future agricultural development. . . .

The land is being subdivided in preparation for the settlement on it of nomadic tribesmen. Villages are being prepared in which to establish the people. . . .

And aren't prospective settlers arriving by the hundreds monthly, to plant crops on the lands to be assigned them? Yes, much in evidence were these pioneer people with their flocks of fat-tailed sheep, goats, camels, burros, little black hump-shouldered cattle, oxen, barking dogs — beautiful husky fellows — and their women, not too particular about remaining in concealment — and romping children — and free men hardened all their lives to struggles for existence

79

in the ruthless, boundless deserts.

Yes, all about is life and an air of hopeful expectancy, and the beginning (we Americans each in our own humble way fervently pray) of a new Afghanistan rising from out of the mysteries of forgotten centuries to become truly a modern "Star of Asia."

Here before the eyes of Jan Mohammed and myself in this vast desert expanse, on a February afternoon, lay remnants of an ancient, powerful civilization — and over there is the beginning of a new civilization — a new way of life abounding in the riches of worthy endeavor.

And look! What is the cause of those rolling dust clouds obliterating much landscape to the northwest? An approaching sand storm? No, it is the M-K-A "catspread" — caterpillar tractors, bulldozers, twenty-five cubic yard carryalls, road graders, ditchers, dragline excavators. As air currents lift the dust temporarily, one sees the bright yellow equipment steadily at work constructing irrigation canals and laterals — preparing the water distribution system for the lands upon which waiting people will soon be settled.

And all this while up the Hellmand *Rud* seventy-five miles, there is rising from the bed of the river and nearing completion at a height of 295 feet, a rock fill dam. This will impound 4,000,000 acre-feet of water, enough to irrigate 1,000,000 acres and more of fertile valley and desert land south and west to the Iranian border.

The other day I was invited into the tent of one of these nomads awaiting, with relatives and friends, the opening to settlement of desert lands to be reclaimed by irrigation. His tent was commodious, flat-topped, opened to the wind, dust and sunshine on two sides.

Failing in an effort to sit down comfortably on my heels, like my friend, I finally assumed a lounging position on a very fine rug covering the bare ground. As if this were not the acme of comfort, a young man provided me with a large pillow upon which to lean.

My host — a man of about forty — sat very straight and dignified. Soon it was plain he knew enough English to make me understand in general what he had in mind.

"Shoo-ma a gentleman," he began.

"Ma Am-ree-kan," I rejoined proudly as a faint smile of understanding passed over his dark-brown handsome face.

A young mother sat close by and behind him, her baby in a hammrock swung between two willow tent poles. The child was tightly wrapped, I noticed, in spite of the heat of noonday. It awakened and cried a little. The mother, quite young but old beyond her years it seemed, removed the child gently from its swaying perch, returned to her seat on the ground, and nursed the baby until quiet again. All the while I tried to remain unembarrassed under her searching but friendly gaze.

One by one, and quietly, boys and girls, some other women, and men of all ages entered the tent until the shaded space was full. An old man with a faded blue turban shook hands with me in a most friendly manner and as I arose, took my right hand in both of his. He could have been the father of my host. All eyed me steadily and soberly.

My friend appeared to be checking information he already possessed about the colonization plan — the number and location of the villages. I said there would be dwellings in each for 120 families — 124, he corrected me — how soon water come? I said June first.

"June — that's three months yet — after August," he suggested.

"No, only about six weeks yet," I said.

"How many days?" said he.

Holding up ten fingers four times and two fingers once, I said, "Forty·two days."

81

"Bes-yar khob (very good)," said he with a pleased look.

It appeared he would soon leave for Madras, India, by caravan, to buy cloth and other goods — would bring back many nomads to settle on this irrigated land. Nomads recognize no boundaries between countries, he said — many hundreds would come with him.

Then a lad came from another tent with a pot of tea and two small cups. Gravely the man poured the tea, adding plenty of sugar. He and I drank, and I calmly studied the faces of these dark-brown people whose steadily penetrating gaze symbolized an air of hopeful expectancy, of patient waiting for something good about to happen to them — and could I volunteer answers to their unvoiced questions?

"You have doctor at Chah-i-anjir?" said my friend as I was consuming a third cup of tea.

"No, just a first aid nurse. The company doctor is at Kandahar, 160 kilometers away. *Fah-mid-i* (you understand)?" said I.

"Maybe you get nurse — she help my wife — she have fever?" he asked, pleadingly.

But here was a situation which I was helpless to relieve. Malaria is prevalent among these people. There are almost no doctors or medical help of any kind so badly needed to combat maladies and plagues. Mrs. Danskin, our company first aid nurse at camp — a splendid woman — on her own time and by herself, had attempted to do what she could to relieve the distress of ill health among women and children who had gahered by the scores on the lawn of her home for medical attention. Finally it had become for her physically impossible to handle the situation alone, much less to furnish the medicine and accessories needed. And finally our company doctor at Manzel Bagh, through necessity, was forced to issue an order as the chief medical director of the company, forbidding the furnishing of medical assistance to any but company employees.

This I endeavored to explain very briefly to this merchant nomad. He seemed to understand, as a look of disappointment passed over his countenance. I tried to console him by saying soon the agricultural commission at Ft. Nad-i-ali would have a doctor of its own to attend to the needs of people settling upon the land.

The woman with the baby seated just behind the nomad did not look especially ill, however. Maybe her husband was talking about another wife in another tent. This passed through my mind.

And then I picked up my sun helmet to leave. *"Mata-shak-ker* (thank you)," and bowed my way out of the tent.

*   *   *

All is not work for Americans in Afghanistan. There is a movie about every week or ten days at this oasis-like camp. We use the white-washed end wall of one of the adobe barracks as a screen.

Here gathers a small group of foreigners — Italians, Filipinos, Americans — in the early evening dusk, and out over the western desert is still the faint glow of the setting sun — a sun that has been on the job over Washington, Oregon and California already for a couple of early-morning hours. The planet Venus is brilliant.

"Mrs. Mike" — scene in Canada's Northwest Territories and a thrilling romance — is the feature picture; and also there is "Dangerous River" (the Colorado). Silently these desert men and workmen for the company — in turbans, loose garments, barefoot or in sandals — form a large crescent on the ground. The English words are not understood, but the joys and sorrows of the theme are closely followed, judging from the looks on their faces and their audible expressions. It is a picture of life in the great Canadian North-

83

west — frontiersmen, Mounties, sled dogs, Indians, an eastern girl, romance, canoe travel, a smallpox epidemic, scarcity of medical aid. These desert men appear fascinated by the western ways of life in Canada and the United States — the, as yet to them, unheard of and kindly manner in which we treat our women — their independence and ability to do things, their attractive dress and good looks.

Somehow one subconsciously hopes — and fervently — that in some measure our moving pictures of life in North America will give impetus to progress toward a higher standard of living that a modern King and his government apparently are attempting to initiate — and this includes, in a mild measure at least, compulsory education for both boys and girls, and the removal of the purdah — to name only a couple of items.

In the midst of these reflections amid such fantastic surroundings, with suddenness a resplendent meteor streamed across the sky from near the zenith and disappeared over the western desert horizon in the direction of the Iranian border leaving a bluish green trail.

This last week Mr. Don Bleifuss, chief engineer from San Francisco, was with us. As far as could be done in three days, we took him over the job, and he also did considerable hiking. From here he was going up the river to the Kajakai Dam under construction — a diversion tunnel was about to be holed through — then he thought to Colombo, Ceylon, where another dam and irrigation canal system is in progress — and maybe to Australia and New Zealand from there, so widespread are M-K's operations. There is nothing conceited about Bleifuss, just as common as the rest of us in suntan shirt and slacks and heavy field shoes. He used his color camera frequently, and among many others got what should be a good picture of a full-arch, gloriously-hued rainbow against a background of the deepest blue-black. It had followed a rare spring shower over the Marja Desert to the extent of what in the distance appeared to be a veritable cloudburst.

One point about the design and construction of the Boghra Canal that had alarmed me since the first week of my arrival was the fact that adequate provision had not been made for checking up the canal flows for making deliveries of water to laterals or other turnouts. Here were drop structures at the lower end of long stretches of canal from which were to be made diversions of flow, large and small, with no means of checking the water. This situation was discussed with "Don," and as a result financial provision was made for the engineering design and construction of the necessary intermediate check structures — also for the addition and necessary revision to the existing drop structures of steel radial gates and attendant lifting devices to check the flow of water to the required depth in the section of canal above. These provisions of course will add several hundred thousand dollars to the cost of the canal, but without them it will be impossible to operate except at full flow, which condition will seldom be obtained, if ever, continuously and adequately.

Another condition also was bothering me, supported by considerable agitation from some quarters for its accomplishment. I, however, had withheld dissenting comment to a time that I regarded most propitious. This came as we were driving down a main wasteway through which the entire flow of the canal at that point could be and was being transported.

It had eroded to bed rock, a thick stratum of impervious naturally cemented gravel — a material as hard and tough as concrete. The agitation was for the installation of a series of reinforced concrete drop structures to lower the grade of the channel and reduce the water velocity to a non-scouring state. This would have cost hundreds of thousands of dollars. As we drove across the desert alongside this waterway, Don heard the arguments in favor with astute silence. Later on, pausing for a respite in which each went his separate way, Don said to me, "Jones, what would you do about putting in these drops? Are they necessary?"

Said I, "In my opinion — no. The water, no matter how swiftly it flows, cannot do damage by eroding deeper — the cemented gravel will not allow that. The water can only scour laterally. To effectively prevent that damage, plant two or three rows of willows or poplars in a straight line at the water's edge on both sides. The cost would be negligible."

Without a word the chief engineer got back into the car, the others joined us, and this was the end of the proposals for what seemed needless expenditures!

*   *   *

Jack and his survey party, and I have been continuing on horses our field reconnaissance of the preliminary line for the Valley Canal. A small percentage of this land in the Helmand Valley is being cultivated — probably has been for centuries, and more intensively than now. These agricultural people live in mud huts. They raise mostly wheat, yet I was surprised to see small patches of alfalfa starting to grow luxuriantly with the coming of spring.

These people maintain large canals by hand — divert the water direct from the river by temporary weirs constructed of cobblestones, sand and brush placed obliquely to the current. They of necessity have to excavate deep trenches where the artificial channel leaves the river, and this channel gradually comes out on grade at ground surface sometimes many kilometers from point of diversion, where they can turn the water on the fields. The banks of earth thrown out on either side of the canal are excavated deposits of silt and sand and these deposits, if allowed to accumulate, will

86

entirely cut off the flow. We saw accumulations of this removed material many times the height of the men who removed it, the results of the work of many generations of gray-turbaned toilers.

In this valley are large herds of camels turned loose on the great areas of uncultivated lands which are rather rough, subject to overflow, and covered with low clumps of tamarisk, or salt cedar. This shrub is very useful. One sees people trudging long distances with bundles of it on their heads, on burros, or on camels, taking them to the small village communities where they are woven into long rolls for use in making fences, thatches for houses — and even to making small flumes to carry ditches across canals. Laid over poles and covered with adobe, this brush makes good roofs for huts. The mud is glazed to shed the small amount of rainfall, about two to five inches per year.

There are also in the valley rather large herds of small partly-humped, rugged looking black cattle, which seem to be good foragers, but probably eat as much as Hereford steers.

Then there are herds of fat-tailed sheep, the big tails probably weighing seven to ten pounds.

Also there are the ever-to-be-seen goats, which feed on the wild vegetation, such as it is, in desert and valley.

All these herds of animals are attended by one to three or four lone shepherds wearing great cloaks of felt about one-fourth inch thick. These shepherds stand motionless, but apparently observe everything, like an owl turning his head but not his body. Or there may be several shepherds in a group in a half-sitting position with their *pustins* spread out on the ground around them like a small tent.

Large areas of this valley land are unoccupied. It is of deep silt, deposited by river overflow, hence very fertile and capable of supporting a large population. One gets the impression that these people, who seem to be decreasing in number (the average life span is said to be but twenty-two years), are the remnants of a more vigorous civilization.

As Jack and I traveled along inspecting the diversion sites and channels of some fifteen of the existing canals, we were impressed with a fantastical sight on the opposite bank of the Helmand. There on the river bluffs, spread along for ten miles or so, were the remains of an ancient civilization, and these were profiled against the skyline. Here was Qala Bist, or Fort Twenty, and toward the northerly end of these series of ruins stood the King's Palace and military compound, Lakhkar-i-Bazaar. And we gazed in wonder at all this. What had happened? How could so many people inhabit these valley lands compared to the few here now?

These valley people have not the slightest idea of what we are doing. They won't until our excavating equipment arrives some weeks hence. They live in small villages of fifty to seventy-five dwellings — mud huts with thatched roofs, which are several kilometers apart with no habitations in between. They use wooden plows and maintain canals with small spoonlike hand shovels. They have no schools and no bazaars, and half the population is in seclusion, surviving on so little.

As we mused about these things, some six or eight boys came over from where a large drove of fat-tailed sheep were grazing. With my toe I drew a semi-circle where I invited them to stand for a picture. They got the idea all right, but pushed and pulled each other all over the place, never standing still and laughing and playing in great glee — until a jackal ran out of some brush at the edge of a wheat field followed by a sheep dog. They cheered the dog on, and I yelled, "Git 'im, git 'im." Then they took up the cry, "Git 'im," and followed after. But by now the jackal was loping safely out toward the open desert. He had been waiting in

88

an irrigation ditch hidden by tall brush expecting to grab off a sheep. Not long ago, we had seen two sheep dogs and a fleet hound under similar circumstances follow and kill a jackal.

This morning as usual we left the car, an old "weapons carrier," with Ja-far, the driver, and Mah-dee and El-yas, who help look after the ponies, with the understanding they were to meet us about sixteen kilometers further on along edge of the desert in the late afternoon.

They met us all right at the designated locality, but as we approached on our tired steeds we noticed something wrong. A small crowd had collected — we could see no truck — and there were subdued chuckles of amusement. No wonder!

Here was the "weapons carrier" up to its bed in soft mud and water, surrounded by turbaned men, who under the direction of Ja-far, were making futile efforts to lift it or push it out of this predicament. We were some sixty-four kilometers from Camp Chah-i-anjir, our only source of help, and we weren't sure any rescue party from there could find us.

Jack was furious. Reason: his three men had left the truck in a dry spot all right, but on low ground along an irrigation ditch. Supposedly, while the men were making friends about the village, the ditch had broken, flooding the ground where the truck stood. So Jack and I left them to live off the village as best they could in our absence, and we started walking. It now being 4 p.m., I estimated we could make camp by 4 a.m. at the earliest.

Well, folks, hiking steadily for four hours, we came to a prominent knoll along the trail where we knew any car would have to pass to reach that part of the valley. It proved to be a burial ground on the bluffs at edge of desert. Jack collected a few clumps of dry camels thorn by groping around in the starlight. With this we had a fire at intervals on top of the highest mound. The cold of the night was getting intense — that is, it seemed so in contrast to the warm and delightful spring afternoon — so I let Jack wear my fleece-lined leather coat.

In the firelight we could make out innumerable long high mounds of cobblestones about, each one a grave. Some showed evidence of caving in with age. Others had slumped into the ground, leaving a depression. Some were all but buried in the shifting sand.

After what seemed hours, lights approached, at first faint and far away. They would disappear for many minutes, only to show up at some angle to the right or left, bobbing and twisting, then disappear for even a longer interval. However, we were encouraged that each time the lights were just a bit brighter. Then they disappeared altogether. We were about to continue on foot, but then thought better of it; for weren't we posted along the only truck and caravan trail leading down the valley? So it was yet another hour before we flagged them down. In the old car were Woody and Ed, both in a jovial mood.

The next morning in returning to the lower valley, we saw approaching along the desert trail a sight strange indeed to Americans and Filipinos. Worse luck, I didn't have my color camera along. For here, traveling briskly, was a tribe on the move to the mountain areas in the north country for the summer. They had wintered in the warmer climes to the south, in Pakhtunistan perhaps. Amazed, we stood by to watch the entire caravan pass, probably 300 camels well-laden and 500 people or more. The column was about two miles long. Women and small children rode on camels. Burros (donkeys) carried small children carefully balanced on each side, or even dogs rode the burros, or chickens with their legs tied together. There were several camel calves, and each of these rode comfortably in a sort of harness strapped to the mother's hump. Many camels carried long black rolls crossways — the tents. Men and boys walked scattered all along. Women — some wearing sandals — led some of the camels. Sixteen-year-old girls traveled in groups abreast in gala attire of many colors and barefoot. About their heads were bands of bronze or copper with ornaments dangling over the forehead, and a bright disk about the size of a dime worn on the left nostril. These young women were really nice looking, the picture of health in deep brown. The camels wore fancy halters of colored beads and expensive looking shell ornaments and trappings about their necks — green, blue and red. These people looked happy and carefree. We all gazed in wonder, and even the Afghans working for us sensed this to be something out of the ordinary.

On one particular forenoon, alone and afoot along the Helmand River and the located line of the Valley or Shamalon Canal, I came upon a group of eight men with shovels who were about to start their day of work on the Ho-sain-a-bad Canal. Soon afterwards another crew of eight came along to work on the Kha-laj Canal, whose diversion was about a kilometer further down the river.

Something strange then occurred. The sixteen shook hands very formally all around. I started to leave. Noticing this they called me back insistently. They began asking many questions. Little did I comprehend except I knew they were anxious to know about the new canal.

So I unrolled the fifteen-foot map I carried. It was on heavy parchment and showed the Helmand Valley from Girishk to below Shamalon, with river, villages and existing canals plainly indicated, together with the new canal whose construction many miles to the north was already getting underway. I laid the map on a level open space. The men stood or sat with their feet around the edges to keep it flat. I was careful to get it oriented exactly as to direction, and then began.

The words I knew were mostly names of their villages and canals. So I borrowed a cane from an old man and proceeded to name these features pointing them out on the map. The men corrected my pronunciation until it was absolutely right. This went over big.

Then I borrowed a shovel and on a smooth sand bar left by a recent overflow proceeded to illustrate more specifically how the new canal would intercept each one of their nine and supply water the year around to each. I would smooth out the sections that wouldn't be used any more, and obliterated their brush weirs, or *bunds* in the river. This they understood. They were jubilant, so much so that a young man grabbed from me the shovel and continued the illustration vigorously. At this all laughed appreciatively.

Yet the leader of one group wore a puzzled expression. Slowly, he held up three fingers and pointed down the river. I said I didn't understand, but he kept pointing and counting very slowly — *"Yek, du, say"* — even more emphatically until he noted in my face a light of understanding. I had left out three of their canals in my illustrations.

So in chorus we named them all over again: "Bash-a-ron — Bolan (long) — Ee-nak (eye glasses) — Kho-sar-a-bad (father-in-law's buildings) — Ho-sain-a-bad — Kha-laj, — Zar-est — Sork-a-doz (red) — Sham-a-lon (north wind)."

These canals were irrigating well over 55,000 acres in this vicinity and each carried thirty to fifty cubic feet of water per second (c.f.s.).

By now all were laughing and filled with merriment. So I had them sit down in a half-circle back of the long map for a kodachrome picture. Just then a little five- or six-year-old child came out from behind the big cloak of her father where she had been hiding all this time. I urged that she be allowed to sit in the center of the group, but she was timid and hid again. At this the father shook his head darkly and motioned with palm of hand saying, "Nay, nay."

Then all wanted to get a close look at the small kodak. Through the range-finder I let them scan the ruins of the ancient city and fortress of Qala-Bist just across the Helmand along a sixteen-kilometer skyline near the junction of the Helmand and Arghandab rivers. Then they all shook hands with me and went vigorously to work again with their shovels throwing high up on the banks another layer of deposited river silt that was blocking the flow of their water, adding to the accumulation of that already thrown there by no telling how many generations of valley people.

And then I sat down to rest and ponder over what that ancient civilization could have been like. There were the gates to the fortress and walled communities. And I visualized the thousands of people passing in and out, camel caravans, military units of cavalry and infantry, traders from distant lands. . . . All this valley land must have been intensely cultivated and irrigated to support this ancient center of trade and conquest. I determined to visit this scene some Juma at the first opportunity.

And then I looked about me again. Just over there where these men live is Surkhduz, a small village of dried mud dwellings basking in the sunshine of this forenoon. There are a few mulberry trees, and but for these the scene is almost invisible against a background of bare fields being prepared for spring crops here and there by oxen pulling wooden plows. And there could be seen women and girls walking about with just their eyes and noses visible to a foreigner like me — at this moment many miles away from any of my countrymen.

So I wondered further if we few Americans were not

93

now, and here, witnessing a period in this part of Asia that could be a balancing point between an eternity of the forgotten past and an eternity of the unknown future!

Was it possible we Americans were tackling a job under contract with the Kingdom of Afghanistan to be accomplished here in the short period of a certain few months — a job unprecedented in the known history of this country.

And then I recalled the remark of Ee-sah, a *jamadar* or foreman on construction who had confided to me haltingly but sincerely: *"Am-ree-kans* much too good — we like *Am-ree-kans — bes-yar khob, fah-mid-i* (very good, do you understand)?"

*   *   *

We were surprised and delighted one noon with guests from Kabul, Italian Ambassador Fontana with his charming wife and pretty daughter — a girl of about sixteen I'd say — and Father Bernasconi.

"This is a big desert," remarked the ambassador. The ladies were dressed for the trip in slacks and sandals.

Our three Italian mechanics, Wally, Leo and Ricardo, sat at one table with the guests in our newly decorated mess hall. It was quite an occasion for them, and we were all pleased to be thus especially honored.

Signor Fontana said he had been in Afghanistan about one year and in the Orient altogether about eighteen years. He had been in Chicago as a consul for some two and one-half years.

The padre, a dark, short, stout man, and very distinguished and experienced looking, had been in Afghanistan four and one-half years. He told the Italian men Christian missions are forbidden in this country. He travels about administering to his countrymen and other foreigners all over Afghanistan. He has special permission to do this, it seems.

94

I was much interested in what Father Bernasconi told me of their stay the day and night before at Qala Bist. A friendly Frenchman is in charge of the archeological excavations and investigations there. It is about twenty-five miles from us across the Helmand River. However, the river is too deep to ford safely; so that the best way to get to Qala Bist for us is via Girishk Bridge, a distance of some sixty-five miles.

"This Frenchman speaks good English," said the padre. "He would be glad to show you around. They are now uncovering the rooms in the ancient king's palace, and finding things at various levels — ancient paintings on the walls — all very interesting. This king apparently ruled northern India, Persia and Afghanistan about the 12th Century A.D., they are finding out."

"Some Juma several of us are planning to spend the day over there, Father," said I.

"Well, when you come to Kabul, we would like you to pay us a visit," said Mr. and Mrs. Fontana.

* * *

This construction job is really opening up a new frontier for the United States in a remote part of Asia. But not in a sense of what most people usually think of as a frontier. What I mean is a frontier or borderland of mutual friendship and practical helpfulness, and reciprocal respect between two peoples entirely unlike in race, color, religion, standards of living, historic background, culture, mode of life — and, I believe, in a number of other ways, which you may note, folks, as we proceed in this narrative.

There was the day I followed the caravan trail along the government telephone line to well below the limits of our valley project. A single wire is supported by willow poles embedded in mounds of dried mud about six feet high. I wondered if anywhere else on earth there might be another such telephone line.

The winding Helmand followed the bluffs on the far bank to the east. Beyond, the sand dunes and rolling desert — the Dasht-i-Poghdar — disappeared over the horizon. To the right was the Dasht-i-Margo extending 400 kilometers to the delta of the Helmand and the border of Iran. (I had carefully studied these areas from the large maps brought from San Francisco and which now adorn the adobe walls of my quarters.)

Lying between these two vast deserts is this fabulous valley of alluvial soils, extensive plains and uncertain water supply. Here the projecting Dasht-i-Margo threatens to choke it. A ways further, seemingly in retaliation, irrigation laterals transport water well out into the lowlands of this desert. There are large expanses under ditch, beautifully smooth but now taken over by that vigorous plant life of the desert, camels thorn, resembling jasmine with luscious green foliage and small pink flowers. Despite its sharp-pointed spines, camels invariably search out this shrub when grazing, especially in the winter when the plants are dead and brittle.

And there were desert areas white with alkaline salts, while immediately adjacent were thriving fields of wheat.

Obviously this land is a victim of water shortage in spite of the high flood run-off of the Helmand and its submergence of adjacent lands. This is because there is shortage of available water at the time of greatest need — in the fall at wheat planting time, often extending into the following spring — an undependable supply. Great areas, however, are covered by existing canals of ancient origin, diverting water from the river with the aid of temporary make-shift *bunds,* which often are swept away by high floods, and after replacement the river level becomes so low as to preclude diversion. And that is why the government and the company

96

have embarked on this reclamation development in this valley.

What's this? Three men, each riding a camel piled high with camels thorn. I shut off the motor so as not to frighten the animals in passing. Fierce looking countenances have these riders, with untrimmed black curly whiskers and beards. Experimenting, I look directly at them stolidly without change of expression, just in the same manner as they are taking my measure.

The Ford ton-and-a-half pickup edges slowly forward, bypassing sections of the trail flooded by water escaping from ditches or adjacent irrigated areas. We venture over ditch crossings scarcely wide enough for two camels abreast and in precarious condition of unsafety. These had been built of willow poles laid across the ditch and covered with brush or tamarisk mats, upon which loose straw and dirt had been placed. A false move sideways, or a hole punched through the decking of this contrivance not designed for trucks, and there would have been another even longer trek on foot for me — and this time alone!

Here was an abandoned vineyard — a large dry ditch — forsaken for lack of water. Dry camels thorn topped the high surrounding walls uninvitingly, as a warning at sometime to would-be trespassers.

And then I crossed what apparently was a main canal. A bank of silt on either side three times as high as the car was mute evidence of the labor put forth by bygone generations in attempting here to maintain a flow of water for vineyards, gardens, orchards, fields.

Again — what's this up ahead? A solitary knoll, or mound, of high ground just off the trail to the left rises conspicuously above the surrounding level fields. I muse as to the possible meaning of this unusual feature of topography. Had it been an ancient site of refuge, or an observation post, or was something of importance buried there? Drawing nearer I observe two feminine figures riding burros and urging these tough little animals up the sandy slopes of the little hill to the top. They wield and apply willow switches with the suppleness of swaying bodies and brown bare arms. Dismounting, they pose gracefully, lithesomely, in silhouette against the grayish-yellow tinge of the distant desert horizon.

The excited attention and actions of these two desert damsels, evidently caused by this strange oncoming outfit in bright yellow, and the foreign driver of blonde complexion in long-billed sun-tan cap and khaki slacks and shirt, and heavy boots — is only exceeded by like emotions of said driver.

Suddenly each throws off the light veil covering head and shoulders — the one of sky blue, fringed with scarlet, the other of light green, bordered with black. Each wears loose pantalets, snug at the ankles and frilled, and of the same colors as the veils but of darker hues. On the slender trim feet of each are leather sandals with golden colored trimmings.

I slow down the Ford to a walk so as to miss no details. Is it my imagination? The one has blue eyes, the other deep brown! Black hair, combed down smooth, glistens in the sunshine. Glittering coin-like adornments dangle over foreheads, and these are suspended from polished bronze or copper head bands. A shiny disk of silver presses tightly to the hollow of the left nostril. Skin clear, smooth, brown. Noses straight, narrow and delicately cast, as were also mouth and ears. Feature oval, patrician.

Revealed here is the loveliness of Afghan feminity personified in two maidens of seventeen and nineteen — sisters, friends, daughters of a chief? Mayhaps; I can't say. But truly attractive, pretty, with all the appearance of high birth, of

98

aristocratic ancestry! Such are these two young women of Afghanistan.

So I lean out the cab and in smiling appreciation touch my cap in salute. This gesture is promptly returned in like friendly manner by smiles, revealing rows of white teeth, and a wave of slender brown hands — palms out, fingers and thumbs extended.

Rounding a turn, the truck passes an isolated group of tamarisk trees somehow especially spared the ruthless devastation of past ages — rugged, gnarled, smoke-colored, venerated and ancient looking. Just beyond at a sharp bend in the deep, narrow canal, nestles a small village in a niche of the desert. Its square huts of adobe with the thatched roofs of long dried grass are almost camouflaged against the gray of the endless desert beyond.

On either side of the life-sustaining canal is a row of beautiful mulberry trees, their leaves now opening forth with the warmth of spring. Wheat fields are taking on green and vigorous life, as are small patches of clover and alfalfa.

Several women are squatted at the edge of the water beating clothes with smooth, well-worn wooden paddles. Others have come down from the village to fill their jugs or goat skins with water. Without looking up, some continue their work. Others partly turn to observe with one eye through a narrow slit in the veil. Several boldly throw back the head covering and peer coyly and cautiously over the canal bank.

Two lads approach, wide-eyed, barefooted, bareheaded, loose black gowns hanging down to their ankles.

Coming to an abrupt halt, *"Een cheez chee-e, unja deh?"* I chance in poor Persian, pointing toward the village where a group of turbaned, bearded figures are squatted silently and solemnly smoking water pipes.

"Shamalon — Shamalon!" both lads vigorously respond.

Here and further along lush wheatfields are being irrigated. Children rush out from the village to be at the road as the car passes, then flee with fear. One woman, working in a field near the road, purdah drawn closely over face, suddenly takes off like a frightened rabbit, but as quickly squats on the ground concealed completely by the black covering. As the car rolls past surprisingly enough she precipitately throws off her veil!

Here comes a youthful appearing man leading a large camel upon which ride two wives, one on either side of the hump in a sort of leather carrier or saddle arrangement. A small child rides between them.

And here the narrow road is deeply flooded from the irrigation of a nearby field. Dry loose sand is to the left — thorny desert growth to the right. A warm wind from the south is springing up. This could mean the approach of a sand storm. The afternoon is late. This is near the southern limits of the project anyway. It is wise to turn back.

Retracing the route, people display the same voiceless curiosity. Now boldly and inquiringly they search one's face. "Hello!" I venture, nodding slightly, and with a faint smile. Their faces light up.

Approaching Shamalon again, but from the opposite direction, I observe twelve men coming out of huts and joining in a file. They walk swiftly toward the road as if to head me off.

One big, dark, fierce-looking fellow deliberately plants himself just ahead of the approaching truck.

"*Estadah shoo!*" he commands with emphasis.

As the truck comes to a sudden halt, eleven men scramble aboard.

"*Kheli san-geen ast, agha; shayed nam-i-shad,*" I admonish as best I can . . . that the load would be too heavy; perhaps it can't be managed.

100

"*Eens-hal-lah ja peda mi-shad,*" . . . as in reply the fierce-looking fellow says he thinks there will be sufficient space for all.

"*Bur-ro!*" those completely filling the space in the rear shout, with a rolling of "r's" as elaborate as in the speech of any Mexican. . . . "Let's go!"

The fierce-looking one who has hailed the truck, they aren't going to allow aboard!

"*Een-ja,*" and I open the door on right side of cab inviting him to a good seat with the driver.

"*Buro-ro, bur-ro!*" and we are off — but most cautiously at that for many kilometers.

Occasionally a resounding bang on the rear of the cab advises me of the desires of one or two men to debark.

"*Kheli ma-ta-shak-ker,*" as each stands at attention while giving the perfect salute of a soldier, and with broad smiles they thank me profusely for the ride.

At last all but two of these self-imposed travelers remain. Here is a long stretch of newly-flooded road. Sizing up the situation, I turn off to the left in detour over what looks to be a smooth piece of open desert. The truck gains speed — up to twenty-five or thirty-five maybe — and I slam on the brakes with all the alacrity at my command! The front wheels are at a standstill on the brink of a six-foot cut — an abandoned irrigation channel through a low ridge — and in the approach there has been nothing whatsoever to mark its presence. The two dusky riders have slid involuntarily the length of the truck bed and been plunked violently against the back of the cab. Although plainly surprised, they also appeared satisfied that jolts like this are common and to be expected in this mode of travel. This idea is further confirmed by their gleeful shouts again of "Burro, burro!" After a time one man gets off where a caravan trail crosses the road and as he swiftly walks away, my remaining passenger leans outward vomiting several pints of green liquid. And then, *"Burro,"* says he weakly, and we are off to camp.

> "The use of traveling is to regulate
> imagination by reality, and instead of
> thinking how things may be, to see them
> as they are."
>   — Samuel Johnson
>   (1709 — 1784)

VI
Pioneers

CHAPTER VI

Pioneers

WELL, here goes for a few pages to show you people in the States how we foreign folks in Afghanistan really live with the passing days.

We have just had supper — beef steak, fried spuds, fresh chard, canned pineapple, coffee. The food is of the best, cooked and served by trained Afghan chefs from Kabul. They could easily and successfully compete, we believe, with some of the best in San Francisco. There are just we six Americans, three Italians and four Filipinos to feed in the mess hall.

Besides this group, six American couples live in three adobe duplexes, and the only children are a baby boy and a boy of six. This boy being of school age, is taught first grade work by his parents. They use the Calvert course of school instruction from Baltimore, Maryland, which is "tops". . . . I found it so with first-grader son Norman in south Texas.

The mess hall is just a long squatty adobe building whitewashed on the outside. The walls are streaked from the muddy water running off the roof during times of infrequent rain, giving the whole a camouflaged appearance.

The roof is supported by heavy skinned poplar poles upon which are spread willow or tamarisk woven mats covered with dried mud in which is incorporated straw to prevent cracking.

The inside really looks fresh and clean. The walls have been painted aquamarine with white trimmings. Over the windows the women have placed bright yellow curtains which they have made from cotton materials purchased at the bazaars. These shades eliminate the bright light from outside, and are objects of decorative beauty as well. We are proud of them as they impart a home-like atmosphere to the mess hall. We have three long tables, each large enough to seat eight.

The kitchen is equipped with diesel oil-burning stoves, and these are spacious. There is storage space for canned goods and non-perishables. There is a deep freeze for meats, eggs, cheese, fresh vegetables, fresh fruits and other perishables. And a snow machine provides coolness for water to take to the field, and for iced tea, lemonade and other juice drinks at the table. Before supper each man is allowed to draw from the company stores two cans of beer if he desires, but this is paid for by the individual and is not part of the mess.

Seated at the tables this evening were Charlie Jones, area superintendent; Fred Long, concrete inspector; Wright Holstein, farm superintendent; John Lindquist, office and camp manager; Hal Craig, general field engineer from Manzel Bagh; Mrs. Hal Craig, nurse in charge of hospital and first aid; Wallace Segurta, mechanic in charge of transportation equipment; Recardo and Bruno, mechanics newly arrived from Italy; Reinaldo Entienza and and Jacinto Sabiniano, field engineers; Tim Fijardo and Don Riva, accountants and general office men; and last (and least conspicuous), the writer, construction engineer.

Well, people, would you like to know what these men are like — their homes widely separated around the earth?

Let's take Segurta — congenial, affable "Wally" — from a large automobile plant in Milan, Italy. Greatly higher pay attracted him to M-K-A. Efficiency on the job and accommodating to the nth degree, he served in the Italian army for seven years including four years as P.O.W. in Africa and England. As to Mussolini, says Wally, "He good for some people. Not for me, no. Not for mechanics!" Captured in Libya and held by the Australians, Wally claims to have been fed fresh corn — nothing but roasting ears — and ever since is repelled by the sight of them. Later he was transferred to England and worked as a factory mechanic. The Italian government taxes him $35.00 each month for the money he sends home to his parents in Milan.

Sabiniano — "Jack" — energy and seriousness adulterated occasionally with levity — at Malpua Technical Institute, Manila, switched from commerce to civil engineering. A guerilla during Japanese occupation, his home is on shores of Lake Laguna, and while surveying for the Philippine government remembers well that memorable day the war began for him. A Jap plane brought down an American PBY aflame over that lake. The PBY was piloted by my nephew, Ensign "Bill" Jones. Bill was returning with his squadron from a successful mission against a Jap cruiser in the China Sea when the enemy plane seemed to appear out of nowhere, as was later reported by a member of this squadron whose plane was ahead of Bill's. Coincidentally enough, Jack remembers this incident. . . . Well, Jack had later worked in Guam, and now here in Afghanistan, far from wife and children. He was working with a purpose — acquisition of a stake for rebuilding his home. It had of necessity, he said, been bombed by American planes when the Japs were in retreat. Jack is gladdened each time by the arrival of letters from his twelve-year-old daughter.

Then there is Holstein from Fresno — well, Wright and Wally are making good progress in assembling a "combine" for harvesting our wheat this summer. You see it came unassembled from the International Harvester Company. That was all right but in this connection here are thousands of small parts all jumbled together in the utmost confusion in packing cases and sacks with no identification. All bolts were in cases by themselves, likewise the nuts — things like that! No labels, no parts catalog, no assembly guide! Wright is from the University of Arizona at Tucson, is an agriculturist.

Here's Mrs. Craig — "Minerva" — the very jolly lady, formerly a nurse with the Columbia Steel Company at Pittsburg, California, and a friend to anyone in need. The day of her arrival from Manzel Bagh — and from the United States after a three months' voyage by Norwegian tramp steamer out of San Francisco — said Ab-dul (Ob-dool), our first aid man with enthusiasm and in confidence to her, "You come here pretty soon as nurse, I know."

"But, Abdul, how would you know that? Until yesterday I didn't know it myself!" said Minerva.

Abdul replied: "I pray Allah you come. So I know sure you come."

And Hal Craig — rough and ready Hal — a Marine lieutenant on the famed Burma Road — from the U.S. Soil Conservation Service in California — a mechanical engineer of top experience.

Then about "Rey" Entienza — a scholarly type, smallest of all in stature — single — one sister a school teacher, the other a pharmacist — smiling and courteous — studied civil engineering at Malpua Technical Institute, attending classes in the evenings, holding down a full-time regular job in the daytime — six hours sleep — this for four years. Rey is in charge of a survey party — all Afghan crew men.

John Lindquist is from the San Francisco Bay region — a former Union Oil Company agent near Watsonville. John is in charge of the commissary and mess, store, warehouses and office. With John on the job, all these activities function smoothly; we have the best of eats — the best of all the four M-K-A camps in Afghanistan, as is generally conceded. And that is why we have so many visitors from other camps on week ends — that's the main reason!

Then there's Tim — not too handsome — but this lack is made up by his ready and understanding smile, geniality and helpful cooperation. Tim is in the office all day with Lindquist — likewise Riva, favorite of the ladies, but "engaged," he says, to a girl in the Philippines; and Jack comments, "I wonder who's kissing her now. As for me, I already have something to work for!" Both Tim and Don spend much of their leisure time at study on their correspondence courses in accounting; they want to be C.P.A.'s.

Well, these four young fellows from the Philippines, even though not aware of it, are splendid examples of how Uncle Sam's protectorate over that island republic is paying off.

About Charlie Jones — he doesn't object to being known as an ex-Seabee — black-haired, dancing eyes — hardboiled when occasion so demands — but good natured — is proud of the construction training he got in Oregon on the Owyhee Reclamation Project under my friend, the late Oscar Boden, later construction engineer on Contra Costa and Delta-Mendota Canals. Charlie is a most practical minded young man.

Fred Long says he'd like to go to Indo-China when this

job is over, to help out in building concrete fortifications for the French and Viet Namese in their war with the communists. Long talks very little, but from his conversation it appears he was at one time a colonel with the U.S. Army of Occupation in Germany.

* * *

For the last couple of days at many of the jobs, I would be greeted by the *jamidor* in charge like this:

"Hello, Mees-tah Pol-i-Jens, *che tor ast* (how are you)?"

"*Besyar khob!* (very good)," I'd reply.

"*Beeg jamidor come?*"

"In a few days he come to see you," said I.

At a bridge, forms were being removed from new concrete. It was noon, however, and the men were eating lunch — tea and bread and a little mutton. As I munched on some cornbread, newly baked, that was offered me, several gathered about to admire the large stone in my gold ring — alexandrite — transmitting the most brilliant scarlet rays of the desert sunshine or the pale blue of the sky — and colors in between, including a sparkling deep green. These men admired the stone greatly, and seemed to have heard about it through others, as well as the story and sentiment connected with the ring; for they would have me turn it to the sunlight at various angles, and several times one or several pointed to the sky saying *"Chee-na,"* and with their hands imitated the deadly crash to earth of an airplane in a tail spin.

At this particular job the men had just been paid. Their pay varies from 700 to 800 *afghanis* per month — $12.00 to $24.00 — which is all the Afghan government allows the company to pay them. Only a very few, such as interpreters, get any more than that. To top government men, 1500 *afghanis* per month is big compensation. Some showed me

110

their bills. I would hold them up to the sun, and there displayed in the transparency would be the likeness of their King.

Then I pulled out a couple of U.S. $1.00 greenbacks, the last of my American money, except for a few traveler's checks. To the some fifteen gathered about, these were objects of much interest. They would feel the texture — *"Khob, besyar, besyar!"* — and then talk about the pictured engraving in Persian words I did not grasp.

Suddenly a young fellow edged forward and over others' shoulders inspected the greenback. "Mees-tah, Mees-tah *Khushal,"* he called to me, "that is General George Washington" — that last in perfect English, I noted in amazement.

"Hey, *Agha,"* I asked. *"Che farm-u-did* (what did you say)? What is meant by that name '*Khushal*' you just called me?" I was determined to find out.

"Oh, Pol-i-Jens, we name you 'Mr. Happy Man,' 'Mr. Jolly," 'Mr. Goodfellow' — just like that — 'Mees-tah *Khus-Hal!* You O.K. *Am-ri-kan,"* the young chap added smiling, while others chuckled softly.

After a diligent search in my Colloquial Persian Vocabulary, I discovered later why this particular greeting was invariably accompanied by an undisguised look of quiet amusement; the words properly spelled are *"Khosh Shal"* and mean literally "Good Shawl." And also in Pakhtu they mean just what the young fellow said: "Happy Man — jolly — goodfellow."

But, folks, the application also has remarkable historical significance, reliably stated as follows: *"Khush-Hal Khatak* (1613-91) is the national poet of the Pakhtuns, known and revered as the 'Father of the Pakhtun language.' His poetry ranges over a wide scope of subjects, including love and philosophy. He even entered the field of orthography reform and introduced several innovations. He was, moreover, a master of the sword as well as of the pen. He sacrificed himself repeatedly in the cause of Pakhtun independence."

And as I was leaving this last crew, Ee-sa in charge called out, *"Far-da beeg jamidor?"* and I replied not tomorrow but soon.

"Yes, the *'beeg jamidor'*," president of Morrison-Knudsen Company, Inc., of Boise, Idaho, with its worldwide construction activities, would be here soon to inspect the work being accomplished by his organization on this tremendous Afghan project.

* * *

The arrival of Mr. and Mrs. Morrison at Camp Chahi-i-anjir was made the occasion for something special. At the mess hall that evening tables were decorated with wild flowers. There was a bountiful turkey dinner. Many officials of the company were out from Kandahar. It was a real Emkayan — Italian, Filipino and American — gathering of welcome to the Morrison-Knudsen International Construction Company president, a man hale and hearty at around seventy.

Among many things Mr. Morrison observed casually was that: "You people here are pioneers, like in our own early west. You are on the firing line. We can do much to help these backward people. Just remember you are from the United States. To these Afghans you represent America. That's why it's important that we all conduct ourselves so as to maintain the respect and admiration we have already engendered among these people.

"Our projects are far-flung . . . from Afghanistan to bleak Labrador where we are building a railroad and dams for getting out iron ore . . . to Montana, where the town of Libby will be moved to make way for a tremendous wa-

112

Community of Russian Turkmen. Helmand River and Valley in Distance.

Standing grain is laboriously cut by hand sickles, bundled, then carried by hand and stacked in middle of field. Here threshing has begun.

Raw desert land yields to the plow and water. Following flooding by irrigation, the seed is broadcast on bare ground. Then the field is plowed and cross-plowed, followed by harrowing with tree branches.

Black stallion is the pride of his owner

Comfortable travel for babe, mother and grandmother together with purchases from downtown Kandahar.

Gateway to ancient city of Ghazni. In both this and the citadel, note the architectural perfection and evidence of massive strength — both are ancient structures.

Modern business block under construction, Kabul. Adobe and poplar poles are the basic materials.

(Above and Below) On a hill above the plains, Parliament buildings are surrounded by old shade trees, spacious lawns, colorful flower gardens.

A scene in the King's Gardens on foothills of Hindu Kush.

The lofty Hindu Kush from Paghman.

Parliament grounds are approached along this poplar-flanked avenue.

The Hindu Kush.

One of the numerous parliament buildings.

A well defined walkway in the green garden of the King.

Rice, meats, cakes and apples are sold to holiday crowds in shade of trees along irrigation canal which borders Chaman.

The purchase of a small cake in the market place.

A veiled woman of Afghanistan. She could be sixteen or sixty. It should be noticed the woman is completely covered.

After a strenuous march, these tired soldiers find restful relaxation within these architecturally and colorfully beautiful vaulted corridors.

Note the pleasing architectural effect — the beautiful archways.

Ancient palace bathing facilities uncovered by French archaeologists.

ter project . . . to Hell's Canyon on the Snake River, Idaho
. . . these projects to cost not just millions, but billions of
dollars . . . to the interior of Peru on irrigation development . . . to the dense green jungles of Ceylon on dam and
electric power plant construction . . . to Venezuela, building a road and railway from the Orinoco River to tap a new
iron bonanza . . . to British Columbia on tunnel construction through the Cascade Mountains for getting out alu-
minum ore . . . to French Morocco on air base construction
. . . to Columbia, building industrial plants and pushing
a highway through jungle mud . . . to a vast power development in Brazil . . . to Japan . . . to Australia . . . to New
Zealand!

"And now having mentioned pioneers, I think of the
West and of my own experiences as a young contractor on a
railroad job somewhere west of Winnemucca, Nevada. Had
traveled a long way that day in a buckboard pulled by a
span of mules. Habitations were far apart. At dusk I drove
into a lonely ranch. A man greeted me from an alfalfa field.

" 'May I stay here overnight?,' I inquired.

"Said the rancher, 'We live in the cabin over there. Just
one room. But I reckon it's all right. Guess you could sleep
with Madge.'

"Taken aback by this gesture, I said, 'Well, if you don't
mind, I'll spread my blankets out on that haystack over there
by the corral and spend the night with the mules.'

" 'Suit yourself, and welcome, partner,' said the rancher.

"Came sunrise I started rolling up my bed. Hearing
merry whistling, I turned just in time to observe a pretty
young lass tripping jauntily through the corral gate, a milk
bucket swinging from one arm.

"Surprised, I exclaimed, 'Who are you?'
"Startled, she stopped in her tracks. 'O-oh-I'm Madge. And
w-who-oo are you?'

" 'Me-me . . . I-I'm just a gawky damned fool!' "

'Midst the outburst of amusement, an understanding look passed between the Morrisons and one wondered if this might not have been the way of their first meeting. Mrs. Morrison (Ann) travels by plane all over the world with Harry. He won't go unless she comes along. She has just finished a book covering her travels entitled, *"Those Were the Days."* Extracts of this book have been making interesting reading in the company's monthly magazine publication entitled, "The eM-Kayan."

Well, Mr. Morrison continued his speech by way of tribute to the women on the construction jobs. Said he: "As to the wives of construction men, I claim to be something of an authority, both from personal experience and from widespread operation in domestic and foreign fields of M-K's operations. A very large number of wives of M-K men, many with their children, are living in construction camps far detached from the normal conveniences of cities and towns. These women are the social and intellectual equals of any like number it has been my privilege to know. Their temporary camp homes generally reflect, not only the best of taste, but astonishing resourcefulness in overcoming the handicaps of their isolation from shopping centers. They are sharing their husbands' lives in a truly mutual fulfillment of the marriage contract.

"Life in a construction camp varies with the nature and size of the job and its duration. It has always been M-K's policy to provide the best housing and facilities the contract makes possible, yet in any temporary community, makeshifts are nearly always necessary. Neighborliness, patience and tolerance are essential to contentment. Community social life requires cooperation and ingenuity.

"Children must attend school, and this poses varying problems; but always they are solved. These schools may not compare favorably with the facilities at home, but many sons and daughters of itinerate construction families stride ahead of their classes after they have become oriented in new localities, their minds apparently broadened by travel at tender ages.

"In most foreign countries our American wives have the partially compensating advantage of low-priced household servants, but the lady must acquire some knowledge of the language, and both she and the servants go through a period of mutual training and adaptation.

"We of M-K's management never lose our gratification at the high types of men who go into the wilderness to run heavy construction jobs — men capable of making their livings in softer occupations at home in the States. But equally gratifying is the devoted presence of their wives, turning the camp into a livable environment, exerting the feminine influence that keeps a man doing his best."

Mr. Morrison stated he is now in Afghanistan during the course of a round-the-world trip, this being one of many similar journeys to visit construction projects of M-K and subsidiaries in foreign lands, including the Pacific Islands.

"The few weeks required to make such trip by air," said Mr. Morrison, "including the slow overland travel between airports and projects, illustrates the world's rapidly shrinking distances and the growing opportunities for international cooperation between peaceful countries for economic improvement.

"M-K is frankly proud of its part in building the facilities of progress in faraway lands. Although our activities abroad, as at home, are strictly those of private contracting firms engaged in engineering and construction work for profit, international friendship is being fostered by our people in the natural course of their performance and their contacts with officials and local citizens. In every case they hire and train native workmen in the construction crafts, generally raising their standards of productiveness, self-reliance and prosperity.

"Our pride in these men — and wives, too — who go abroad as the company's able representatives, can hardly be exaggerated. At such distances from their home base every problem is intensified. All their needs for principal materials and supplies must be anticipated far ahead when shipments take from one to three months to arrive by sea and then by truck or train.

"These traveling 'envoys' of M-K are chosen, of course, with all possible care as to both skill and adaptability. The extremely small percentage of error that has shown up in such selections is a tribute to the dependable character of engineers and constructors to whom our business owes its existence.

"The most important purpose of this trip around the world is to visit, consult, encourage and thank these people who personify, not only M-K, but the United States, in countries that have favored us with their confidence and have staked their aspirations and their precious dollars on our performance."

*   *   *

At this reception, on my left sat Ja-lal-ud-deen (Light of the Religion). I had seen him at various conferences acting as interpreter between our English-speaking officials and those of the government, most of whom spoke Persian or Pakhtu. He is a tall, dark, bearded fellow — these beards make an Afghan lad of twenty look like a man of forty-five. He seemed to be liking our food — a very fine turkey prepared by Abdul and his helpers — as who wouldn't — but nevertheless seemed a little out of place. So I ventured, "Have you ever been in a Texas oil field?" Just why I said that I'll never know.

"Oh no," said Jalaluddeen, "I've never been in the

United States. I've been in India, Pakistan, Iraq, Saudi Arabia, Turkey, Egypt — have you ever been in the Nile Valley?"

"Only to look down on it from an airplane," I answered. "I could see canals, cultivated fields, orchards, villages — somewhere between Alexandria and Cairo, it was. There were a few scattering white clouds below us, and beyond there was so much green — a beautiful sight!"

"Since you mentioned oil fields," continued my friend, "I was once with an American geologist when we discovered oil close to the Russian border. This man represented an American oil company. He claimed he could just smell oil in that valley. I told him there never had been any prospective evidence of oil reported in that area. The geologist told me he would bet anyone 50,000 *afghanis* there's oil close.

"So I, or we, went on a search of inquiry to many villages. No — no one knew anything about oil. Finally I showed a chief a roll of *afghanis* . . . you get the money when you show me oil! Right away the chief led us to to a spot where oil was seeping out of the ground. He showed us heavy oil-soaked rock — what you call it?"

"Oil shale," I replied promptly. "Say, Julaluddeen, take me along sometime when you go back up there, won't you?"

"Who's that Afghan across the table?" I heard one of the women whisper to Chief Engineer Hohlweg, who sat next to her.

"The wilderness and the solitary place
shall be glad for them; and the desert
shall rejoice, and blossom as the rose."

— Isaiah 35-1

117

VII
They Were There

CHAPTER VII

They Were There

April 19th

WELL, folks, today Gordon King, a dashing young man
from the United States embassy at Kabul, and hardy
Allen Stanley, our M-K-A hydrographer, returned to Chah-
i-anjir from a trip they had made into a wild and little-
known country near the terminus of the Helmand River
along the Afghan-Iranian border. They had traveled between
remote villages, and eaten and slept in the crude adobe
dwellings of local people for the last three weeks.

Stanley makes this trip regularly in a sturdy truck
equipped with two-way radio and hydrographic equipment,
taking along the necessary assistants. He supervises the river
gaging stations whereby we are able to obtain a fair estimate
of the volume of water passing down the river at certain
points. Near Yuma we do the same thing on the Colorado
River to find out how much water passes the international

boundary into Mexico and the Gulf of California; and down the All-American Canal into Imperial Valley. Only over here the Helmand River has no outlet but terminates in a wide area of overflow lands, marshes and lakes on both sides of the international boundary — a region comparable in size to the state of New Jersey — and at least half of this lies in Afghanistan. The whole region has potential possibilities of development by flood control, drainage and irrigation in varying degrees. The largest lake and marshy area is about eighty miles long, lying in Iran, and is now called on the map Hamun-e-Hirmand. Not so long ago this broad district, historians tell us, was subject to more rainfall than now, and greater productivity, and supported a large population. As a part of the Persian empire and later that of Alexander the Great of Macedon it was termed the "Dragiana," and the basin or sink into which discharge many local streams as well as the Helmand River was known as the "Sistan."

*   *   *

"Well, Al, do you ever have any difficulties down there — how do you get along? I'd like to go with you sometime," said I to Stanley.

"Oh, the people know me. I always stay with the village chiefs. Sleep on the ground — eat the same food — have no privacy whatsoever," said Al.

Said I, "Do you ever have any real trouble?"

Said Al, "Well, one time some soldiers stole our horses. Down in that country I always take with me a big Afghan — weighs about 225 lbs. He traced down the guilty pair, gave each a sound beating, and got back the animals," said Al.

"Well, that paid off well . . . to have a man like that you could depend upon," said I.

And, folks, this was Shir Ah-mad (sheer ah-maud), Lion of Mohammed. His name well signifies his aggressive and courageous character. Months later, on hazardous occasions, these factors stood both Shir and me in good stead.

Continued Stanley, "Another time the motor went 'haywire.' I radioed back to Kandahar for help. After a few days here comes Charlie Jones packing in from Farah a reconditioned motor on the back of a camel."

"How do you get down into that country, Al?"

"We go to Farah, on the main road from Girishk to Herat — stay overnight at a hostelry in Farah — then travel southerly to the Helmand River delta and a caravan center called Chakhansur, a distance of some 100 miles. Then near Qala Kang we come to a wide canal. Here we leave our truck and take to horses. You just do as the Afghans do and get along fine," continued Al.

"There's one place though where I invariably get stuck with the truck. Afghans in the vicinity prepare their camels when they see us coming — to pull us out. Their help this way generally costs about 150 afghanis — $4.50. Further along we pass through an ancient city for about eight miles — paved streets, ruins of buildings are yet to be seen. This place was recently written up in a current magazine as a new discovery. May be related to Qala Beest, where the French archeologists are excavating right where we measure the discharge of the Arghandab River as it flows into the Helmand — thought to be 3,000 to 4,000 years old — existed prior to Islam. Traces of this civilization are found at various levels."

"Tell us about your stream gaging in that strange land — and anything else you have found out about it, Al," said I, becoming more intrigued from his description about this wild and forbidding part of Afghanistan.

Al said, "We have measuring stations on the main river and in its various delta channels. Local people help us keep records on these. I see them every two months. The British were in there years ago. They were the people who put that boundary line between Iran and Afghanistan right across the delta lands of the Helmand. At one time they had 1,000 men down there engaged on survey work."

Thinking of the Colorado River delta and the Mexican border, I said, "That's a strange way to locate a boundary between two countries — right across the delta of a river. How come? This could easily lead to serious trouble through disputes over the diversion of water upstream for irrigation — diversions that would be to the detriment of people in Iran — could cause war. Already we are finding indication of some such difficulties on the Boghra Project."

"Yes," said Stanley, "the situation is causing friction. The British were playing up to Iran, or Persia, at the time."

And now I was looking at my maps stapled to the adobe wall of my quarters — nine World Aeronautical Charts prepared by the U. S. Army Air Force, all neatly fitted together edge to edge, forming one immense map of Afghanistan and the frontiers of the adjoining countries on a scale of 190 miles to the foot — the U.S.S.R., Iran, Pakistan and around to China. These I had obtained at the suggestion of my niece Elizabeth at the last moment in San Francisco from the U.S. Coast and Geodetic Survey, and that was a most opportune idea.

"About how much is the river flowing at Girishk now, Al?" I inquired.

"Around 35,000 c.f.s."

"With that flow," I mused out loud, "70,000 acre-feet per day — let's figure — that would take only around two months to fill our 4,000,000 acre-foot reservoir behind Kajakai Dam when completed in the spring of 1953. Do you realize that's enough water to irrigate 1,000,000 acres of Afghan land in the valley of the Helmand and the Sistan? Wheat, cotton, rice, corn, alfalfa, clover, sugar beets, fruit, livestock and other crops we haven't dreamed of yet. What potential wealth this Helmand Valley and Sistan possess under present day scientific development and management. A fine modern civilization should thrive here. By the way, Al, what kind of people are living on the lower river and basin lands now?"

"Very poor people," Al rejoined ". . . even poorer than elsewhere in Afghanistan. A sort of feudal system prevails. Only wheat is grown extensively. People here have a name for the winds and sand storms that last up to 120 days at a time — 'Shamal'."

"Oh, I see what you mean — 'northers,' 'Shamalon' — a land of north winds," I added explanatorily.

And then I read aloud and with a stick pointed on the map to strange names like Fa-rah, Cha-khan-sur, Qa-la Kang, Nuk-ju, Cha-har Bur-jak . . . all along the easterly or right bank of the Helmand River, and the international boundary . . . and to other places scattered over this vast Dragiana or Sistan basin, like Sohren Qa-lat (ruins), Qala-i-Alzel (desserted), and to one place in particular seemingly centrally located in the delta with caravan routes leading to it from six directions like the hub and spokes of a wheel, a place just over in Iran named Zabol which even yet was indicated to be a center of trade . . . and to other villages — I counted eight or nine — marked "deserted," and to whole areas and places, a dozen or so in number marked "deserted villages," or "deserted villages and forts," or just "ruins." There were large areas designated "subject to flood," and "dasht" (desert).

The whole set-up indicated an abandonment of large regions by ancient civilizations . . . how old, will we ever know?

And at this juncture, said Stanley, "Oh, we go on horses

125

as far south as Chahar Burjak. A river gaging station is there."

And then we discussed and speculated on what we knew of the history of the area. To help out at any time along this line, I had brought from the states with me a number of the National Geographic Magazine maps, and one in particular bearing on the subject was on the wall over my bed. It depicted the empire of Alexander the Great in the year 325 B.C. All of these maps displayed in my room were proving to be a center of interest to the many persons visiting or living in our camp . . . to Afghans as well as to Americans, Filipinos and Italians. Charlie Jones had already told me confidentially:

"Say, Paul, about those World Aeronautical Charts in your room that show the Afghan-Soviet frontier country. Members of the Afghan Commission a couple of years ago saw similar ones we had on the wall in the 'Rec' Hall. Would you believe it, they got excited and resentful, and from their attitude and expressions of surprise as much as said, 'Why that's a map of Russia! Get it out of here!' "

"Well, Charlie," I had said, "there's no point in hiding one's head in the sand. The more the Commission, as well as we, know of the Russian frontier facing Afghanistan, the better we will all be prepared for the inevitable. Besides, we're not spies!"

So Charlie had smiled in his pleasant way and with emphasis had said, "You're damned right, Paul!"

So here were Stanley, King and I poring over these maps and discussing ancient history bearing on the parts of Afghanistan in which our daily work was taking us, or with which we were otherwise concerned and interested. For weren't we associating and working with these people whose manner of living evidently hasn't changed one iota since Biblical times? And profiled against the desert horizon

126

everywhere weren't there these remnants of ancient fortresses? How strikingly evident it was that they had been well and carefully planned by the ancients as to strategic location, advantageous topography, inter-visibility, pleasing architectural appearance, and engineering design and construction? Weren't we seeing these strongholds throughout this Helmand delta country, and all along the Helmand River northeastwardly to the sources in the Hindu Kush near Kabul . . . and likewise up the Arghandab to Kandahar and on to Ghazni and Kabul? And these were the routes traveled by the battling and conquering Greeks under Alexander the Great from the time of their defeat of Darius, King of the Persian Empire, at the battle of Karbala on the Euphrates near Baghdad in 331 B.C., to the battle of Hydaspes and their conquest of the Indus River valley, in 326 B.C.

Yes, swift messengers had sped forth from the camp of Darius to the far corners of his empire, summoning fighting men from all quarters of the compass. And they had responded by the scores of thousands . . . "Men in such numbers as the world had never seen before," the historian states.

And from northern Afghanistan and Baluchistan the satrap of Arachosia led his clansmen and mountaineers. Out of Afghanistan and Turkestan, from Bokhara and the steppes of Kara-kum, poured the wild horsemen of Bactria and Sogdia under the satrap Bessus. And they came as allies, not as subjects, men who fought for the love of battle and danger. Of deadly accuracy and enormous range were their U-shaped reverse bows. Formidable were their curved swords. And out of Afghanistan and Aria came shaggy tribesmen upon shaggier ponies, and they trotted for weeks along the desert roads converging on Baghdad and Babylon. And down the Helmand Valley and into and across this Sistan basin and on westward over deserts and mountains of Iran, came

127

armored war elephants. With a contingent of bearded Pakhtuns, Rajputs and Punjabis from India, they had stalked through the mountain passes south of Kabul and into the valley of the Helmand.

But the ponderous hordes of Darius did not prevail against the forces of Alexander, fewer in numbers but swift moving and well disciplined. And Darius himself, in the fiftieth year of his age, died a fugitive from his conquerors, "a king," historians agree, "imprudent and inept both in war and in peace, who succeeded to the throne by fraud and murder, and left it the same way."

It was Alexander, himself, personally in command of a small but swift moving cavalry unit, that overtook the fleeing column of Bessus just southeast of Damghan in Iran and 450 miles northwesterly of Herat. Darius stubbornly refused to leave his chariot to ride a mount with his faster fleeing cavalry. Frantically Bessus and his commanders pleaded with him. Then in desperation and "exasperation they drove javelins into his body, hastily gathered six hundred men into a squadron, and galloped away" toward Herat and their homeland of Bactria in the Hindu Kush Mountains.

It appears Alexander in pursuit of Bessus, whom he feared as a possible successor to Darius, moved swiftly into Herat. All people bearing arms were put to death; others were made slaves. Realizing Herat's strategic importance as a trade center, and its value as capital city of the Arians — the original Aryans — Alexander improved, enlarged and strengthened it, and posted there a strong garrison. And today, as then, Herat — ancient beyond knowing — is the center of trade routes from all directions out of Afghanistan — to Turkistan, Iran, Pakistan, India, China — and up the Hari Rud into Bactria.

Hearing that tribesmen under Barsaentes in the Sistan Lake country were raising an army of defense, Alexander

128

marched his forces southward to Farah and onward to a place marked on my map as Zabol, or a nearby village of Nes-rat-a-bad. He called it Prophthasia. However the historian says, "the most probable site of the ancient capital is the ruin known today as Shahristan, some sixteen or eighteen miles southwest of modern Nasratabad."

Well, as the conquering army marched south, Barsaentes fled, but was later seized and delivered back to Alexander, who had him slain.

The historian states that "within the last few decades it has been discovered through various means that . . . the Sistan and southwest Afghanistan were, in that day (of Alexander) rich lands with vastly greater population than today. The lake itself was correspondingly greater, includ-the whole of the desolate sink today known as the Gand-i-Zirrah, now a curved depression, partially occupied by salt swamp. The whole of Asia was, in that period, demonstrably much less arid than today, a truth especially applicable to this section. The rich lake delta and lowlands were an obvious source of large food supplies; the many populous villages and towns equally prolific sources of potential enemies. Both of these would have remained untouched had Alexander bent his steps along the Farrah-Girishk caravan road. But food was needed for the army, and the population must be subdued and subjected if for no other reason than the necessity of again leaving only chastened and cowed people in the rear."

Well, folks, this conquest of the Sistan took place in the year 330 B.C., the historian Lewis V. Cummings tell us.

*   *   *

But to get back to our reclamation project —

It now so happens that 2,280 years later — in these years of the 1950's A.D. — another "conquest" has begun . . . this time in reverse.

129

AFGHANISTAN VENTURE

The conqueror: His Majesty, the King of Afghanistan, and his Government.

The army: M-K-A, Inc., with its thousands of Afghan workers.

The enemy: A recalcitrant Nature.

Cause of war: Nature's enforcement of its decree that a vast region be doomed to drought forever.

Field of battle: The Arghandab and Helmand River valleys and Sistan basin.

Battles won: Near completion of Arghandab Dam; Kajakai Dam; Boghra Canal and Nad-i-ali laterals; and Shamalon Canal.

Reinforcements summoned: Technical guidance; money.

*　　*　　*

So, folks, that's the way the three of us pondered about things past and present — King, Stanley and I — until our reverie was broken by Al:

"Say, men, I've got to turn in — a long trip to Kajakai Dam awaits me tomorrow. Got to measure flow in some canals on way upriver — gaging station at Kajakai and above reservoir site, too — where we'll measure the river."

Said I, "Very interesting — your work, Al. Several of us leave early tomorrow morning also — the Governor's barbecue at Panj-wa-i. It will be an unusual day — it's Juma, you know."

And as Gordon prepared to retire, he enlightened me some about life with the U.S. embassy at Kabul.

Said he, "There are about thirty American families living at the embassy, including the military and teachers. The Russians have more — perhaps fifty families. They keep pretty much to themselves. The city's population is variously estimated, and is perhaps 200,000."

"The teachers instruct in colleges through interpreters," continued King. "Any school in Afghanistan is called a col-

130

lege. Seldom do any of these extend beyond the 11th or 12th grades. One such college is sponsored by a German, where students are given limited technical training for work under foreign technicians. There is really only one university in Afghanistan. That is at Kabul. Here is taught medicine, law and agriculture."

King told of the Afghan army furnishing certain officers — majors, captains — to M-K-A one summer to learn how to do topographic surveying. This did not work out successfully. These men had not the basic training, he said, to grasp this work.

I said, "Well, around here we have had splendid results in training Afghans to handle heavy construction equipment, like Caterpillar tractors, bulldozers, carryalls, air compressors, dragline excavators, ditchers, well drilling outfits, concrete mixers, heavy duty trucks, aggregate plants, grain harvesters, explosives, radio equipment, machine shop equipment — to repair cars, trucks and all other equipment — to read blue prints and boss construction jobs — to do surveying . . . to do satisfactorily everything connected with this vast American engineering undertaking."

"More about these Afghans," said King, "If you want something made that you can't buy in Afghanistan, just show the Afghan a picture of what you want. He'll make for you a pair of shoes, a table, a suit of clothes — just like is illustrated, for instance, in a Sears, Roebuck catalogue — a perfect job."

And then we talked about other things.

Said King, "Twice I had experiences with trigger-happy soldiers near Kabul that I wouldn't want to repeat. For over an hour they held me at the points of eight fixed bayonets until I could be identified to their satisfaction."

"They probably mistook you for a Russian," I said.

Three weeks ago they had stopped en route down the valley.

AFGHANISTAN VENTURE

I was very glad for the visits with these two young men. Bearded now, muchly so, they had eaten enormous stacks of hot cakes and much other good food prepared by our excellent Afghan cooks.

I have a double room with extra bed for any guest, so am fortunate in this respect in getting acquainted with people temporarily in camp. The last had been Mr. Berry, office manager and assistant to the project manager at Manzel Bagh, a former professor of history and economics, he told me at Golden Gate College in San Francisco. Said his wife is leaving San Francisco by boat and will arrive at Karachi in about three months. Berry said he had been on the bridge of a flag ship in Japanese waters the hour the Japs had signed the surrender papers on the "Missouri" a short distance away.

And that's all for tonight, folks.

"Alexander wept when he heard from
Anaxarchus that there exists an
infinite number of worlds. Upon being
asked by his friends if an accident
had befallen him, he returned: 'Do
you not think it a matter worthy of
lamentation that, when there is such
a vast multitude of worlds, we have
not yet conquered one?' "

— Plutarch (A.D. 46-120)

"Astronomy compels the soul to look
upwards and leads us from this world
to another."

— Plato (427-347 B.C.)

VIII
The Governor's Barbecue

CHAPTER VIII

The Governor's Barbecue

THIS will be an account of one day's events, more or less, as I took notes on same at the time, folks. Quite a day, this Friday in April, 1951, our time — Juma in the month of *far-var-din* in the year 1330, Mohammendan time.

My awakening at daylight was partly due to early retirement last evening after a long day's work in the increasingly warmer weather. Also from hearing a mullah at the labor camp, not more than 300 yards from my quarters, calling the faithful to prayer at about 5:30 a.m. . . . "Allah, Allah — God is one! There is no God but Him! Mohammed is the Apostle of God!" . . . a weird chant, almost a wail, with rising and falling inflections, repeated three times.

Four of us dressed in sun-tans rolled forth at 7:30 a.m. in a company "Chevy," on a smooth road made so over the desert by M-K-A, Inc., road graders, to the wide high banks of the Boghra Canal, on top of these some twenty-five miles to the diversion works at the Helmand River.

135

We were headed for Panj-wai (ponj-wa-ee) — Five Waters — and the estate of Mohammed Rafiq Khan in the valley of the Arghandab Rud, some ninety miles away.

Our four Filipinos and three Italians had gone on to Manzel Bagh last evening in order to attend a special Catholic mass service this morning; also to be present at the homes of Messrs. Traverso and Comosso, where a reception was to be held at 10 a.m. "in honor of His Excellency, the Ambassador of Italy, his charming wife and daughter, and Father Bernasconi." So had read the announcement. They would join us at at Panjwai about noon.

The Helmand was nearing full flood, but was well under control here at the diversion weir, where its chocolate-colored turbulent waters rolled majestically over this long low concrete dam. This a job of beautiful construction completed only recently by American engineers and constructors and thousands of Afghans working under their supervision — the M-K-A, Inc. Toward the easterly bank of the wide river channel, a heavy submerged rock weir is being over-topped its full length by the swirling currents. This rock work, at lower stages of the river, forces the stream flow entirely into the main channel of the river leading to the diversion weir. But for this arrangement, a flood flow crowding against the eastern shore could scour out a channel which might take the entire river flow as the floods receded, leaving the elaborate diversion works high and dry. As we viewed this situation, it was agreed that as the floods went down these works would be inspected to note any possible breeches or settlement that might have developed in the rock revetment, and plans made for repairs.

Water was being diverted into the Boghra Canal, but not a full head, and a large part of this was being turned back into the Helmand under the two huge steel automatic radial gates at the wasteway structure, which we had crossed this morning some four miles downstream from the canal headgates. By running a large stream of 1000 to 1500 c.f.s., and unchecking frequently at the wasteway, deposits of sand and silt can be sluiced back into the river.

The watchman at the weir and Boghra Canal headgates we found living in a small hut nearby with his wife and children. His pay from the Afghan government is so meager it's pitiful. He wanted "bakh-sheesh."

In this early morning the valley countryside was green and beautiful with fields of growing wheat separated by low adobe walls in lieu of fences, and long rows of spreading mulberry trees. Patches of blooming white poppies appeared in corners of some fields. People traveled the canal banks in gala attire on little ponies, bullocks, burros, or camels.

Over there valley meets desert — a steep ascent of perhaps a hundred feet. Here for about four miles the desert scarf is surmounted by the adobe ruins of an ancient civilization which governed this land — compounds, quarters, defense works — ending in the huge and well preserved fortress commanding the town and surrounding valley countryside and endless desert stretching far to the northwest toward Iran.

And among the dwellings and compounds and gardens close to the road were children, and women and girls with black head coverings, peering covertly over mud walls and from behind trees at these strange foreigners, and here as we turn out on the main road past a public school building, a woman turns sharply to look us over, a white lattice affair over her face. She could observe us plainly without being embarrassed by our return glances — a girl of sixteen or a woman of sixty-one — how was one to know? Such is the Moslem custom. This, the purdah and all it implies over here, is a major barrier to progress as we Americans size up the social situation.

137

Off to the north side of the bridge over the Helmand, stands a series of huge piers and brick arches remnants of a bridge built by the Germans. They had erred on the foundations. The piers had been undermined by the floods.

Then we come to the villages of Zambuli and Yakh-chal (the place of ice). In this vicinity live hundreds of the families of the Turkistan Russians forced (?) across the border into Afghanistan by "Joe," so it was said. All men and boys over fifteen were promptly imprisoned by the Afghan government and held for eight years. While among the prisoners were a few who had wrong intentions, the great majority were potentially good citizens, and when freed were allowed to settle down as such with their families. It appears, however, there had been actually some among their leaders who were planning annexation to Russia of the lands occupied by them. These were found out and liquidated. The men are tall and straight and of huge frame. Their features are Mongol, with high cheek bones, and their appearance is classic. Many of them work on our project. One I'll always remember — Taghi, the truck *jamidor* — always so friendly and genial, attending strictly to his own assignment.

Well, folks, this morning Charlie is driving fast. Rounding a sharp turn in the road, we narrowly miss a herd of thirty-four camels grazing peacefully nearby. One, partly grown, a cute little fellow, runs in panic to its mother, but she calmly continues munching on camels thorn. The desert is partly green from meager spring rains. We overtake a caravan of forty or more with six cameleers. On the leeward side of the animals, the scent is strongly musk. They move easily along in file, some tied by ropes from the rings in their noses to the tails of the ones ahead. To me, in a camel caravan there's always something of enticing interest. There proudly walks one in the lead with a fancy pair of twins, one on each side.

138

Something prominent is looming up on the landscape ahead. It's an orchard within a mud wall — and there's no visible source of water. It developed that this once belonged to a prominent man now dead. It is being taken care of by a mullah. The water reaches it in a small ditch whose source is that line of *kareeses* extending from the mountains down that little valley.

What a resemblance to Arizona is this land of mystery. One glance at the humans and their activities, however, and you come out of your reveries. Besides, there is no cactus or sage brush, but wild red poppies are in evidence.

We pass through Khugiani (koog-i-onee), a string of bazaars on each side of the road, a school building, a district governor's office and a scattering of adobe huts. A prayer platform gives a touch of religious atmosphere. A grove of mulberry trees through which winds an irrigation ditch with running water looks cool and inviting. This place has been dubbed "Kansas City" by the Americans, being easier of pronunciation. We cross the dry bed of a wide deep arroyo just beyond this village. It is called Kushk-i-Nakhud (koosh-ki-nak-hood) Rud, and following heavy rains in the mountains to the north during the spring it severed road connections with Kandahar for days at a time. Here some time ago was located one of our road survey camps. They used the peaks flanking this desert corridor for triangulation stations.

That mountain scarcely five miles to our left is fascinating — a chrome yellow mass, gnarled and jagged against the deep blue of the sky. It rises precipitously from the desert plain some 3,100 feet. The air is so clear, it seems one could almost reach out and touch it. I did not know that some months later I was to have an unusual experience behind it and at this town of Khugiani.

This is a land of fantastic mirages. That peak to our

left across the desert seems to be detached from the earth's surface, like a huge ship on a great lake.

On the right some miles is the low-lying Arghandab River valley with what appear to be green wheatfields and rows of poplars. And the river appears to be surmounted on its far shore by a bluff which could be twenty feet or a hundred feet high due to the mirage effect; one cannot be certain.

Beyond these bluffs is an impressive sight — what looks to be a turbulent yellow ocean the vastness of which is emphasized by the level horizon where it meets the blue sky far out to sea, as it were. But this is not water. It's a region known as Registan, reaching from the Arghandab to Baluchistan — 130 miles and equally as wide — comparable in size to the combined areas of Massachusetts, Rhode Island and Connecticut — the Dasht-i-Poghdar, a trackless waste except for a few caravan trails. The myriads of shifting sand dunes appear as waves. They gleam with reflected yellow sunshine and dark shadows form their background in the late afternoon or early forenoon. Drifting blow sand in the gentle breeze appears as yellow spray.

At Haus-i-Madat (a place for the help), groups of men with turbans wrapped about their heads, and wearing light, loose garments, sit upon their heels in serious demeanor. No women are visible.

And a ways further are goat herds. This is the season when the young are being weaned and are herded in separate droves. They are surely cute little fellows in black and white. The black tents of nomads who own these herds are seen in the distance, and nearby their camp is a camel on the end of a rope, being driven around and around at a trot.

Truly this is a land of wide open spaces reminiscent of our great Southwest. Only now the desert is meagerly cov-

140

ered with a variety of short grasses and a plant that hugs the ground and has cylindrical watery leaves salty to the taste, and the rank-growing camels thorn.

And then the painted desert, a rolling region reminding one of our own Western deserts and range lands in the springtime. As in California, the blue and gold of the lupine and poppy, in Texas the bluebonnet, in Oregon the yellow buttercup, in Imperial Valley the purple desert verbena — so here in faraway Afghanistan, in Central Asia, the smiles of God are also on this landscape. For here, as it were, a huge paint brush has spread about haphazardly, but radiantly, the colors of royal purple and sage gray — masses of low bushy sage arrayed in full bloom with multitudes of small reddish purple flowers. And mingling and alternating with this brilliance are plots of a waving silvery grass emphasized by a light breeze and the Afghan sunshine. And, as though to complete this colossal work of art, nature herself had harmonized the whole against scattered bare patches of chrome yellow earth. This scenic landscape extended for some ten miles or more.

And now to our right beyond the river the yellow choppy sea of dunes and blow sand is giving way to jagged peaks rising half-submerged from this desert wasteland, isolated from each other, coal black, pinnacled and mysterious against the golden skyline of this early forenoon — finally forming a continuous range of mountains, high, black and saw-toothed.

We cross the Arghandab on an unassuming but substantially adequate simple timber trestle bridge built by our company at the beginning of its operations in Afghanistan. Flanking this on our left are the remains of a bridge built by the Germans years ago, imposing piers of granite blocks but unable to withstand the rush of spring floods. And on our right likewise is an impressive but unfinished beginning of a masonry arch bridge — Japanese. The reports concerning these two structures and the one across the Helmand at Girishk are vague.

Up a steep and tortuous grade and past a tax collection station, we cross over a main canal and pass by a shrine where the traveling faithful stop to face toward Mecca in worship.

Already we have met some six or eight lorries this morning. These are large trucks with staked bodies piled high with freight and people. The passengers ride in tiers or on top of the freight. Several of these lorries had stopped for repairs beside the road. The passengers patiently wait aboard the stalled truck, or lie around on the ground in relaxation. Over there is a man in reverent prayer, his prayer rug spread out under him. The driver may be overhauling the motor — the wait may be for a day or longer — but no, fortunately, it is only a stop for tire repairs. A man is patiently using a foot pump to put air in a big tire. Some trucks are loaded high with 200 lb. sacks of wheat, last year's crop. People are disposing of this now due to the nearness to harvest of the new crop.

We pass a roadside well. Two men with a bucket on a windlass are alert to serve water to travelers. They live in a mud hut nearby, the only sign of habitation for miles.

An hour more and we near Kandahar, passing people en route to the city by camel, burro and bullock — and nearer the city, in two-wheeled carts are purdah-covered women and girls facing to the rear, men to the front.

The Arghandab Valley is on our left now, broader and greener, with gently sloping desert on either side of the narrow cultivated areas.

We enter an area of many small vineyards. We see them through openings in the mud walls. They are pruned apparently as on our Pacific Coast. "The grapes here are better than in California," my Oregon friend in the front seat maintains.

142

THE GOVERNOR'S BARBECUE

The vines are rooted in ditches on the northerly side of mounds, possibly four feet high, over which the vines spread out and bear their fruit. These mounds take the place of the wire trellis supports in the vineyards of our Pacific Coast. Wire is scarce in Afghanistan. All metals are.

But, let's forget this. We are on our way to Panjwai — and the governor's picnic, with Morrison-Knudsen Afghanistan, Inc., employees as guests. "Emkayans" we call ourselves, and it is a big event for us "foreigners." We leave the main road and head south among a jumble of those projecting black-pinnacled peaks. My map shows they rise 1,200 feet and more above the plains — straight up in places. They border the city of Kandahar on the west and north.

Now we are entering the governor's feudal domain. Here is a large two-storied adobe building, a granary for wheat storage. Nearby is a cluster of mud huts. Then open wheat fields, the wheat in head. There are small orchards behind adobe walls, too; one can just see the tops of the trees.

The governor has told us he owns some 20,000 jeribes (10,000 acres) of land; he just isn't certain how much. A *rais* (rah-ees), superintendent, looks after the land and tenants — sharecroppers. The governor and son had once been stopped by an overseer.

"You'll have to get out of here fast," said the overseer. "If the governor ever finds out you're here, he'll make much trouble."

In this vein the man had protested at length, failing in his plea to get the supposed trespassers to move on.

Finally the son said: "But this is my father and he is the governor!"

The overseer's apologies were then lengthy, much to the amusement of father and son.

We park the "Chevy" in a grove of beautiful mulberry trees. A group of Afghans greet us reservedly. One indicates in a friendly manner, "Follow me."

143

AFGHANISTAN VENTURE

This seems to be a small village — this Panjwai. We progress through narrow, winding, walled lanes and between adobe dwellings. Curious children peer out from entrances to courts, followed by unobstrusive glances of older sisters and mothers who are not veiled.

Through an opening in one mud wall, I smell and see goats, sheep and several black cows and work bullocks, quietly feeding.

We cross an irrigation ditch, carrying possibly twenty c.f.s., flowing along and under walls, hiding and reappearing . . . a baffling network of narrow alleys, courtyards and dwellings . . . and finally we come to a beautiful open area.

Here are many shade trees, fruit trees, flowers, sunken gardens and wide graveled paths.

Facing these grounds is a long, one-story adobe residence with archways, patios and beautiful landscaping. The architectural effect is marvelous. The irrigation lateral flows in front flanked by flowers and shade trees and an adjoining patio. This is adorned with beautiful rugs. Large mulberry trees provide cool shade.

The governor greets us in a most friendly manner, shaking hands all around. In gray suit, black karakul cap, with polka-dotted kerchief and broad chin whiskers, he looked impressive, as he seated us at small tables in the patio.

Then we all chatted and nibbled large raisins, some of black and some of green varieties — very tasty — and parched dried peas, and drank hot tea. The governor's two sons, lads of around eighteen or twenty looked after the guests. They wore neatly pressed tailored blue suits with pin stripes, and karakul caps, and in their lapels what looked to be medals for rifle marksmanship. Several other young men in loose garments helped serve the *chay*.

The governor seemed occupied with the men preparing the barbecue in large pits nearby.

While relaxing in these beautiful surroundings — they

144

seemed especialy pleasant and cool after the dryness and dazzling heat of the desert — my gaze inclined upward into the wide spreading branches of the mulberry trees, and the foliage and heavily-laden twigs of growing fruit. I was thinking why don't they produce silk here as in Japan — when I spied, not twenty feet away, looking over the top of the wall from the roof next to the end of the patio, the heads and shoulders of a line of eight or ten of the darlingest little girls. They were about ten or twelve years old. They were getting a general view of the party, even though not invited. Later they were in the gardens. They looked so gay in colorful little filmy kerchiefs worn partly over head and shoulders — red, green, yellow — and long silky pantalettes of black, or in color, with broad white lace anklets, and little black sandals, or slippers.

Then the musicians took their places, seated upon rugs. There were three of them, one with a long keg-shaped drum, another with a large stringed instrument something like a heavy mandolin, and a third with a sort of accordion laid flat on the rug. Now this music is difficult to describe — totally different than any kind I'd ever heard.

The man with the accordion sang a strange melody interspersed at intervals with a series of high-pitched guttaral notes accompanied by a violent trembling of throat and head, alternately similar to the whinnying of a horse and the bleating of a sheep.

While taking in all of this, and while the others — American men and just a few American and Italian women, and the Italian men and Filipinos chatted — my gaze again wandered covertly to the overhanging wall. The little girls had disappeared. Now women with black purdahs were attentively looking over the foreign women. These were so busily engaged in conversation that the Mohammedan women were unnoticed. Taking in this situation, I sensed that these veiled ladies were charmed with the attire, man-

145

nerisms and independent bearing of this alien femininity.

During all of this I drank about six cups of most delicious *chāy*, and then looking around more closely, noted some who were not showing this same appreciation. Then I observed men carrying platters of meat inside, under the watchful supervision of the governor, himself.

Wright Holstein, Reed and I and several others moved toward the entrance to the dining hall. Here several men had jugs of water which was poured on our hands, accompanied by lathering with soap. Then a towel was offered. We walked into a spacious T-shaped hall. On the floor were long narrow strips of canvas upon which the food was placed. All around were rugs close to the walls. There were platters and bowls of mutton, fowl, beef, *palau* (rice), greens, curd, pudding, and thin slabs of bread shaped like snow shoes, and bottles of water. Also there were other foods I did not recognize.

Due to crowded conditions it was an effort to get adjusted to a cross-legged position on the rugs. In these maneuvers, I planted one foot directly into the plate of the man next to me. He didn't mind.

The food was not passed. You just reached out to the platters and helped yourself by aid of your fingers. The rice, being half dry, was easiest to eat. I tore off a chunk of barbecued beef and found it delicious. I also helped myself to fowl, greens and bread.

During this repast one of the governor's sons came walking along among the heaped-up platters. He was seeing if all was well with the guests. Later Mohammed Rafig Khan, himself, came along in like manner.

An American woman near me whispered loudly, "My mother would never let me walk on the table like that!" From the semi-darkness, a man's voice rejoined, "Your mother wasn't modern!"

Upon leaving the dining hall, men again poured water

146

on your hands and gave you a towel. I noticed many Afghan men in alcoves adjoining the main dining room, doing a neater job of eating — less messy, I mean — than had the foreigners. Also, they had removed their shoes and placed them in a pile at the entrance. Beyond the large outer archways one could see outside to the gardens where there were groups of solemn men squatted on the ground eating out of large common platters of rice and barbecued meat. These diners had also placed their shoes in piles nearby.

My companions and I were filing out pretty well to the rear of the crowd. I suggested to Wright and Reed, "Why don't we look around the building and gardens before we join the others in the patio?"

Seeing a door slightly ajar along one side of the main corridor, and thinking it led possibly to an orange orchard or sunken garden, or the like, I said, "Why don't we see what's out this way?" and no sooner said than done.

Well, folks I pushed past this heavy door. Behind it, but until then unseen by me, was a dark brown man, high of stature, with jet black well-trimmed beard, and clad in immaculate white. He scrutinized me darkly and questioningly, as I walked briskly past him. A quick glance behind showed me to be alone — Reed and Wright had not followed!

The dark fellow followed and brushed rapidly past me, shouting something I did not comprehend. I followed him at a rapid pace thinking, "Out here's something interesting. Maybe the camels are stampeding!"

Coming to a right-angled turn in the passageway, the white-clad one hesitated, and then gesticulated and admonished in no uncertain terms at something beyond. Still puzzled and determined to see what went on here, I rushed forward. Amazed I suddenly found myself in an open courtyard, off from which led a dozen or more doorways with a small low patio in front of each. And in each patio

147

were young unveiled Moslem women, just sitting there talking maybe, or like they had nothing else to do.

Surprised and abashed at this uninvited and apparently rude intrusion, many scurried for the doorways. Others, noting no offense was intended, lingered, or seemed to be leaving reluctantly. I had rushed squarely into the midst of a Mohammedan harem!! — probably an unheard of violation of Moslem etiquette — more serious since it was done by a foreigner. . . .

Then there was time before the afternoon entertainment when I began to stroll about the premises. Looking over low walls towards the south, one saw a vast expanse of wheat fields, now turning from green to the straw color of ripening heads. A light breeze caused silvery wave movements of the standing grain. Canals diverting water from the Arghandab Rud made this splendid crop possible. Later I was to learn more about this river, and the canals and people living along them.

There was an orchard of pomegranate trees, apricots, almonds, apples and a vineyard.

Maple trees along the ditches planted close together were forced to grow with a single branch, tall and slender, with just a bunch of twigs and leaves at the very top.

While thus engaged during the early afternoon, I would reflect on the late after-dinner episode, momentarily expecting serious and unfavorable action from high quarters. None came!

Soon further entertainment was being provided in an open space near some tall Italian cypress trees.

A man entered this enclosure beating a drum. Its beat was steady. Men began to enter from all sides doing a steady dance around and around the drummer in the center of the circle. First there was a long hop to the right followed by two short ones. Then a repetition of same to the left. And all the while there was vigorous waving of arms overhead,

148

turning about, advancing backwards and forward. The rhythm steadily increased, accompanied by weird singing and shouting. There was recruiting on the sidelines. Others were urged to fall in, young and old.

An old man, seventy-five at least, fell in, starting out with a slow and easy movement. Finally one at a time many were dropping out from sheer exhaustion, until just two remained, one of which was the old man.

It appears this dance is based upon a legend: men are marching off to battle; slowly at first they bid farewell to loved ones. The fast movements and shouting and singing represent the heat of the engagement. To drop out of the dance in its early stages is considered disgraceful.

Beginning the next feature, two men locked arms. This represented a bridge. A third man, the bridge keeper, would dart about to prevent anyone from the sidelines from springing upon the back of either of the two men. Soon, however, one of the bridge men was supporting two other men on his back, one on top of the other. The ones who failed to reach the bridge would endeavor to regain the sidelines without receiving a violent kick from the keeper.

Well, we left Panjwai about 3 p.m., thinking to get back to Chah-i-anjir about dusk. It was a hundred miles about.

I thanked the governor for a "mighty fine time." In doing so I removed my sombrero, something the other Americans were failing to do, bowed, touched palm of left hand to breast. At once the governor smiled appreciatively, removed his karakul cap and did likewise; and this I knew to be good etiquette.

Getting back to the main road we four discussed a black precipitous mountain mass on our right. A well-beaten path extended part way up to the foot of a flight of steps, at the top of which appeared to be a shrine. Said Charlie: "A legend has it that Marco Polo was married up there to an Afghan woman. Since then it became customary for women,

149

especially wanting boy babies, to climb arduously up and then down those Forty-Nine Steps on hands and knees." I was to climb these myself and learn more about them at a later time.

Well, we ran out of gasoline after three hours of driving. This happened on the bank of the Boghra Canal three miles below Girishk.

Said Charlie — CMJ, Charles "Mohammed" Jones, we jestingly dubbed him — "I'll walk back to Girishk and see Yo-sef (Joseph) about getting gas."

"I'll go with you," I promptly rejoined. It was nearing sundown.

We met many men on foot, on donkeys, camels or bullocks, that we had just passed in the "Chevy" along the top of the canal bank. Some seemed to know us; undoubtedly they were M-K-A workmen walking twenty miles back to Chah-i-anjir after a holiday in Girishk, for greetings went like this:

"Ma-da-na-bashi," a man would cheerily say in wishing we would never get tired.

Not to be outdone, I would answer, *"Zandah bashi,"* in wishing him long life. Viva!

In meeting one I definitely knew, *"Che tor asti?"* or "How are you?" I would inquire.

The answer: *"Besyar khob!"* — very good.

Or, *"Salam alekom,"* a man would say to Charlie ("Peace, be upon you"), and then Charlie would respond similarly; *"alekom-o-salam* (upon you be peace)."

And some would just say "Hel-lo, mees-tah," or give a hand salute in a friendly manner.

Well, all this seemed to make shorter the distance we were hiking.

Pointing to the opposite bank of the canal, "Charlie, what is the meaning of those broken-down archways over there?" I said.

"Those were erected when Engineer Shah had completed the Boghra Canal to this point. The arch fell down the day before the prime minister arrived for the celebration," said Charlie.

"Well, who lives in that nice place over there?" I wanted to get the lowdown on some things I had often noticed, Charlie having been in Afghanistan for some five years or so before I arrived.

"The former governor of Girishk," Charlie continued. "We put that small flume across the canal for him. Wouldn't have done it had we known at the time he had turned Chaman over to the British." (I did not know what he had reference to, so said nothing.)

"Why are there so many graves back there — thousands of them?" and I pointed toward an extensive burial ground along the Boghra.

"We think they are the graves of workmen — those who were digging the canal by hand when the Japanese were overseeing its construction," said Charlie, as we neared the bridge crossing the Boghra at Girishk.

We found Mr. Yo-sef and a dozen customers, or employees, relaxed in the front of his establishment. Here was a new and neatly-constructed adobe building with sixteen stalls for bazaars and a large compound inside — and a gypsum plant, brick yard, orchard, alfalfa field, tea shop and garage.

"He has all kinds of money," said Charlie.

Mr. Yo-sef shook hands and had us sit down outside near a line of potted flowers. It was the cool of the evening; the sun had just set; and it was very pleasant here, accepting Yo-sef's hospitality at *chay*.

Then a young man approached and sat down to have *chay* likewise at a nearby table after greeting Charlie.

In a low tone said I, "A fine-looking chap — a college boy — Yo-sef's son?" I suggested.

151

"No, he is the mayor of Girishk," said Charlie.

The mayor wore a karakul cap, light sport jacket and typical Afghan trousers, white and sort of gathered and pulled up between the legs.

"Well, Charlie, I believe Yo-sef is a good example of a self-made business man," I said.

*   *   *

And now, folks, in order that you may understand "harems," here are rules governing marriage relations in Afghanistan:

"Respect women, for God is watching over you."

"Take in marriage of such other women as please you — two, three, or four — and not more. But if ye fear ye can not act equitably towards so many, marry one only."

"Men shall have the pre-eminence above women, because of the advantages wherein God hath caused the one of them to excel the other, and for that which they expend of their substance in maintaining their wives. . . .But those of whose perverseness ye shall be apprehensive, rebuke; and remove them into separate apartments, and chastise them."

"Now are the true believers happy: who humble themselves in their prayer, and who eschew all vain discourse, and who are doers of alms-deeds; and who keep themselves from carnal knowledge of any women except their wives, or the captives which their right hands possess (for as to them they shall be blameless: but whosoever coveteth any woman beyond these, they are transgressors)."

"They who accuse their wives of adultery, and shall have no witnesses whereof besides themselves, the testimony which shall be required of one of them shall be: that he swear four times by God that he speakest the truth, and the fifth time that he imprecate the curse of God on him, if he be a liar. And it shall avert the punishment from the wife, if she swear four times by God that he is a liar, and if the fifth time she imprecate the wrath of God on her, if he speaketh the truth."

"If ye be kind towards women, and fear to wrong them, God is well-acquainted with what ye do. Ye can by no means carry yourselves equally between women in all respects, although ye study to do it; therefore turn not from a wife with all manner of aversion . . . fear to abuse your wives."

"O prophet, speak unto thy wives, and thy daughters, and the wives of the true believers, that they cast their outer garments over them when they walk abroad; this will be more proper that they may be known as matrons of reputation, and may not be affronted by unseemly words and actions."

"Thou mayest postpone the turn of such of thy wives as thou shalt please; and her whom thou shalt desire of those whom thou shalt have before rejected: and it shall be no crime in thee. This will be more easy, that they may be entirely content, and may not be grieved. It shall not be lawful for thee to take other women to wife hereafter, nor to exchange any of thy wives for them, although their beauty please thee; except the slaves whom thy right hand shall possess."

"By the star when it setteth, your companion Mohammed erreth not; nor is he led astray: neither doth he speak of his own will. It is no other than a revelation which has been revealed unto him. One mighty in power, endued with understanding, taught it to him: and he appeared in the highest part of the horizon."

So admonishes the Koran as translated into English immediately from the original Arabic about 1734 by George Sale — "a gentleman of extraordinary learning, and a perfect master of the languages, customs, habits, manners, laws and traditions of the Eastern nations."

AFGHANISTAN VENTURE

"The task and triumph of religion is to make men and nations true and just and upright in all their dealings, and to bring all law as well as all conduct into subjection and conformity to the law of God."

H. J. Van Dyke

IX
Stirring Events

CHAPTER IX

Stirring Events

FOUR MONTHS BY WATER, rail and truck from San Francisco. What? That large steel, strap-bound box which greeted me a few days ago as I came from the heat of the desert into the soothing coolness of our adobe quarters. Inside, carefully packed in layers of shredded paper, were my locker trunks and S72L Hallicrafter Radio set.

During this 120-day interval, I had gotten along famously on the clothes included in the sixty-six pounds of baggage allowed me on the plane. In this there had been three sets of underwear — very simple, just briefs and shorts — two pairs of khaki slacks, four colorful checkered shirts, a long-billed khaki cap, heavy field shoes.

The Afghans had liked the looks of the green, black and red rayon shirt — their national colors.

Fortunately, Lawrence Kelsey had arrived this same day from Manzel Bagh. He had gotten the radio set adjusted and functioning properly, and was evidently quite impressed with it. Also, in our recreation hall, he was installing a wonderfully new and powerful long distance short wave receiving set. It was now bringing in programs from every continent . . . none of them regularly or continuously, mind you, but surprisingly frequent.

In this wild and remote country, radio communication between far-flung construction jobs is of extreme importance. It is Kelsey's responsibility to install, maintain and operate the company's radio facilities extending from Kandahar to Kabul to each of the construction camps, to company cars anywhere carrying transmitter and receiving sets. Kelsey trains and oversees the Afghan operators, sees that all communications go through promptly day and night. He has his central station, shop and quarters in the King's Palace at Manzel Bagh, and is doing a marvelous piece of work.

Something about Lawrence, himself — really a young man of notable traits. When first seen by our men in Quetta en route to Kandahar, Kelsey presented the appearance of an English explorer — all in white — sun helmet, blouse, shorts, socks, shoes and, in contrast, a growth of long black whiskers. Although California-born, somewhere Kelsey has acquired a pronounced British accent — possibly in New Zealand — with which on occasion he unaffectedly delights to provide entertainment.

It seems in the spring of 1947, Kelsey shipped from Beaumont, Texas, with Finn Ronne's expedition to the south polar regions. In *Antarctic Conquest*, the explorer himself states regarding Lawrence: "For radio operator we had Lawrence Kelsey, a Californian, who was studying radio engineering in Washington when he heard about the expedition. Although not quite twenty-one, Kelsey had already had four years' experience as a merchant ship radio operator. As soon as he presented his credentials, I gave him the job of getting our radio frequencies and licenses from the Federal

Communications Commission. Later in New York, we worked out the radio and radio photo transmission technicalities with the North American Newspaper Alliance and *The New York Times*. Weather reports, scientific messages, communications with field units, and regular traffic left him little free time."

As Kelsey was relating his experiences, I pointed to a map of these polar regions — one of the *National Geographic Magazine* — stapled to the adobe wall of my quarters. With a quick movement he was in front of the map carefully tracing the course of the expedition and noting where corrections and additions should be made in accordance with information acquired by Commander Ronne and his men. Here were features named after members of the expedition. Here was a bay named "Kelsey Inlet."

After that, Kelsey worked for M-K-A a couple of years, and then spent two years on an archaeological survey in India — again without pay, so he said. And then Afghanistan beckoned again. Hence here he is now, a handsome young man, about 6' 4" and 201 lbs., clothed in green shirt, green shorts, green beret — straight as an arrow — telling English jokes that make people chuckle long before the point is reached (because Kelsey is telling them using English terms scarcely understood by Americans).

And so, folks, that's Kelsey . . . !

           *   *   *

There has just been another one of those border flare-ups . . . skirmishes near Chaman between guerillas — Pakistani vs. Afghan or Pakhtun. It seems in the clash some women were stolen. The information comes to us underground — *jamidors* get it from their men — and there are rumors of impending war.

This meager news reached our general manager at camp one morning a hundred miles west of Kandahar. Our rail supply line to Karachi and the coast could be severed summarily. There promptly followed a radio conversation over the M-K-A network somewhat as follows: —

G. M. (turning to John Linquist, office and camp manager): "Have Kelsey call Schenk at Kandahar. Get the latest."

Linquist: "Say, T. J., Kelsey's apt to be taken for a British spy! Then we'll all get into trouble. Right?"

G. M.: "Hadn't thought of that. I'll radio myself." (Picking up mouthpiece.) "Hello . . . Hello . . . Hello, Schenk? Well, listen to this carefully. Did our supplies come through this morning from Chaman?"

Voice from loud speaker: "Sure, T. J. Why not?"

G.M.: "Well, do you expect the rest from Karachi in a couple of days?"

Schenk: "Sure. Why not?"

G.M.: "Say, Schenk, I want you to take a ride down through Kandahar — the streets and environments, right away. Radio back to me what you see unusual!"

Schenk: "What in hell are you driving at, Ted?"

G.M.: "You mean you don't know what's happened? Why you . . .!" as T. J. handed back the instrument to the amazed Re-za Goo-lee, and grinned broadly as he stalked out of the radio room.

*   *   *

After retiring early, sometimes immediately after supper, one often arouses for an hour or two at midnight, or after, to tune in on world events in the "rec" hall. This is most delightful entertainment to anyone in the back country of a far, faraway land; and often at this time the night shift is coming off work at the machine shops and garage and there are coffee, tea, cold drinks and sandwiches available in the mess hall.

Well, folks, there is the day's news from London over the B.B.C. — not much American news. American stations are heard only occasionally. The Italians, enraptured, listen to opera in Milan and Rome. Swiss yodelling is at its best.

160

There are loveliest strains from Scandinavia and Holland. The meleodies of Spain are softly sweet and romantic.

One could listen by the hour to the alluring, enchanting notes from Ankara — wildly mysterious, suggesting Turkish harems, I guess. And then the strange and wildly sweet melodies out of India — the same from Colombo, Ceylon, alongside of news in English and Western records. From China and Thailand come a weirdness of sounds out of this world.

The prolonged squawk and and cackling of the kook-a-burra introduces an Australian station with news, song and instrumental music from "down under," together maybe with an account of agricultural development in the Darling Downs.

Our Filipinos are entertained with programs from Manila. There is news in English from Tokyo and songs by Japanese radio stars, skits in Spanish from Buenos Aires, messages from a Christian missionary in Quito, fandangos from Mexico City, accounts of doings in Canada from Montreal, news from Cape Town — U.S. Armed Forces programs from Germany, the Voice of America relayed from Tangiers. And not far away the Kabul station broadcasts sounds that to us are wild, outlandish, unearthly — followed by news in Persian or Pakhtu.

Yes, most of these broadcasts, although not audible regularly, and often then only after prolonged periods of silence, are heard with keen interest by all of us far out in these wide open spaces bordering on central Asia. They are entertaining, educational, wholesome, and — in so far as we could determine — were accompanied by a spirit of good will. One pondered about this modern miracle — radio.

And you can tune in on Moscow or Tashkent almost any hour of the twenty-four — their stations are nearer and powerful — and be entertained with Russian opera on occasion, magnificient in the extreme. But they'll also keep you informed on the latest worldwide developments — in

161

AFGHANISTAN VENTURE

English and right off the Pravda press, if you please (you can imagine!). You'll learn the most recent on "germ warfare" — oh yes, you can't doubt it, for they read extracts from letters and conversations with American prisoners of war — all experts, it appears, on the distribution of deadly germs over North Korea — giving name, rank, branch of service and home address by town, street and number They'll tell you about their love of "peace," about the pleasantness of existence in the Soviet Union, about the imminent crack-up of the United States. And they'll proceed further to excoriate us in terms subtle, lying, deceitful, vicious, hateful! And this happens every day, if you care to listen.

Say, folks, some of us purposely turn off the radio and start playing pool when outbreaks like this occur . . . don't like to get too worked up.

Most have just experienced disappointment, disgust and bitterness over the fiiring of MacArthur.

Scorn, contempt and denunciation from these rough-and-tumble Americans in Afghanistan has been heaped upon the perpetrators of this traitorous, treacherous act. And here in Asia, Moscow and Tashkent are further encouraged to insult us openly before the world without the slightest fear of reprisal.

Appeasement, conciliation, cringing behind a Russian bear already in retreat, fighting a war according to the enemy's rules, the disastrous retreat from the Yalu. . . .Why, why?

There were those who maintained the bear should be shot summarily.

As for me . . . in fields infested with rattlesnakes in southeastern Nebraska during my early youth — hadn't I helped my three older brothers shock oats and wheat behind the old-fashioned binder? Alert for the warning whir, one cautiously approached each bundle as it lay in the tall stubble. Was the reptile rendered harmless by a pass at his

162

rattles? Ridiculous! One whack on his hissing head sufficed!

So now in Washington, could it be possible that a modern Benedict Arnold at top level in government— on a boldly grand scale — was attempting to deliver his country into the power of an enemy?

Folks, these speculations go through our minds and are voiced by hard Americans in Afghanistan, in strong lanage and no uncertain terms.

And one believes Senators William Jenner of Indiana and Pat McCarran of Nevada are right in preparing to introduce a resolution in Congress to sever diplomatic relations with Russia and other Communist countries. Say they: "The conscience of the world demands that this nation, as the last great bastion of freedom, take the lead in expelling from the family of nations the tyrants of Moscow. This course of action would give notice to the enslaved peoples of the world, and those who are threatened with enslavement, that we will no longer welcome their vile oppressors at the council tables of the world to spew forth their venom in mockery of men of good will."

*   *   *

Mohammedan Ramazon ended on panj-shambe (Thursday). This is the month of fasting and prayer for all men and women over fifteen. Excluded are any sick, and those on journeys. There was no eating of food or drinking of water between 2 a.m. and 8 p.m. Although men went to the field to work, on our jobs there was a complete slowdown. On such a fare, can ayone imagine a man working effectively in the intense heat? However, the requirements were painstakingly observed. Then there followed four days of feasting and joyousness.

On one of these days, accompanied by two surveymen as interpreters, I made a special trip to a little place known as Babaji (ba-ba-jee) in the Helmand Valley. We parked our car along side a mulberry grove — a picnic ground near which flowed a rather large canal, the Babaji. Then we walked along the Lui Manda (big arroyo) and across cultivated lands to the fringe of the salt cedar. This is a low bush growing in clumps on the overflow lands. We passed small groups of mud huts with thatched roofs, each surrounded by a wall to form a compound, and all about were fields of wheat the harvest of which had begun. There were rice paddies in the low ground where running water was available for flowing slowly over them continuously at constant depth. There were small patches of cotton and of corn — not in rows as we would plant it, but broadcast in contour basins which could be readily irrigated by flooding.

We stopped for a few moments to watch the operation of a flour mill. Here a stream of water ran from a pond kept full by water flowing into it from an irrigation ditch. The water ran down a chute made from a hollowed out half-log of cottonwood — possibly three cubic feet per second — set on an incline of about 45°. About ten feet lower than the pond in elevation, the swiftly-flowing stream impinged on wooden blades projecting from a vertical wooden shaft. This shaft revolved rapidly from the impact of the water, and turned a circular granite slab, about four feet in diameter and about four inches in thickness, and which revolved on a nether stationary slab of similar dimensions. The grain, that is, wheat or corn or mixture of both in varying proportions, was fed in between the stones from a hopper by a very crude but efficient regulator. This was a little inclined wooden trough whose slope was varied by a cord arrangement and which was vibrated by a trigger device in contact with the revolving stone. The smaller the stream of grain the finer the texture of the flour.

The finely-ground flour centrifugally was driven to the periphery of the revolving stone and dropped into a bin made of adobe, and holding a couple of bushels.

Under the brush covering the inclosure, some fifteen men

lounged about in the shade just taking it easy while awaiting their turns in use of the mill. Some were sleeping on a
pad spread out on the bare ground. Others were talking in
groups. One was smoking a large water pipe in the far
corner — tobacco, charss (marijuana), or opium, which in
any case seemed to lose the noxious effects due to the smoke
being drawn through the water. A man with a sharp-pointed
black beard, noting my interest, explained to me in Pakhtu
the workings of this water pipe. Meanwhile my two helpers
each took a draw. As we were leaving, two men arrived with
camels bearing sacks of grain to be ground. These animals
were promptly caused to kneel and the heavy sacks removed,
after which the animals were tethered nearby on dusty
ground, where they enjoyed rolling.

Nearby in a field, three ox teams were plowing. These
plows are of wood, shod with a short conical iron point.
Farmers here know nothing about plowshares — yet. One
team plowed crossways; the other lengthways of the field.

Here irrigation is by contour checks, this valley land being of deep silt with a gentle slope down the valley and
away from the higher levels along the river channel. Corn
and cotton, both broadcasted in contour checks, were coming up nicely.

We walked over the lands and talked to many farmers.
Our object was to observe any damage from high ground-
water conditions. *"Es-ter-e-mache,"* ("May you never get
tired") was our greeting in Pakhtu. Re-za talked in low
tones to these people, and as best he could, conveyed their
ideas to me. A dozen or more complained about too much
water flowing down the Lui Manda. We were using this as
a waste channel from the Boghra. However, the benefits
seemed to outweigh the damages. Many wanted this water
for growing rice, even though it raised the water table and
did damage elsewhere. All were friendly and good-natured.

165

AFGHANISTAN VENTURE

The valley language is Pakhtu — not Persian — although some seem to understand that also.

One man said the ground water had risen so high the foundation of his dwelling had crumbled, that he had had to rebuild it on higher ground at a cost of 4,000 *afghanis,* or about $120.00 U.S. — a lot of money to these people, and equal to wages over a period of ten months.

Another man led us to a rather pretentious looking building. By word and gesture I got the idea a rise of ground-water was beginning to affect the base of the walls, or would shortly if allowed to continue. Inside on the hard, but damp, dirt floor were rugs, and a neat rectangular basin in center, evidently a fireplace, and above it was a large opening in the roof. There were high open windows where birds flew in and out, and false arch-shaped windows near the floor — no other furnishings. The one door to the place hung on two wooden pegs for hinges and was of wood ornately carved. I decided this to be a club house or meeting place of some kind. Outside grew a luxuriant patch of alfalfa and nearby another that had been cut meticulously to within one-fourth inch or less of the ground surface!

Also in an adjoining area, I noticed growing wild, large clumps of hemp which I recognized as marijuana, whose dried leaves and flowers are smoked as a narcotic.

"Nam-i-en-che-hust?" said I pointing to a clump of this.

"Charss," was the reply.

In the spring I had seen patches of white poppies growing in corners of the wheat fields, as much as two acres in a place. At the proper time the stalks are scarred and as the milky white sap exudes, it dries into small, black, waxy globules. This is opium. The people eat the poppy seeds as a delicacy when they are in the milk stage.

Well, as we looked over the situation further, it became evident that the high water table situation was due to the rice growers' insistence on an excessive water supply from

166

our wasteway, much more than needed for other crops. This we tried to impress upon the people. We could cut down the flow to meet some demands; leave it "as is" to meet others. Which did they want?

By now, it was well past mid-forenoon, and I had been observing groups of women and children crossing the fields toward a spacious mulberry grove and grassy area beside the running stream; they carried lunch baskets. As we passed in meeting them, the women deliberately stepped to one side of the trail and waited for us to pass, and in doing so very pointedly turned their backs on us! Upon first observing these strange gestures, I felt somewhat abashed and insulted. At times, however, perhaps one of a group would deliberately throw off her face and head covering, and, looking interestedly our way, almost muster a smile!

As we approached our car there were groups of men and boys gathering for a picnic of their own at this other grove. Strange customs these!

*   *   *

In the valley, people are harvesting their wheat now. They cut large fields of it by hand. Do they mow it down with a cradle scythe? Oh, no, nothing so modern! A small curved sickle is used with fine teeth like a pruning saw; and they tie it in bundles with long stalks of wheat or wild grass; carry the bundles to a stack in the middle of the field. A pair of oxen is driven around and around the stack, dragging brush and boughs tied firmly together. A man on the stack throws down the bundles ahead of the moving oxen, and with an all-wooden pitchfork also keeps the threshed straw raked away from the path of the circling animals. After many days, there remains a ring of chaff and threshed grain, the grain mostly on the bottom. The driver is careful to remove all cattle manure before it can pollute the grain. On windy days, chaff is separated from the wheat by

167

tossing all against the breeze. The final product is a long pile of cleanly winnowed wheat some four feet high and triangular in cross section. Caravans bear away the crop to market in bags holding 200 lbs. or more, two or three of these to the camel. If left in the field long, the pile of wheat is temporarily protected by a light covering of straw upon which soft mud is spread, smoothed out, and allowed to dry, to shed any possible rain water, or to otherwise protect from the elements. If kept on the premises, the wheat is stored in tall cylindrical bins made of adobe.

Men are seen in the wheat fields, under the burning sun, offering prayer for as long as twenty minutes, unmindful of anything around them, facing westerly towards Mecca. And about sundown likewise about the premises of their humble dwellings, groups of white-turbaned, bearded men lay aside the water pipe and join together in evening devotions to Allah — a long line of them, forgetful of their hard labors of the day in the harvest fields, their minds, their visions in faith reaching far beyond the wheat fields, the lonely deserts — far beyond the setting sun to the Great Beyond and the comforting presence of Allah.

*   *   *

On the company wheat farm of 1,600 acres, we have two International harvesters busily engaged. This crop is for use of the Afghans employed on the irrigation project. The grain is milled at the company's plant and flour at the rate of four *sears* per employee (about one bushel) is rationed out.

As the harvesters pass along, old men, women and children follow behind picking up and putting into sacks scattering heads of grain missed by the machines — even loose grains that have been scattered on the ground. These poor people are from the waiting camps whose assignments to blocks of irrigated land have been delayed. In the meantime they have so little to eat.

168

And in view of these conditions, I am almost apologetic in relating to you home folks what we had for supper in our camp on the evening of July 8th: fresh baked rolls, carrot and raisin salad, cucumbers, tomatoes, fried potatoes, gazelle steak, sweet corn on the cob, tapioca pudding, watermelon. All vegetables but the tomatoes came from our truck farm within four kilometers of where the gleaners were so painstakingly and anxiously following the harvester combines. As gazelle are abundant, we have a liberal supply of venison in the deep freeze, and the men enjoy hunting these fleet-footed animals. One morning about sunrise, I saw seven of them in scattered places.

*   *   *

Yesterday being a holiday, I went with three men who had come down from the Kajakai Dam job, to the ancient bastion of Qala Bist (Fort Twenty). It is only about twenty miles from our camp on a beeline, at the junction of the Arghandab and Helmand rivers. It is near a village by the name of Corez.

The villagers cross the Helmand to watch our construction equipment at work on the Shamalon Canal. The river is still high and wide. The men cross back and forth with the help of two or more large dry gourds tied by thongs under their arms pits, and in front of chest. This way they can float upright and work their way to the far shore with a minimum of swimming effort. I haven't had the temerity yet to try this, so we drove sixty miles around by way of the bridge at Girishk to get to this isolated ghost city.

It is strung out for some ten or more miles on the high lands above the Helmand. My companions were in a hurry to get back up the river to Kajakai Dam that evening. So far as I was concerned this was just a preliminary reconnaissance. I expect to go back a number of times to examine things more closely, for these were not just ordinary people that lived here so long ago.

169

AFGHANISTAN VENTURE

The northern part of the area is known as Lakh-kar-i-bazar, meaning "army division's exchange or headquarters," and here are the extensive remains of the elaborate palace of an ancient king. Not far away is an area of perhaps sixty acres surrounded by a massive wall still fairly well-preserved, and adjacent to it are the remains of a long and extensive two-story structure, the military compound and army barracks apparently. Scattered along the river bluffs to the south, toward the ancient fortress, are the remains of other rather large and important looking buildings, all of adobe. We did not have time to do any more than drive through this area.

Our main objective was the fortress, Qala Bist, for this was visible on all sides for many miles. The crumbling walls of adobe surrounding the place were at least fifty feet high and fifty feet thick at the base, tapering to about a twenty foot width on top. These walls had been laid up in small slabs about two inches thick by eight inches by twelve inches. Massive turrets surmounted and projected outward from the walls at intervals of possibly 500 feet. The walls surrounded a place containing, I would estimate, about forty acres that probably had been level at one time but now is a mass of broken tile, and in among this debris are bits of broken pottery. It looked like there had once been tile-covered buildings in this area which by some circumstance had been smashed to fragments.

But in the midst of this scene of havoc stood a most amazing object — a beautiful archway, perhaps eighty feet high in the clear and sixty feet between abutments with thickness of twenty feet. And looking up at this from directly beneath, with the clear blue sky as a background, are series of panels or plaques with a network of beautiful yet simple designs, so symmetrical, so carefully molded without a flaw, the like of which I have not seen in modern architecture anywhere. And in perfect harmony among these were

170

ten-pointed and five-pointed stars. One could, and I did, study these patterns for a long time in overwhelming astonishment.

Then from the arch we walked on debris up a steep path over what may have been terraces along the outer walls of this fortress Qala Bist. Reaching the top, we had a commanding view of this ancient city of Lakh-kar-i-bazar and the staggered system of smaller forts now crumbling on both sides of the Arghandab and Helmand rivers. One could see for miles up and down both river valleys, fertile and productive, and well-populated without a doubt by subjects of this ancient king who is said to have ruled from Qala Bist all of Northern India, Afghanistan and Persia.

And standing on top of this prominence, with hundreds of square miles of valley and desert lands spread out along radii extending to the distant yellowish horizon in all directions about us, we recalled a certain autumn 2,281 years ago. For it was in the late October, or early November, of the year 330 B.C., historians tell us, that Macedonians under Alexander began their advance up the Helmand valley. For months, they had occupied Prophthasia in the delta lands of the Helmand River. From there they had dominated the then rich Sisten Lake basin following their conquest of Herat. This center of operations apparently was in the near vicinity of what is now the village of Za-bol, where five different camel caravan trails converge from as many directions. Zabol is within Iran about sixteen miles from the Afghan border, and about thirty miles from the Afghan village of Cha-khan-sur, from which many people are now coming to settle on the irrigated lands of the Boghra Project.

There seems to be some doubt among earlier historians whether the army of conquest actually followed the Helmand valley. But later a preponderance of evidence indicates this is true, that the marching forces crossed southwardly over the many delta channels and then turned eastward and

171

then northeasterly up the valley on the southerly side of the river, passing the site of what is now the village of Garmsel (hot place), near where there eventually may be constructed a diversion weir from which to divert water, originating at Kajakai Reservoir, to the lands on either side of the Helmand. And the main body continued onward up the valley and opposite our project villages of Kirtaka, Shamalon, Surkhduz and Zaras, and then crossed the Arghandab just above junction with the Helmand at Qala Bist.

It appears some earlier historians reasoned that the army followed the site of the present main road from Farah to Girishk across the desert, but recent evidence indicates this was not the case, insofar as the main body of the forces was concerned at least.

The first clan encountered was the Ariaspians, an independent and self-governing people. Their caliber and organization greatly impressed Alexander, just as had their hospitality a long time before impressed the army of Darius when here and in difficulties. So Alexander gave them additional territory nearby which they had long felt the need of, but not to the extent of going to war with the neighboring tribes.

One of these tribes was the Gedrosians which inhabited what is now Baluchistan. They surrendered at once to the invader, their lands being but a short distance to the south of Alexander's route. This they believed better than having him pay them a visit and enforce submission.

The other tribe was the Arachosians, whose country along the Arghandab River the conqueror was now entering. Likewise they saved themselves much trouble by submitting at once. They allowed the Greeks, in their onward trek, to found the city of Alexandria — Arachosia — on or near the present site of the city of Kandahar, third largest city in Afghanistan. Here Alexander left a satrap by name of Menon to govern the new city and province. Menon was given an army of 4,600 cavalry to beat off and put an end to the frequent raids from India. These raiders came through the several mountain passes debouching on the area.

Well, folks, we tried from the ramparts of Qala Bist to visualize those events of long ago. Those subsidiary forts in staggered formation on both sides of the Helmand, each visible from the nearest one on either side or across the river; these elaborate works of ancient military engineering — did Alexander build those to hold this empire in subjection, along with this Qala Bist, upon whose ramparts we four were standing on this July day centuries later?

Perhaps we'll know, as the French archaeologists continue their work of excavation in this area.

And we marveled at the valley scene below us, now of a scanty population with limited agricultural development. What's become of the gallant Ariaspians whose attitude and orderly civilization in this very area so impressed two ancient emperors? And, here we Americans from the other side of the planet, in just a few years are expected, and destined, to change for the better the existing order of things for these poor people!

And then I began looking about our immediate surroundings and spied openings in the rampart, one of which I entered. It led to a winding, gently sloping ramp, or stairway almost obliterated with debris. And overhead were arched ceilings.

I then walked across two large corridors with arched ceilings perhaps twenty feet high. It looked as though decorative tiling had been removed from the walls and ceilings.

My three companions now having rejoined me, further along we came to a balcony overlooking a vertical shaft possibly thirty feet in diameter. The sunlight of midday shone down to the bottom through an opening in the canopy above. So I could see the bottom five stories, or about 125 feet below, which we decided was at or below the level of

173

water in the Helmand River several hundred feet away.

At each story level opening out to the shaft were four archways, each shaped like the one outside, and possibly twenty-five feet high, and they led to two parallel corridors encircling the shaft at each story level.

Then we all walked over the debris along the ramp to the next story below, and there was evidence that at some of these levels, tunnels or corridors led out like the spokes of a wheel to the terraces or parapets beyond the outer walls and overlooking the valleys. From the outside, the crumbling walls and debris had all but obliterated any semblance of the outward facilities or architectural form of this marvelous stronghold. However, from a distance, one could readily make out from the portions remaining intact, something of the appearance of the original.

And then apprehensively we went down another flight of this spiralling, debris-choked ramp. Disturbed in their security, bats by the thousands swarmed past us on their way out. . . .

And so, folks, in this way ended our first inspection of an ancient masterpiece of engineering and architecture, and bulwark of military subjection over what was once no other than a marvelously productive garden land.

Thrilling it would be to peer back through the centuries on this ancient seat of an empire at the height of its power and glory!

And thus went the early part of my first summer in Afghanistan.

Often have I wondered if those wheat harvesters in their evening devotions had anything like this in mind — to them a solace — as in the hymn, "Sweet By and By," for I would like to think so:

> "There's a land that is fairer than day,
> And by faith we can see it afar:

For the Father waits over the way,
To prepare us a dwelling place there."

You people at home may not understand, but life in these wide open spaces causes one to ponder deeply. And we Americans in Afghanistan were forcibly affected by the words of General Douglas MacArthur in his address to Congress on April 19th of that year:

"In war there is no substitute for victory. . . .
Appeasement but begets new and bloodier war. . . .
Why, my soldiers have asked of me, surrender military advantages to an enemy in the field? — I could not answer. . . .
The Korean people have chosen to risk death rather than slavery."

So through our minds stirred profound resentment — better expressed in the words of the patriot, Henry Ward Beecher (1813-87): "A traitor is good fruit to hang from the boughs of the tree of liberty!"

X

Progress

CHAPTER X

Progress

WELL folks, we're in the midst of an Afghan summer, and today it's Juma, a fine time to stay in one's air-conditioned, one-meter-thick walled adobe quarters out of the intense heat of the desert. Ordinarily from 11 a.m. to 5 p.m. it's 105° to 113° F in the shade, with a few exceptions of 115° to 120°. The nights are 70° to 80°, a cool contrast to the afternoons when a light breeze is like the blast from a furnace.

We are disturbed by the drastic curtailment of construction operations. All diesel burning equipment is shut down — tractors, air compressors, dump trucks, graders, dragline excavators — just the work that can be done by hand labor will proceed. This includes a lengthy reinforced concrete siphon which will carry 750 c.f.s. under the Bacheron Manda for the valley canal, and numerous smaller concrete structures. On this work, concrete must not be poured when its temperature exceeds 90°F. Actually, due to this latter con-

179

dition, there has been only a negligent cessation of activities.

The real slowdown is because of the Iranian oil dispute and international political conditions in this part of the world. But you folks at home are undoubtedly much better informed about these matters than are we, here so close to the scenes of disturbance.

There may be a complete shutdown soon. However, our general manager has optimistic views. These in spite of the border forays — regardless of the apparent intent of the Anglo-Iranian Oil Company to shut off oil supplies to this part of the world. The proposed nationalization by the government of Iran of this British oil industry is being countered by this threat.

Yesterday, I attended a meeting of our men from each project at Manzel Bagh to talk over the situation. Most of the work at Kajakai Dam is stopped already.

Of what may be in the offing, we only obtain fragmentary information via the Afghan "grapevine" and from the English language newspaper, *The Dawn,* edited and printed in Karachi, Pakistan.

As to British-Afghan relations in the past, we know that the British in India viewed these with utmost concern. Sir William Barton expressed the opinion, shared by his government, that: "The North West Frontier (Province) is not only the frontier of India — it is an international frontier of first importance from the military standpoint for the whole empire."

The "partition of India" was based solely on religious considerations — a Hindu state and a Moslem state. The fate of the Afghan and Pakhtun tribes was not clearly defined. Pakistan assumed that since these people are Moslems, their land should be included in Pakistan territory; to confirm it called for a referendum. The terms proposed, the tribes considered most unfair, and would have nothing to do with it. They met in national assembly in Tirah close to the Khyber Pass and passed a *Declaration of Independence*:

" . . . the National Assembly of Pakhtunistan having formed the first nucleus of a free and democratic Moslem Government amidst the lofty mountains of Tirah, hereby express the hope that, with the help of Almighty God and the support of the brave and freedom-loving Pakhtuns, this young plant may in a short time grow into a sturdy and fruitful tree which will not only benefit Pakhtunistan (from Chitral to Baluchistan, and from Khyber and Bolan to the banks of the Indus) but will also fulfill its obligations to the cause of progress and world peace.

" . . . the people of Pakhtunistan have an unswerving devotion to the cause of freedom . . . will eventually defeat the dark forces which threaten their cherished goal; independence.

"The masses of Pakhtunistan . . . have repeatedly and successfully beaten off the advances of imperialistic power; have gallantly defended their beloved soil from foreign subjugation. . . . evil forces under guise of religion and false promises, would like to trample upon your hard won freedom . . . bring you nothing but slavery, misfortune. . . . to have what is rightfully yours you have fought to ward off your evil enemies from taking possession of your beautiful mountain abode. These lofty mountains and long green valleys which are dumb witnesses of your unforgettable devotion and sacrifice in the past, now once again await your heroic intrepidity and reckless devotion. Your mothers and sisters look to your courage and devotion to guarantee their future happiness in freedom and self-rule. . . . step forward . . . stand united behind your national representatives!

"We . . . extend our heartiest gratitude to the people and government of Afghanistan . . . who have given us moral support. . . . our past assistance to Afghanistan in the hour of her need has won us a special place in the heart

181

of every freedom-loving Afghan. . . . Now that we are in need of help, we turn to our Afghan brothers. . . . we are certain no sacrifice will be withheld from us. . . . we beseech our Afghan brothers to stand shoulder to shoulder with us in this great struggle for liberty and justice."

The attitude of Afghanistan was expressed by the Afghan House of Representatives: "The Afghan nation is deeply alive to the dangers of Pakistan's creation of hindrances and obstacles affecting Afghanistan's political and commercial affairs, as well as Pakistan's efforts to oppress the independence of Frontier Pakhtun Provinces from Chitral to Baluchistan." The Afghan Parliament resolved to co-operate fully with the government in overcoming commercial and political difficulties and achieving the independence of all Afghan brothers.

And there it is, folks — Afghan and Pakhtun will continue fierce resistance against all foreign aggressors just as in times past they gallantly withstood Cyrus, Alexander, Genghis Khan, the British Empire (for 100 years).

But here is our immediate concern: Astride a big construction job well beyond this formidable northwest frontier region, our supply line — some 660 miles of railroad from Karachi, port of entry in Pakistan — could be severed in numerous places at any time by raging conflict! Something to ponder, folks!

Fortunately, water is now available for stock and domestic purposes the full sixty-mile length of the Boghra Canal, and for irrigation purposes on a part of the 16,000 acre unit. It is quite a sight to view this stream of water — blue from the reflected skies — reaching far out into this hitherto almost uninhabited desert — uninhabited except for isolated camps of the nomads, many miles apart, with their flocks of camels, sheep, and goats. And months ago, I would give such camps a wide detour because of the wildly charging dogs, followed by running children, and men waving me away vigorously — or so I thought — with their arms and long sleeves. But recently, much to my satisfaction, I've learned that an Afghan's gestures for "go away" and "come here," are exactly the opposite of ours!

So now as these camps move nearer to available water for their herds, as caravans en route to markets reroute their itineraries to take advantage of this first stage in the development of a national asset — a dependable water supply — just so will we Americans come into closer contact with these people; and especially so will I, since this management of the water distribution is another one of my engineering responsibilities from here out.

And in this matter of water distribution, folks, the agricultural commission is assigning to me an assistant, an intelligent appearing young man by name of Saif-fu-din (Si-foo-deen'). He chuckled as I first pronounced his name.

"What does it signify?" I asked.

" 'Sword of the Religion,' " he said, smiling, I thought, rather proudly.

"Very dynamic — in fact you look to be a man of action!" I added.

And then Saiffudin confided he'd like to get back into the British army — the air force — how could he go about it?

"See the British Ambassador in Kabul — at least that'd be a good start," said I.

Saiffudin said he liked in the army the "good fellowship." Those were the words he used. If the Russians continued to act up he wanted to get back into the paratroopers, where he'd served eight years with the British in the Middle East during the recent war. (We're now only 240 miles from the Russian-Turkestan border.)

And then, we slowed down to estimate the number of camels of all sizes comprising three herds that were crowding into the canal for fresh water.

"About 1,000 altogether is my guess, Saiffudin. These people are wealthy. In American money those camels are worth at least $150,000.00 — 6,000 afghanis apiece for the grown ones.

Nearby were nine large black tents, the temporary abode of the owners, all open on three sides to the morning breeze and sunshine. This camp, true to practice, had a commanding view for miles around. And on the far bank of the canal from us were three young women or girls, dipping up the fresh water. Their men keep the women timid in this country, and a foreigner (of all men) isn't supposed to notice them — but, well, you know how Americans are, folks!

The first of these three suddenly squatted on the ground and covered up with her purdah completely from shiny copper disc-adorned hairdress to graceful brown bare feet.

The second returned my curious interest with one eye peering through a slit in her face covering.

The third was openly and frankly filled with curiosity, until suddenly she bethought to place both hands over her face, peering with both eyes between widespread fingers.

By this time three dogs, powerful and handsome fellows, were excitedly barking and moving swiftly to and fro on the far canal bank. Typical were they of protectors of the flocks from marauders and wild animals — wolves, jackals, hyenas. Their fur is yellowish white and slightly curly. About the head and neck it is tipped with black. Reminded was I of dogs similar to these I had seen staked out on the snow at 67° below zero near Hay River on the Great Slave Lake and opposite Providence on the MacKenzie River — Canadian sled dogs. And above these howling huskies, across the jet black northern sky, arched the brilliantly white aurora for half of the long winter night until it disintegrated into dangling curtains of seemingly whitest mist floating gently southward just above the tree tops of this vast Canadian wilderness.

Invariably these dogs of the carefree nomads of Afghanistan recalled to me vividly those wintry white scenes in the wildness of the Northwest Territories. And this strangely enough, but for these fine dogs, nothing about this hot desert scene in these boundless wide open spaces of Afghanistan bore the slightest resemblance to that far distant Canadian landcape.

And following the dogs, came racing from the tents almost clothesless children out into the hot sunshine.

A man left his 200 or more fat-tailed sheep to drink water in the canal and invited my companion over to the camp to take several drafts of tobacco smoke from his long-stemmed water pipe. In lieu of this he gave me a drink of sheep's milk from a flat copper bowl. These sheep were worth about 630 *afghanis* each or $18.00 U.S., Saiffudin said.

Downright handsome was this young fellow. His brown, finely-shaped features, his black eyes that looked right through you, his stern look but ready smile in response to your greeting in Persian, his erect carriage, his air of complete independence and pride — all bespoke patrician ancestry.

People are coming from afar to go on the land, irrigate and plant crops. The government, however, is slow about providing leadership in this matter, and because of this some waiting tribesmen seem stranded in camps nearby on the desert.

So Saifuddin and I proceeded to investigate this situation. Stopping at a large camp, one is quickly surrounded by tribesmen mostly barefoot, or with sandals made from old automobile tire casings. We say nothing as they gaze solemnly and pentratingly at us, while some make way for the chief to come forward. A pleasant word of greeting in his language — just this simple gesture, and a smile, and the faces of the people light up in welcome, with broad smiles,

185

twinkling eyes and a show of white teeth. The women and girls are in the background in front of the black tents, this time unveiled, their black hair combed smooth and ornamented with copper or silver discs of various sizes arranged about, and one the size of a dime over the left nostril.

The chief would have us come to his tent for *chay*, but this time we decline. We are here to inquire why they are not over there with other newcomers putting in summer and fall crops. The irrigation water — plenty of it — awaits their use.

And Saiffudin, having sized up the situation, endeavored to get the tribesmen's reactions by expounding, as near I could understand, in this manner:

"Bes-mel-lah! O chand vaght digar inja mimanid Khal-a-fam chi-e?" (In the name of Allah! And how long will you stay here? What is wrong)? "Those tribesmen over there — Kharoti! Beyond Durrani! They're putting in vegetables — corn — fall wheat! What will you eat? We want you to get busy!"

At this last their brown faces light up further in perceiving that some one is interested in their welfare.

The chief explains they are waiting for the government to assign them land units . . . and that's what we wanted to know!

*   *   *

Around Fort Nad-i-ali and the experiment station I check with Jan Mohammed about the colonization program. Jan is in charge of construction, the building of adobe quarters to house the people in eight or more villages. This work is under the agricultural commission, whose offices are in the long building inside the fort. Yes, it is true, Jan told me, that 500 families are expected in by camel caravan from Ghaz-ni in the near future — Pakhtuns. Ghazni is 270 miles distant. Jan has their quarters ready. Noor Mohammed is president of the agricultural commission and has general charge of all this land settlement, agricultural development and experiment station work.

"Is Noor Mohammed here now, Jan?" I ask.

"No, His Excellency is in Kabul," Jan rejoins . . . but alas, it develops he is seriously ill in Europe, and no one of equal authority is presently acting in his behalf.

*   *   *

Listening to the Voice of America in the recreation hall last evening, three soldiers entered. The army has guards posted about the camp and environs day and night. These men like to wait outside the window to listen, and often will follow me into the hall. They are most impressed with India music — Turkish, or the like — and of course especially with that of Afghanistan. So I dialed to an oriental station and there came forth a wild chanting, sweet at times, but interspersed with gutteral tones not unlike a combination of a horse's neigh and a goat's bleat. *"In-dee, Ind-dee"* — the three were delighted and swayed in unison, slapping vigorously in time. Then one wanted to compare Persian script to English writing. So I would write down some word like 'sheep' and he would write in Persian below it *'gusfand'* and hold it up for all to see . . . when, *"Bas-bas!"* All became very alert, looking questioningly at each other and then at me.

"Shu-ma fah-mi-di?" said Ka-reem excitedly ("Do you understand?")

"Ba-le, ma fahmidam cum!" It was the Kabul radio broadcasting station. . . . Yes, I understood just a little, and the soldiers explained with vigor. . . . The Korean cease-fire talks had broken down. The Iranian oil dispute negotiations were deadlocked. Stokes and Harriman were going home.

And then, folks, again I thought, well, this is surely a strange situation with which to be surrounded.

Afghanistan at odds with Pakistan — there are border

raids; Pakistan and India mobilizing troops along the boundary between them — something about the status of Kashmir; Afghanistan helping in the formation of an independent state out of Chitral, Northwest Frontier Province, and Baluchistan, to be called Pakhtunistan, and thus have an outlet to the coast — be done forever with Pakistan domination. Pakhtu is largely the language of eastern Afghanistan and Pakhtunistan. Persian is that of Western Afghanistan and Iran. This explosive situation could well be the powder keg of the Middle East.

And there are the Russians beyond their border, 240 miles away, waiting to take advantage of any such situation.

And as I further analyzed the set-up, I remembered hearing recently about a member of our engineering staff — a sort of American adventurer and soldier of fortune — carrying out an exploit in Pakistan. Kingleigh was his name, or something like it. He was a bold, impertinent cuss, for one day along the road he stopped Mr. Ludeen, a top official close to the prime minister, and not knowing his identity inquired glibly as to what was his "game" — what sort of a "racket" was Ludeen engaged in? Ludeen likes to tell Americans about this incident.

Well, Kingleigh goes over into Pakistan, recruits an army division, places himself at head of it — and as such carries on quite successfully for a time. Unmindful of the price on his head, this ex-Ranger mingled freely on occasion with the enemy undetected! Finally, cornered in Karachi, by the grace of the British Consul there he was allowed to escape to sea — so the story goes.

But good news, folks — in spite of all these threatening rumors, we are now getting diesel fuel oil and all other supplies in the quantities needed; so full speed ahead goes the construction!

*   *   *

According to the Koran, folks, Afghans have a decided

188

view about warfare when they as Moslems are involved:

"Fight against them who believe not in God. . . . And if ye fear want, by cutting off trade and communication with them, God will enrich you with his abundance. . . God directeth not the unbelieving people . . . The provision of this life, in respect of that which is to come, is but slender. . . . Unless ye go forth when ye are summoned to war, God will punish you grievously; and he will place another people in your stead. . . . "

* * *

And over 200 years ago here's how the translator, George Sale, regarded this guide to Moslem faith:

"The Koran is universally allowed to have been written with utmost elegance and purity of language. It is confessedly the standard of the Abrabian tongue. The Moslems believe, and are taught by the book itself, that it is inimitable by human pen; and therefore insisted upon as a permanent miracle and alone sufficient to convince the world of its heavenly origin."

XI
Kandahar Celebrates

Spirit of Freedom
Siphon at Bacheron Manda
Gardens of Kandahar
Approach to the City
Camels and Burros
Deserted Streets
A Policeman?
Festive Throngs
What, No Women!
The Lone American
Bazaar Wares
Shall We Eat?
No Thieving?
The Pavilion and Arena
Me — A Russian Agent!
Military Hospitality
The Dancing Quartets
Tribal War Dance
Portrayal of a Legend
Desert Road by Starlight
The "Legend of Vaihund"

CHAPTER XI

Kandahar Celebrates

PERHAPS you would like to hear, folks, about my jaunt to the festivities commemorating Afghanistan's independence. I hadn't planned to attend this celebration at Kandahar, but it came about anyway in the natural course of my work.

We are crowding the completion of a reinforced concrete siphon of the valley canal where it crosses the Bacheron Manda, a wide, dry arroyo ordinarily. However, in time of spring floods it may become a roaring river, and at other times also should there be freak storms and cloudbursts on the desert. It is dry now; that is, on the surface. In the excavation for the structure, however, we have been right down in water, muck and quicksand. The water was drained into sumps and then with centrifugal pumps removed from the excavation. This was a dangerous place in which to work for a while on account of the earth caving in from the sides, and great care was taken in sloping the banks to pro-

193

tect the workmen and equipment. The excavated material was removed down to grade by use of the dragline excavator, Caterpillar tractors and 25-cubic-yard carryalls. A thick-bed of river gravel was then hauled in to completely blanket the bottom width of the excavation, and upon this the concrete for the floor of the siphon was poured. So it is highly important that we get through and get out of there — to take no chance on the occurrence of unusual weather conditions — as much money is at stake. The siphon is some 650 feet long, and the barrel about twelve feet deep by fifteen feet wide, the top being arched. It will carry 750 c.f.s. of water.

The layout of the steel reinforcement is intricate and exacting. The Afghan workmen putting this together take great pride in placing the bars just as shown on the blue prints. In fact every man on the job takes an interest. The barrel is constructed in thirty-foot lengths, the floor having been poured from end to end of the structure first. A pre-fabricated steel sheet form supports the roof and walls of green concrete. After the concrete is set up twelve hours or longer, this steel form is partially collapsed and moved forward as a unit to the next section so as to be in place and in readiness for the next day's pouring. This moving is ordinarily accomplished during the night and before 4 a.m. An entire section of walls and roof can be poured by about 4 p.m.

So now we have arrived at the section lowest in elevation, where facilities are to be installed for draining the siphon by pumping should necessity ever require it. A heavy steel flange ordered from the company shops has not arrived. It must be in place before tomorrow's pouring. So there's but one answer: I'll go in this afternoon and get it myself. Then the job will proceed without delay. September 30 is the deadline for completion. I'll leave at 1:00 p.m.

By 4 p.m. I was nearing the city of Kandahar. There's

194

not much that I can write to adequately describe the strangeness of these "Gardens of Kandahar," so aptly named, and the evening's events I was to witness in the city. One could almost imagine stepping into the pages of history and life as it existed some 2,000 years ago. I had traveled in this yellow Ford pickup some 100 miles over a desert road of continuous "wash board" corrugated surface, the main road between Herat, Farrah and Kandahar. Now the landscape, bathed in the lemon yellow sunshine of this September afternoon, was changing to scenes of rich beauty.

Here were rugged mountains, barren and black, rising precipitously to great heights from the surrounding level plains of the Arghandab River valley. And all about was verdant with fields of corn, alfalfa, clover, grain; and with vineyards, vegetable gardens, orchards; and rows of poplars and groups of wide-spreading mulberry trees.

Fortunately for me the machine shop at Manzel Bagh had the flange ready. I ate a bountiful supper. Directly I was driving the two miles into Kandahar. Delighted was I that the turn of events had made possible my attendance at the evening's festivities.

By now, the sun was setting and dusk approaching. The evening coloring was mythical. A hazy mist of gold enveloped the saw-toothed ranges, jet black against the sky, and merged into a velvety gray down their slopes, and into deep blue shadows out upon the plains.

And, I mused upon what strange events in dim and unrecorded history must have occured on the gardens and plains of this ancient setting — the Mongols — the Macedonians — the Persians — a thousand years before them — Who? — What? And how much to the valor and brave spirit of ancient tribesmen does Afghanistan owe its independence? Have these qualities been passed along to modern generations now living in these ancient surroundings?

And now, the massive outer walls of the ancient city loom

up dimly in the gathering darkness. Preceding me through the north gate are hundreds of little burros driven in droves by men on foot or riding burros. Each animal is laden with four or five conical-shaped baskets filled with vegetables, grapes or melons, perhaps 250 lbs. altogether, a tremendous load for such small animals. And behind me come trains of camels, each animal burdened with large sacks of grain — 600 lbs. or more of cargo. The camels are led in a file, tied nose to tail of the one ahead, and the one in the lead is led by one of the drivers. Other drivers walk in the rear or beside the animals. They shy a little and the drivers make them give way for the few passing automobiles.

Glancing right and left, I drive along narrow streets and past the entrances to narrower alleys and the homes of people behind low adobe walls. Lantern lights — a thin scattering — soften the night darkness. In this part of the city the streets are becoming all but deserted.

A young fellow hails me from out in the darkness and rides along on the running board. He directs me where to turn. Is he a policeman fearful I will get lost, or that I am a lone foreigner needing his protection? No, he states in perfect English that he is a first aid assistant to Dr. Colburn in the hospital of M-K-A out at Manzel Bagh.

We turn right and along a main business street, lighted only dimly with electricity. There are many people shopping in front of the bazaars. A few blocks of this and we come out into the bright lights and the streets are thronged by thousands moving in all directions; and I gingerly drive past policemen in low boxed-in stands at street intersections. They sound whistles and wave me to come ahead. An impatient driver in a lone jeep wants around and dashes madly past through the crowd. I pick my way cautiously through this jumble of pedestrians, fancy horse-drawn carts, occasional automobiles, camels, burros, bullocks. And after many blocks, we get to where the crowd is thickest. This appears to be the center of festivities, and here are large open grounds. I park the car along the street in the midst of the passing crowds, lock up the large chest in which are carried tools and loose articles, and after thanking the young Afghan, who is fearful that something may be stolen, join the throngs.

Half of Kandahar's population of 60,000 must be on the streets and festival grounds tonight; the other half, the feminine portion, is safely at home in strict seclusion. Well, how do you like that, folks? I don't! But such is the Moslem custom. Oh, there are little girls, possibly up to ten or eleven years of age, walking hand in hand with their fathers.

An American far from home, alone in throngs of dark brown people in loose white garments and turbans; not another white man or even the resemblance to one do I see. I am eyed curiously but politely and strive to be nonchalant. Occasionally several walk slowly behind me, to satisfy their curiosity, I decide. A fair complexion, sun-tan clothing, boots and sun helmet; one can't well hide these distinguishing characteristics of an American.

Well, folks what's to be seen in the bazaars? In your reverie let's take a look. Here are huge stacks of watermelons extending out on the unpaved sidewalks — and strangely shaped and as strangely colored canteloupes and other of the muskmelon family, and everywhere fine-looking grapes in big plies on rugs spread out along the street, and bakeries with heaped-up piles of golden brown bread, slabs of it shaped like snow shoes or tennis rackets on stands along the sidewalks, or in front of charcoal ovens. You don't enter the bazaars. Just point from the sidewalk to what you want and the proprietor will bring out the article, and then you bargain perhaps as to the price.

An old man washes his face and drinks water from the palms of his hands, as he dips down for water in the *jui* (ditch) flanking the street.

And here are eating places doing a lively business. Let's

197

look at one from the street. There's the center aisle along which the proprietor walks to serve the customers. These have seated themselves on the platform about two feet above the ground that exends along both side walls. They may lean against the wall with feet extended toward the aisle, recline, or sit upon their heels singly or in crescent-shaped groups. The man sets a pot of tea on the platform with cups, and food in platters. He pours water on the hands of his customers before they begin to eat and offers them a towel. Each eats with his fingers along with the others from a common dish — meat, rice, vegetables, and sops up any liquids with a slab of bread.

Having eaten a good supper already — at least this is a good excuse — I don't feel hungry just now. The bunches of beautiful grapes — blue, green or golden — do look most tempting, but I remember the old man using the water from a near-by *jui* in which the vendor may have dipped the fruit to keep it fresh.

In front of a candy stand a customer returns my look of inspection of his person and clothing by looking me squarely in the eye without wavering, sizing me up from helmet to boots, never taking his eyes off me until somewhat embarrassed, I turn away.

I find my way back to the parked Ford pickup, outstandingly yellow in the electric lights. To my surprise the young Afghan is still there! — says he was afraid to leave it for fear things would be stolen. I say never mind, that no one will bother anything, people don't steal like that here — and he gives me a questioning look as I thank him.

Not far away, in a large public park, is an open-air pavilion strung generously with electric lights. I edge through the dense crowd and cross several open ditches filled with water and reach the outskirts of this center of activities. A canopy covered area at the far end appears to be reserved seating, and I continue to edge forward to a nearby point of vantage. Here from an oblique angle I can view everything taking place in the cleared area.

A man out in front is delivering an oration. Other speakers follow. Some read from notes. The people stand with rapt attention. I doubt if all can understand what is said, there being no microphones. I can not comprehend the speeches, but in my attitude and bearing give every indication that I do.

Suddenly, I observe an armed soldier breaking his way through the crowd toward me. He motions for me to follow him. Through my mind flash alarming thoughts. Am I about to be arrested on suspicion of being a Russian agent? My passport — I hadn't thought to carry it! But it's O.K. I'm escorted to a seat in the midst of a group of military men. On my immediate left are two four-star general officers. The one with gold stars I believe to be a major, the one with the silver stars to be a lieutenant colonel. All about are officers and soldiers of various ranks. I begin to feel relieved, and then embarrassed; for here I am, disheveled, sweaty, dusty from my long ride in the glaring heat of the desert — I'm quite out of place — but that's all right too, for I catch a glance from the colonel, who nods curtly and smiles reassuringly.

The program continues. Patriotic fervor marks this occasion as expressed in oration, music, song and dance.

Two hundred young men have entered the arena. Snappily attired, they dance in quartet formation around a large circle. Rapidly side-stepping left and right, whirling, bowing, advancing, retiring, each man clicks a pair of hardwood sticks he carries, one in each hand, against those of his neighbor to the left and the right in rapid succession, and over his head. Nearby the army band plays in continuous accompaniment the refrains of tribal music, animated, wildly sweet. This all has lasted close to an hour. The people in loud acclaim signify their approval and enjoyment of this picturesque and unique production. The arena is cleared.

There is heard the slow beating of drums that look like kegs. Singly from all sides come men dressed like tribal warriors. They form a circle and go into a slow dance. Faster, faster — more irregularly beat the drums, and more loudly! Now there's a large circle of dancing men in file shouting, shrilly singing — there is great excitement as they go around and around the ring, each man side-stepping, advancing, retiring, bowing, whirling with increasing vigor, chanting, yelling in apparent utmost confusion — and in the background is the harmonious music and steady accompaniment of the army band. After half an hour or more men begin dropping out from sheer exhaustion. There are old men, young men, and — would you believe it — two small boys keep right up with the others. Suddenly with a loud flourish the music stops and the men walk firmly away. This was an act expressive of men leaving home to engage in battle, the conflict, victory. And during this performance the expressions on faces in the audience were intent and thoughtful, tense and serious. Ringing applause followed this portrayal of tribal patriotism!

And next some thirty boys, possibly twelve to fourteen years of age, march snappily into the arena. Stepping to one side, one of the number selected for his good appearance and vocal achievements undoubtedly, begins to sing a verse of song in Pakhtu — folklore or a legend of a religious and patriotic nature, as is explained to me later. As the boy finishes the verse, the whole group take up a repetition of it in refrain. After about five verses are sung in this manner, the army band takes up the refrain, its trumpets and other wind instruments putting great expression and animation into it. As the band plays in quick time, the boys mark time with one foot in place, swinging their arms smartly forward and back. Series after series of verses are executed in this manner for the space of about an hour. The song and music have a wildly sweet melody, and an appeal that resounds in my ears and mind for days afterward. The production comes to a climax with the boys marching briskly from the arena to the accompaniment of a loud flare of trumpets and a long roll of drums — and the crowds go wild with applause!

This concluded the evening's entertainment in celebration of Afghan independence.

As I was about to leave the pavilion, a lieutenant had me go with him to some large tents nearby where were extensive displays of Afghan rugs, karakul caps, ornaments and clothing typical of the country. But it was getting late.

On the way out of the grounds a fellow whose looks I didn't exactly like edged up and seemingly wanted to talk. He resembled a prize fighter and must have weighed all of 225 lbs. I nonchalantly turned and said as best I could in Persian: "Good evening. The program over there in the pavilion was indeed excellent."

To this the man responded in Persian: "I do not understand Persian well. I speak Pakhtu," and then added in good English, "Yes, mees-tah', it was mighty fine, mighty fine! Good night." And by this time, I was fading away from a gathering audience that was chuckling in low undertones of mirth at this (to them) amusing dialogue.

And as I drove out through the dark streets of the city, again I met many camel trains and droves of burros laden with produce for early morning distribution in the city.

And then out on the long lonely desert road to our camp at the "Well of the Fig Tree" in the "Desert of Death" — 100 miles. A pitch black but starry night, and at long intervals I would meet or pass small groups of white-clad figures walking swiftly along in the coolness of the night, and an occasional lorry beside the road piled high with bales of wool or sacks of wheat, or two-decker lorries that carried both freight and passengers, the latter being in deep slum-

201

ber in various postures around on the ground. And I shivered in my shirt sleeves after the intense heat of the day. Then there was the hot shower at 4 a.m. and a tumble into bed in my comfortable adobe quarters, only to be up at 6 a.m. ready for another strenuous day!

And such is the life of one American in Afghanistan.

*   *   *

But list, folks! Don't sign off just yet. About that folklore in Pakhtu depicted so wonderfully in music and song in Kandahar: The refrain of it still lingers pleasantly in my memory.

I've found out that this production commemorated a legend of long ago. In a nutshell it runs about like this:

It is sunset on the plains near Panjwai. The shadows of the mountains creep over the earth. The breezes that cooled the day have come to rest. At dusk all is silent — except for the cry of a lonely maiden in agony. She is fettered with ponderous weights and lies beside a kneeling camel laden with a load of bread.

Two horsemen appear over the horizon. She prays they will see her. Could they be bent on an errand of mercy? A halo encircles the head of the one and his presence seems to illumine the earth!

He reins up and listens, as his charger paws the ground; then he locates the girl. What's the cause of her pain? It's his duty to relieve the oppressed, he says.

He may not have the patience to listen, she tremblingly tells him. Besides, she warns, he'll also lose his life should he interfere.

The stranger dismounts and loosens the girl's fetters, while Kumber, his helper, holds the reins of both mounts. He tells the maid that he will chance that peril; that he has met nothing yet, in the lands in which he has traveled, but what he has subdued by sword, arrow and lance through the favor of Allah, the one only God.

202

For nine years, the girl tells him, this Arghandab Valley — this land of the Arachosians — has been cursed by a serpent with seven heads. When he first burst into the valley none could withstand his fury. He carried away cattle, men, women and children. He laid waste to the fields. Survivors took refuge behind the walls of Vaihund (ancient Kandahar). To leave the fort, no one dared. There was famine and despair!

Then the serpent deprived of prey, every morning thrust his head over the walls, seized seven victims and bore them away.

The king finally found a way to appease this monster, continues the girl, so that people could plant their fields and not be molested any more.

So every evening at sunset, she says, out upon the open plain there is brought from the city a virgin, a camel, and a load of fine bread with which to feed the serpent. The virgins are chosen by lot. The girl says she is almost the last one remaining.

"At what hour does this monster appear?" asks the stranger.

"At midnight," says the maiden. "He glides out from a cave on the other side of the mountain and up that hill right over there, coils, thrusts forth his heads, feeds on the victims and retires."

Said the stranger, "By the grace of Allah, I'll give him his supper tonight! Trusty Kumber, tether the horses that they may feed." And then to the girl, "Awaken us at midnight!"

The strangers sleep.

The hour arrives. In the night's darkness the foul light of the serpent's track is plainly visible as he ascends the mound. His scales glare with evil luster. His bristling mane stands erect. His fiery eyes glance about.

The girl is dumb with fright. In but a moment the

203

monster's cruel head will wave, then thrust forth to seize his spoil. Fearfully she awakens the men.

"Trusty Kumber, stand ready. I'll rely on my bow!"

As seven heads thrust out, seven shafts speed in succession from the stranger's bow. Each shaft pierces a head. In fury the monster hisses, rebounds, falls dead!

"Speed to the city. Tell the people this curse to their land — this foul spawn of hell — lies dead!"

"Whose arm shall I say won this conquest so rare? Come with me!" said the girl.

"No. I go east where the heathen are strong. I'll see you and your king ere long. Farewell for now!"

The girl calls to the guards on the walls. The people are jubilant. The king is skeptical, and waits until dawn to see what has happened.

The stench of the rotting carcass is carried by the breezes over the beautiful Arghandab vale. A pestilence breaks out. The countryside and the city streets are littered with the dead and dying. A blight sears the fields and orchards and fouls the water.

The king consults his sages. Yes, the maiden is responsible for this. She has offended the skies, the many gods. She slew the serpent by aid of a fiend. What has she to say?

To die, she is willing, if that will relieve the distress. But no fiend killed the serpent. She dares to believe it was the favored of Allah, the one God, the Most High!

The girl is sentenced to execution and is thrown on a pile of faggots in the public square. A garland of lilies is placed on her head and a torch is uplifted to kindle the pile — when, "Hold," cries a voice of command in the crowd. "I am he who slew the serpent by the favor of Allah, the one only God!"

The stranger lifts the girl from the faggots, and turning about says to the king and his sages, "You have by error been misled. Know now that he whose shafts felled the ser-

pent is Ha-zar-at' Al-ee, the Lion of God — that God who
should be adored by all mankind — great Allah, the one
only God, the Most High! Acknowledge His power, and His
mercy will remove the horrors from your land.

Yes — the king and his sages crave the pardon of Allah.

Then Hazarat Alee, the maid by his side, and Kumber
in front leading the proud Dul-dul, lead the king and his
sages and the crowds of people to the hill where lies in
stench the carcass of the monster.

Drawing forth the blade of his bright sword Zool-fee-kar,
Hazarat Alee smites the carcass. The mountains recoil at the
shock. Lightning flashes afar. Thunder roars. The serpent's
foul carcass becomes a part of the rock!

*   *   *

And so, folks, that is the legend of the "Serpent of Vaihund," the incidents of which took place so long ago in this
very Arghandab valley where we Americans are now engaged
in the construction of a great irrigation project.

And thus is explained the vein of black outcropping
rock on the hill commanding the plain near the ancient
city of Alexandria of Arachosia, named such by the invad-
ing Alexander, but known by the ancients supposedly as
Vaihund, and presently as the ancient city of Kandahar on
the road between modern Kandahar and the present boom-
ing locality of Panjwai. This outcropping winds tortuously
up the hill to its summit and on the eastern slope branches
out into seven parts, thus the petrified seven-headed serpent.

As to the cave where the serpent lay hidden in retreat,
local residents now speak of it ominously. Men have ventured within its portals to look for treasure but have never
returned to the light of day, so I was told most seriously one
day by Me-tab-bud-deen as we passed there en route to
Panjwai.

And so then I'll always remember the interpretation by
music, song and recitation in Pakhtu this legnd of the tribes-

men of ancient Arachosia so animatedly depicted in Kandahar's celebration of Independence Day.

> "God declareth his signs unto you that ye may consider."
>
> — Koran

XII
Miracle of Irrigation

CHAPTER XII

Miracle of Irrigation

THESE November days are glorious — like Arizona at the higher altitudes. No frost yet. Chilly at night and in forenoon. Sometimes a north breeze prevails — out of Siberia maybe.

After a long day in the wide open spaces, it is nice to return to comfortable quarters around 4:30 or 5:30 p.m., have a hot shower and then a cold one, and enjoy an evening meal of our own beef and vegetables from the company farm at Fort Nad-i-alee, fresh roasting ears, carrots, turnips, eggplant. During the evening and night two oil-burning heaters make the quarters pleasantly warm. The vaulted roof and the meter-thick walls, all of adobe, hold the heat very nicely, and besides my room is on a southeast exposure with sunshine the whole day. We leave camp for the various job sites in the morning right after breakfast, or about 7 a. m.

While writing one evening, I was interrupted by Azizullah (A-zeez-ul-lah') — Dear-to-God — who came in to say that Sayed and his survey party had not yet returned from the valley.

Azizullah is the young Afghan from the agricultural college at Kabul who is now my protegé; appointed by the government to learn all he can about this reclamation development — agriculture, irrigation, construction, surveys, water distribution, etc., and has been with me about three months. He speaks Persian, Pakhtu, Urdu and English, the latter quite understandably. So we drove in the pick-up toward a rising full moon and the Helmand valley. After a time we met Sayed and his men in the old "weapons carrier" coming out. Conscientiously, they had remained quite late near the river in the area of salt cedar brush to finish a drainage survey line in the Babajee area. So as we turned about to follow them into camp, Azizullah said, "Will you please stop for five or six minutes?"

"Of course," said I.

Spreading his cloak upon the ground, he said, "Now which way is west?"

"That way is Mecca," said I pointing a stick about twenty-seven degress south of west.

Taking off his shoes, the young man stood up very straight, put thumbs into both ears with palms spread out in a hearing position. Then for a moment he stood with head bowed and hands clasped in front at the waistline. Then he bent forward with both hands on his knees. He went down on his knees and held his forehead to the ground with hands, palms down, spread out on ground to the front. Then he rested erect with knees to the ground, hands on knees, in a few moments of meditation. Then he stood up again in the position of a soldier at attention. After that he went through these positions of devotion twice again, while I stood beside him uncovered and with head bowed in an attitude of reverence. And far away toward the west, the

desert landscape and evening sky were illumed with the lemon yellow afterglow of the sun now well below the horizon, and the shadows cast by the desert vegetations were becoming sharply distinct on a land bathed in the light of a
brilliant moon.

Turning about sharply, but smiling, said Azizullah, "Do
you believe Jesus Christ is the Son of God?"

"That is what the Christian religion teaches," I returned
simply, not desiring to become involved in a discussion of
the relative merits of Christianity and Mohammendanism.
Moreover, I remembered the mullah's admonition in his
call of the faithful to prayer: "Allah is the one only God,
and Mohammed is his prophet." In other words Moslems
do not believe in the Holy Trinity.

This Sayed is a man just coming into his own as the
chief of a survey party. Right now he is taking the place of
Ghulam Dast-i-gar, who had to leave today for Kabul due
to the illness of his wife. You'd be surprised how well Sayed
can run a transit or wye level and keep the notes. Jack
Sabiniano and Rey Entienza had trained Sayed for this work
and to be available for just such an occasion as developed
today. Jack and I have spent some time in the field going
over this drainage situation with Sayed. He has been lined
up to get the survey data I am needing for early rendition
of a report to the general manager on what can be done to
correct the high ground water conditions under the Babajee
Canal and along the Lui Manda (big arroyo).

While eating our lunch in a grassy swale at the edge of
a cotton field, some of Sayed's men said to me in their own
language, "Pol-i-jens, we want you to stay a long time in
Afghanistan."

In reply I took occasion to state a few ideas I had in
mind. "Well, I can't do that," said I. "But sometime what
I'd like to see around here is this: In Babajee over there and
at Chah-i-anjir and Fort Nad-i-ali and in each of your vil-

211

lages, a school attended by both boys and girls (not just boys), a mosque, a hospital, a doctor, a dentist; for the children to be in school for eight years and learn to read, write and figure arithmetic, and to learn all about Afghanistan and the neighboring countries — and about every country on the earth. That's the way schools are in Kabul — something like that? Well, here they should be the same, with four years of high school where you learn to do things like growing good crops — good cattle — make cotton and woolen cloth, leather goods — and make these into comfortable clothing, and where the girls learn to cook and be good wives. Also, you should study how to sell your produce to Pakistan and India and get rupees in return, and with the rupees maybe buy radios or good cows from *Amrika.* And then maybe some of you could go on to the university — like the one Jan Mohammed says will be started on this project — learn to be doctors, teachers, agriculturists."

"Engineers also?" said Ka-zeen.

"Oh, of course, engineers," I continue, "and learn to build dams, canals, electric power plants, sugar factories, cotton and woolen mills, to process food — and oh, just lots of things. All this and more I want you to do — just like our boys and girls in *Amrika!*"

"How long this take?"

"Oh, fifteen to twenty years, Jan Mohammed believes. Jan is building the new villages over there under the Boghra Canal — dwellings, schools, mosques, hospitals, hotels, bazaars — many things. You know Jan?"

They nodded assent, and appeared to get the general drift of what I had said, as they had listened attentively, and Sayed had helped make clear my meaning.

*　　*　　*

Recently I was alone inspecting some finished lateral structures. Several Kharoti tribesmen gathered about in a friendly manner. These people had been assigned some 5,000 acres as their own to put under irrigation and raise crops and already had made a good start.

Would I have *chay* with them? *Ba-le,* yes, I would.

They led me to their temporary quarters, a camp of mud huts with thatched roofs, and low adobe walls to fence in (or out) the camels and burros. They had me be seated on a fine rug spread out on the bare ground — brought pillows for me to lean against, while I indicated that wasn't necessary — *la-zem na* — that I could sit on my heels like the rest.

Some fifteen men, bearded, serious-looking fellows, seated themselves on the ground entirely covering the floor space of the hut. They had come from places in Pakistan by camel train — from Sibi (apples), Shik-ar-pur, Suk-kur. Yes, I had been through all these towns en route to Afghanistan. My heavy fleece-lined leather jacket, they greatly admired. With all their *goos-fand* (sheep) and *shoo-toor* (camels), they could just as well be wearing jackets like this, too, I told them.

After about twenty minutes, two maidens brought in a large pot of tea with sugar and cream. The host first poured me a small cupful and then passed the teapot around to the others.

Glancing over their shoulders, I observed several women and girls peering modestly over nearby walls, and their faces were lighted with animation in contrast to the grave demeanor of the men. However, in accordance with custom, outwardly at least, I took little note of these manifestions of interest in a foreigner.

Leaving this hospitable environment, I invited my host and as many others as could squeeze aboard, to go for a ride over the barren lands that were now becoming beautifully verdant with fall wheat. Approaching a new village prepared by the government and soon to be occupied by the Kharoti, I observed a *zan* hurrying out to draw water from

213

the irrigation ditch which paralleled the road. Being an American and doing as any American would do under similar circumstances when prompted by curiosity, I was in the act of giving her the once over, which she was quite obviously returning in kind, when I felt a gentle tapping on my right shoulder. *"Na, na!"* admonished my host moving both hands to and fro before his eyes.

Catching his meaning, and again being desirous of adhering to Moslem custom, I muttered, *"Oof — woof,"* and thereafter in his presence looked straight ahead as far as interesting looking *zanha* by the roadside were concerned.

And one day a row over water distribution between the Kharoti and adjoining tribesmen threatened. So Azizullah and I went out to correct the situation by first asking the Kharoti chief to go for a ride with us.

"Good morning, chief," said I in English, just like that.

Azizullah and my friend talked quietly together for a moment, and then Azizullah said, "Mohammed Ak-bar wants to know what you meant when you called him 'chief'."

As Azizullah explained that the word "chief" signifies "the head man, the big man of the tribe," Ak-bar's eyes twinkled merrily.

We put a *"mir-ab"* (water tender) on each lateral — the chief suggested the name — and this man, by patrolling the ditch early and late, maintains an orderly distribution of the water.

*   *   *

Well, folks, since late summer and early fall, we have been witnessing the Afghan version of the American covered wagon days and the settlement of our western irrigation projects. However, in place of wagon trains, these people come on long trains of camels from far away places, like Ghazni, 290 miles; Baluchistan, 225 miles; Cha-khansur, near the mouth of the Helmand, 100 miles.

One outfit was strung out for several miles. There must

have been 500 camels and a like number of burros and oxen. Many people were walking barefoot, or with just light sandals. The majority riding were women and children. A child fell, or by accident slipped off, one camel right in among twenty or more other camels herded together and walking swiftly. Quickly and fearlessly, the mother slid down to rescue the child. Not one man appeared to notice the incident or made the slightest gesture to assist the woman!

There were groups of women together, and girls in their teens — some in brightly colored kerchiefs, or adorned with silver or bronze ornaments worn about their slickly combed black hair or over their foreheads or as earrings or wristlets, and ones especially bright and about the size of a dime rested flatly over the left nostril.

The tents — long black heavy rolls — were carried crossways on camels. Plows were strapped to the backs of oxen.

Many children and dogs rode in special saddles or bags strapped across the backs of burros and balanced on both sides of the animals. And there were chickens tied by their legs to trappings on the backs of the animals.

Big, classy looking sheep dogs, white or yellow, bob-tailed and as big as wolves, trotted along happily.

An occasional camel carried her offspring in a special harness behind her hump, carefully balanced and in perfect contentment. The young animal's head and long neck swung like a pendulum in unison with the swaying motion of the mother. Some camels were provided with fancy halters or neckpieces of rope or leather ornamented with bright yellow, red, green or blue beads.

I started to take kodachrome pictures of these unique sights with my 35-millimeter kodak. I would get directly in front of rapidly approaching groups of camels and the miscellaneous assortments of other animals, men, women and children. In this, I was doing all right until stopped by a warning shout "Zanha Zanha!" from several advancing men with their arms uplifted in protest against photographing any women.

Luckily for me, on the sidelines were several Kharoti. The Kharoti had been intently observing these passing people of another tribe who were shortly to be their neighbors on a large area of adjoining land reserved by the government for their occupation.

"*Khoshal — Khoshal —* Mees-tah Pol-i-jens!" shouted these Kharoti in chorus, and with this identification established, I continued taking pictures unmolested. And this was the manner of my introduction to the incoming Durrani tribesmen.

Their camp was established in a central locality awaiting assignment to quarters in the nearby new village. The black tents were set up and mud walls were built around them and thatched roofs provided. The menfolks of each family started occupying the land reserved for them in the wide open spaces; or two or more families would work together, each family utilizing from 25 acres to 125 acres, or perhaps more, under a lease system.

The land is a smooth plain for the most part, with gentle slopes, and for these people no leveling is required; besides, they have not the equipment to do this. While one group is putting up temporary shelters of mud hovels in the fields for the men and dried mud mangers in which to feed the animals, others are preparing the land for seeding. In this preparation they flood the land in checks or strips bordered by low ridges to confine the water. These ridges are put up with a shovel operated by two men after the ground is made damp and soft. They work facing each other. One sticks the shovel into the ground. By means of a short rope the other man pulls it full of earth on to the ridge. They work steadily and ridge about one-half as fast as an ox team can walk.

When the soil is soft and mellow as it dries from the

216

first irrigation, men with ox teams pulling wooden plows begin to break it up for the first time. The plow simply consists of the fork of a tree. One stub is sharpened to a blunt point and upon this is fitted a cylindrical piece of steel brought to a point. The other stub constitutes the tongue of the plow and is attached to the yoke which the oxen support in front of their humped shoulders. Small areas the size of a check are prepared at one time by plowing both ways. The wheat is broadcasted by hand. The plowed surface is smoothed and the seed is covered by dragging a log over it by ox team. In just a few days, the weather being warm, the field becomes green with the growing grain.

Most primitive, you say. Yes, unbelievably so in these modern times — typical of Biblical days. But their basic food, wheat, is thus produced. And surprisingly enough twenty ox teams working like this for a month can seed 500 acres, and this, increased several times because of the large number of tribesmen, really produces a miraculously green appearance over large areas of hitherto barren desert.

There are amusing incidents. The oxen move slowly, and at regular intervals the drivers in tones that carry far, admonish the animals to keep moving and crack whips loudly by way of emphasis. At a turn the wooden yoke happens to slip from the neck or shoulder of one ox. This is a signal for the animal to lie down on the soft damp ground to rest. Ordinary prodding does not cause him to arise from this comfortable posture. What does the driver do? Bites his tail! No response. Moves to head of the ox. Bites his ears! No response. After several trials— tail, head, ears — the animal reluctantly stands. And then as the driver spits hair and filth from his mouth, the plowing proceeds.

One day I saw a lone camel pulling a plow.

The sub-laterals are laid out on a straight line at a low gradient, following approximately the topographic contours, and 500 meters apart. They are provided with the necessary checks — each just a pre-cast slab of concrete with rectangular opening and metal slide gate, and a provision for overpour. The turnouts are of similar design, only smaller, and are spaced at regular intervals along the sublaterals. Each of the field ditches from these turnouts discharges into a shallow surface drain where provision is made to prevent erosion by means of a small, simple, brick-lined chute. Provision is made for the excess water from each sublateral to be carried away in a drain or waste channel, by which the water is conducted to lower lying areas for re-use.

Topography permitting, the main laterals take out of the main Boghra Canal at intervals of one kilometer.

*   *   *

A few days ago, I was out to where one of our engineering parties was surveying for the extension of a large main wasteway. Also at work here was a five-cubic-yard Northwest dragline excavator and several RD8 Caterpillar tractors and 25-cubic-yard LeTourneau carryalls. In this vicinity the waste water from the Boghra Canal had partly flooded a widespread area in which was a series of large shallow lake beds and interconnecting sloughs. These together with the surrounding swamplands are making a perfect paradise for migrant waterfowl. Also nomadic squatters have been taking advantage, during last summer and fall, of the water and moist land adjacent for raising small fields of wheat, corn and melons, and to feed their flocks of sheep and goats on the succulent wild grasses and brushy vegetation.

It is now the time of year when the nomads are trekking southward from central and northern Afghanistan into the milder fall and winter climes of Baluchistan. And there in this oasis-like area was temporarily encamped a large assortment of big black tents, each open to the weather on two sides. Advancing closer, we saw many people just sitting about under the tents, or lounging on the outside resting, and all around were thousands — literally thousands — of

218

sheep and goats in flocks; and camels, both loose and hobbled; and burros. Tall dark bearded men in turbans and white loose garments, and sandals of leather thongs, attended these animals. Camels rolled in the dust, or strolled about seemingly taking especial delight in rubbing their chins on Jack and Rey's grade stakes and knocking them down right and left.

As Azizullah and I pulled up, here came the huge dogs overtaking the car in great arcs of a circle, and children almost clothesless, for it was warm, and larger boys and many friendly men. The rest of the population without veils gathered not far away in groups at the sides of the tents. I could not understand what was said, but they plied Azizullah with many questions. Where were we bound?

We were going over there where those big machines are at work. Well, could they go along? Yes, O.K., we told them.

They filled the back of the pick-up — even jammed into the cab — as Azizullah in Persian or Pakhtu admonished them to take it easy. They even argued in a playful way as to where else they might want to go, as I headed the car toward the big dragline with its boom towering above the salt cedars a mile or two away. Soon they subsided — but suddenly with a yell, the ones on the running board broke out into a medley of wild songs the like of which I had never heard anywhere before.

"What's this all about, Azizullah?" said I apprehensively, but he only chuckled mystifyingly. The car was slowing down from sheer exhaustion. I visualized getting stuck in the soft treacherous surface of the apparently dry sloughs and lakebeds.

So we abandoned the car and walked on, and I counted *bist nafari* (twenty men) that got off; they laughed in great glee and thought it a great joke, and they followed right along with me afoot to the dragline and watched that for a while, seated solemnly on the wet banks of newly excavated earth.

It was so boggy here that the machine had to work on mats made of our precious 8" x 16" x 20' pine timbers cabled together. These beams had been shipped from the States. Charley Dale had put these to good use as supports for the concrete form work on the big drop structures of the Shamalon Canal last spring and now they were being broken to pieces in the mire; but this could not be avoided. And the tractors and carryalls were also excavating a shallow cut in the nearby marshy ground.

Leaving this job to walk back to the Ford, my newly found nomadic friends and tribesmen promptly trooped again by my side. Downright handsome were they — tall and rather lanky with classic features of patrician origin, so it appeared, and dignified, independent looking. They probably represent some of the happiest people in all of Asia, wild and carefree like the original North American Indian, and well-to-do with their valuable flocks. Also, they are respected by the governments of all the countries they may temporarily inhabit largely because they are peaceful and attend strictly to their own business.

So before we could get the car underway, all twenty again climbed aboard as mirthfully boisterous as before. With our gain in speed, however, the black tented camp to the rear was swiftly becoming a part of the cat-tail clad wildfowl refuge amidst the green marsh lands of the distant horizon — when, with a shrill yell, followed by the unrestrained hilarity of those remaining aboard, each tribesman began bailing out. The first one hit the ground just to the left of the cab and rolled over and over; then another, and still another all around in rapid succession. I slackened speed, but surprisingly enough all were getting up laughing and unhurt and waving a friendly good-bye: *"Bes-yar khob, agha, mar-ha-mat ze-yad!"* they shouted.

"Azizullah, what is that they are saying?" I exclaimed, giving them a military salute by way of farewell.

Azizullah, sides vibrating and tears flowing down his cheeks in uncontrolled mirth, responded in jerks, "They say 'Very good, sir. Goodbye and highest respects!' "

*   *   *

These are the weeks when hunting is a recreation for all of our camp having guns and ammunition; Les Crane, Jim Brownfield and Wallace Segurta, especially. Not everyone is a hunter; ammunition is scarce and so are guns; but the camp is kept well supplied with fresh meat by these hunters. Just a few days ago, Les made an excursion toward the plains at the base of the high mountains to the north and brought in four gazelle. Said he could have slain fifty. Ducks; big fat mallards, redheads and teal are plentiful everywhere there is water. And sand grouse by the thousands — and pheasants, something like our prairie chickens, geese, and some strange birds of several varieties that are edible; and there are huge eagles coming from somewhere in great numbers.

Chief Engineer Don Bleifuss from San Francisco has been on the project for several days, together with W. A. Hohlweg, chief engineer for this entire Afghanistan project. Both are very friendly men of few words. We have been looking over all of the construction jobs under the Shamalon and Boghra canals, the new lands being brought into production, and the contemplated new development.

On the Helmand valley work, from a high bank of excavated materials deposited there by numberless generations of the past along the Ainak canal, I called attention to the dangerous nearness of the new Shamalon canal to heavy erosion underway on the outside of a sharp bend in the Helmand River. During conditions of high flood in the spring and early summer, continuance of the scouring could breach the canal and even change the course of the river to the westerly side of the valley. We looked at topographic

221

maps of this bend country prepared by Jack's engineering party and discussed possible remedial measures.

This valley canal had been located on paper by our engineering office in San Francisco from the topographic sheets furnished from the field. As locating engineer, however, I could not be bound rigidly by this "paper location," and found it necessary to depart therefrom in a number of instances. The main object sought, of course, was economy of construction following the higher overflow lands paralleling the Helmand and utilizing to fullest extent the channels of old, existing canals right on down the valley. We would locate the new canal, for instance, by widening and deepening the Bolan canal for several kilometers below its point of diversion from the Helmand, then cut across open country in a completely new channel to a point on the Ainak (eye-glasses) canal well below its diversion point on the Helmand, and then widen and deepen this canal for several kilometers, and so on down the westerly side of the valley to below Shamalon. Jack Sabiniano's parties were handling this relocation work in the field in a most efficient manner. Also Jack was looking after the engineering work connected with the construction of all structures on this Shamalon canal, the chief ones being reinforced concrete chutes, drops, checks and turnouts.

On the Boghra canal, Rey Entienza was handling the field engineering connected with the location and construction of laterals and drains, and miscellaneous unfinished work on the main Boghra canal. Rey was doing an excellent job in following through to completion a mass of details connected with the land subdivision, and the layout and construction of the irrigation distribution and surface drainage systems.

And in the upper valley area, Sayed and his party were getting the necessary field data from line locations and cross sections, to enable me to make the required report on the location, cost and possible need for the Lui Manda waste-way extension to the Helmand River, and the high water table situation connected therewith.

And with the approach of winter, the need for distribution of irrigation water has practically ceased.

Knowing that during next spring the Arghandab Dam will be complete and water will be available to furnish a continuous supply for the irrigation of some 130,000 acres in the Arghandab Valley, I was not surprised when Bleifuss and "Holly" requested that I come to Kandahar for a time on an additional assignment which was to prove of much interest — and, on several occasions, of near tragedy.

This will have to suffice, folks, as a Christmas letter. As you may conjecture, greeting cards of any kind — much less, Christmas cards — are simply not available in Afghanistan. And this should not surprise you, for neither are there, as of now, any airlines or railroads in Afghanistan. That's the way it looks from here on December 4th. May each and all of you have a merry and joyous Christmas season.

> "Forests and water are perhaps the most vital internal problems of the United States."
>
> — President Theodore Roosevelt
> December 3, 1901

A team of workers, using modern equipment, harvest wheat at Ft. Nad-i-ali.

— Photo by M·K·A, Inc.

— Photo by M·K·A, Inc.

Northwest power shovel and Euclid carryall loading earth for Arghandab Dam embankment.

Work at Kajakai Dam.

— Photo by M-K-A, Inc.

Spillways under construction as caravans reroute trails around reservoir.

Hydrographic party prepares to measure streamflow of the Helmand River.

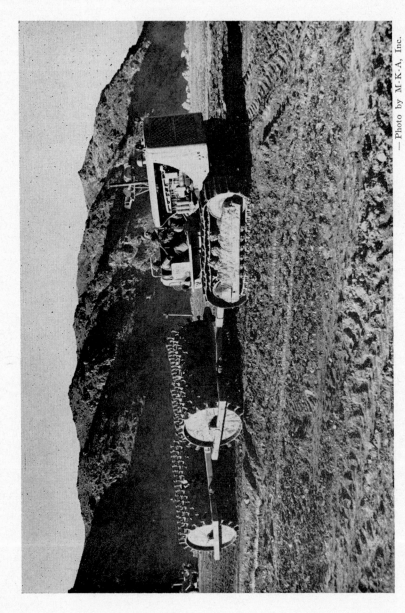

Caterpillar tractor and sheeps-foot roller compacting growing embankment at Arghandab Dam.

Tribesmen follow bank of newly constructed Boghra Canal.

Outlet tower and gate for release of reservoir water.

Rey (left) and Jack, engineers from the Philippines, pose in front of Qala-i-Fateh, remnant of ancient civilization in Helmand Valley.

Rey and surveymen make topographic survey of irrigable lands near Iranian border.

Boys' school at Girishk takes up after recess. Teachers stand above on platform. Outside large cities education of girls is neglected.

"Operation Nomad," trailer survey camp on the move in lower Helmand River Valley.

Crack infantry company and cavalry troop.

Military gathers for observance of Eeds.

Overlooking historic plains of Chardeh. The King's summer home is nearby.

Ancient citadel overlooks walled city of Ghazni and dominates region "beyond the North-West Frontier."

Afghan labor and supervision have erected this intricate steel reinforcement for barrel of siphon under Bacheron Manda.

An Afghan laborer stands inside the network of steel, revealing its size.

Construction of outlet works, Arghandab Dam.

— Photo by M·K·A, Inc.

Diversion weir across Helmand River near Girishk. Diverts flow from Kajakai Reservoir seventy-five miles upstream.

Boghra Canal headgates at diversion weir. This canal is sixty miles long, and will irrigate 165,000 acres of arid Afghan land.

XIII
Plans and Reconnaissance

CHAPTER XIII

Plans and Reconnaissance

THERE STOOD THAT 6,000-foot high mountain dominating the plains of the lower Arghandab River valley. Rising abruptly from the desert, of gnarled and warped stratification, deeply indented with precipitous ravines, barren of vegetation, in this early forenoon of mid-December it was clothed in shades of bronze, brown, yellow, gray, merging into the coal black of the main range. In the clear cool atmosphere and the brilliancy of the lemon yellow sunshine, it appeared within stone's throw. But on this particular morning, the mountain's serene stateliness and aspect of profound mystery concerning stupendous events in history and geology of the dim and distant past, to which it must have been a witness, served only as a background for my reflections on happenings of more immediate concern.

En route to Kandahar, I had just crossed the irregular mile-wide sandy channel of an arroyo known as Kushk-i-Nakhud, at the village and trading center of Khug-i-ani.

AFGHANISTAN VENTURE

Suddenly feeling alarmingly faint and nauseated, I had pulled off to one side of this lonely desert road to rest and refresh myself . . . and to reflect.

Yes, life in Afghanistan had been good. These strange people had been most kind to me and co-operative. In return I had given them the best I had in effort and hard work, had helped to forge a mutual understanding of the common objective . . . the development of vast areas under irrigation where many thousands of families, so inclined, could settle down to the growing of all their own foodstuffs and be otherwise self-supporting, happy and independent on land of their own, where life could hold a worthwhile future for their sons and daughters — just like in *Am-ree-ka,* I had told them.

The Company management had been good to me. Oh, there had been minor altercations among individual Americans through not understanding the other fellow's problems. But this was only to be expected among rugged individualists in far-from-home places. Most such difficulties had been remedied by the application of mutual forbearance. Frequent meetings had been held — weekly, in fact — of all Americans, Italians and Filipinos where the progress of the work was reported upon, discussed and helpful ideas for its improvement advanced, and where "gripes" of all kinds had been aired in a frank and friendly manner. At higher levels— headquarters at Manzel Bagh, on each of the two dam jobs, on the canal project — there had been many conferences attended by the supervisory personnel directly concerned. Afghan government officials had maintained a close and friendly working relationship with the company management.

Construction of main canals and laterals was making steady progress. A start had been made in establishing wandering tribes — people on reclaimed areas for which there was ample water supply.

228

PLANS AND RECONNAISSANCE

The great dam at Kajakai, a tremendous undertaking, was rapidly gaining in volume and height above the bed rock of the Helmand. Set for completion fifteen months hence, potential storage capacity of 4,000,000 acre-feet of water assured the wondrous development of 1,000,000 acres of desert land in the valley of the Helmand and the old Sistan Basin.

In the coming spring the Arghandab Dam would begin impounding the flow of the Arghandab River in a 350,000 acre-feet reservoir, enough to give an all year around supply to the 90,000 acres already under irrigation, and perhaps 40,000 or more additional.

Yes, these units of a great Afghan engineering project, true to the traditions and with the help of American ingenuity and efficiency, were moving steadily along toward final achievement.

And my reflections then turned to events of a more personal nature.

The home folks had been well and managing quite nicely during my absence of almost one year.

Health conditions on the job for foreigners had been surprisingly satisfactory. Oh, there had been several attacks of dysentery. This was in the spring before we got to raising our own vegetables on the truck farm at Nadi-ali, just a result of carelessness on my part in eating greens purchased by our chief chef, Abdul, from the bazaars at Girishk, vegetables that had been kept fresh in piles along the dirt sidewalks by liberal sprinklings with the all-purpose water bailed up from the *jui* on either side of the main street. Such attacks had been all but annihilating to the unfortunate and, at first, unsuspecting victims.

Scourges of the deadly malaria, so widespread among the Afghan people, had been prevented under the able direction of Dr. John Colbert, physician and surgeon for M-K-A at Manzel Bagh. Anti-malarial tablets had been placed beside one's plate, as a reminder, at the noonday meal on each Juma. Use of these, for me at least, had been 100% effective in warding off the disease.

But in the recent fortnight, influenza had struck with deadly effect. Yesterday the victims numbered two-thirds of the foreign personnel at the canal camp.

The only two women in camp, Mrs. Jim Brownsfield and Mrs. Bob Pechner, had performed meritorious service in caring for the stricken men hospitalized in their quarters. Faithful Abdul, the medical aide, and understanding Abdullah in charge of the commissary, both had helped in this work untiringly. Unfortunately our nearest doctor was stationed at Kajakai, ninety miles or more away over roads frequently blocked by flooding from the irrigation of adjoining fields, or by run-off down the innumerable arroyos.

I had been feeling perfectly well myself amid this scourge, but how long this state of well-being would continue was indeed questionable. Work of importance was awaiting me at headquarters . . . better get there on my own power while yet able to do so! That's why I had left for Manzel Bagh this morning immediately after an early breakfast.

And so, folks, gazing in subconscious interest at that calmly inspiring mountain, seemingly so near to touch yet actually twenty miles away, I became aware of numerous good reasons for feelings of gratitude to Allah above for His beneficent care during the preceding months.

*   *   *

"Say, Paul, the Arghandab valley situation is worse than we expected. Don and I attempted to look over some of their canals today. There are no roads through the irrigated areas, only trails for animals and people. We traveled a caravan road — barely passable for cars — skirting the desert; couldn't see much, but know the canals are subject to complete washout at every high flood from cloudbursts on the desert where they cross the ordinarily dry arroyos. There are no checks or turnouts, as we know them, to control water distribution. The canals are many and their alignments are poor; each takes out of the river at a rock and brush weir subject to damage or obliteration by river flood flows. One hell of a mess, I'll say!"

Along these lines our chief engineer, W. A. Hohlweg (Holly), had just spoken, as he seated himself comfortably at his desk after a day in the field with Don J. Bleifuss, vice-president and chief engineer of the International Engineering Company, Inc., of San Francisco.

"That difficult?" I interposed questioningly.

Until now full time duties had engaged my attention on the 155,000 acres Boghra Project in the Helmand Valley 100 miles to the west as resident construction engineer. My responsibilities now were also to include a field investigation and study of ancient canals and lands soon to receive water from the new Arghandab reservoir. Our job was to rehabilitate this irrigation system along modern lines.

There was to be constructed a concrete diversion weir across the Arghandab River at head of the Patow canal. This latter would serve as a main canal for bottom lands to the south of the river and for these higher areas sloping gently away from the precipitous bluffs around an area known as King's Gardens, Dand, the Gardens of Kandahar, and desert lands beyond Manzel Bagh and areas beyond the Tarnak River. The Patow would be enlarged as necessary and more favorably relocated in places.

An entirely new canal would leave the river at the Patow diversion weir and skirt the higher desert slopes above the presently irrigated land to the right and northerly of the river.

Also a system of deep wells would be developed in the lower areas of the valley. Water pumped from these into irrigation laterals would be used on additional reclaimed areas. Electric power would come from the plant at the dam. By this arrangement a high water table waterlogging lowlands would be lowered sufficiently to allow profitable production of crops.

From the two main canals, especially constructed laterals would convey water directly to each of the existing ancient canals, some thirty in number. No longer would it be necessary to maintain *bunds* in the river at the head of each canal for diversion purposes. A year around supply of irrigation water will thus be assured from the Arghandab reservoir.

It was apparent Holly had been viewing this water distribution system — which undoubtedly had been operating much as now since Biblical times — as something needing radical revision to fit into our plans.

He leaned back in his chair with feet high on the desk, meantime filling his pipe and lighting it, taking long puffs in deep study.

His company I had always enjoyed. A man physically hardy though small of stature, of serious mien, young in appearance, Mr. Hohlweg had already seen much of life in the Middle East, he had told me, on railroad location, construction and operation during World War II in Persia. As man to man, he conversed in Persian with the Afghans most understandably. Prospective buyers of fine Afghan rugs among the American colony invariably sought Holly's advice.

At this juncture in strode Mr. Bleifuss. He had just been conferring with General Manager Johnson in the adjoining stone office building. To this calm and reserved engineer, Holly's reactions to what they had just seen of Afghan irrigation systems was of much interest. Seemingly of Scandinavian origin, a large well-built man of the outdoor type, he was now giving evidence of having formulated in his own mind a plan of orderly procedure for attacking this rather unusual problem of engineering and agriculture combined.

"Hohlweg is right, Jones," said Bleifuss. "A chaotic situation does exist among the canals in the Arghandab valley. But — this is where you come in! — we want you to lay the groundwork for a workable tie-in from the Arghandab reservoir to the ancient valley canals, doing away with the individual diversions to each from the river."

I nodded assent.

Continued Mr. Bleifuss: "You will need to become familiar with the layout of all the canals, how these Afghans operate and maintain them — get to know the *mirabs* in charge — learn their problems, estimate under each canal the area devoted to each crop, get actual measurements of the amounts of water diverted, and that returning to the river. You will need to explain to the *mirabs* our proposed plan for the construction of Patow weir, the two main canals, the tie-in laterals. During the interim period, you will have to attend to the release and distribution of Arghandab reservoir water in the right amounts to each canal, with no flow or waste below the lower limits of the project."

In this manner was outlined to me the job I was to undertake in the Arghandab valley, together with similar assignments on the Boghra project, which Mr. Bleifuss was now ready to discuss.

Said he: "In a few days, Paul, I am leaving for our project on the island of Ceylon — Colombo. Before I leave, will you get out for us to study a plan for handling the operation and maintenance of the entire Boghra project under conditions of full development?"

Having already given this subject much thought, I said, "You'll have this by 3 p.m. the day after tomorrow."

So on that day we discussed the proposed set-up at some length. Mr. Bleifuss, evidently being well versed on these matters, was in general assent, adding a few essentials that I had overlooked — like the *bakh-sheesh* clause. I had drawn freely on my experiences along the Mexican border with the Imperial Irrigation District for six years.

*   *   *

Yes, it was agreed that for purposes of systematic control, the Boghra project will be operated and maintained in seven divisions, designated as Girishk, Nad-i-ali, Upper East Marja, East Marja, West Marja, Upper Shamalon, Lower Shamalon — and function along the following lines:

The *project manager* will be in full charge.

A maintenance superintendent will have full charge of maintenance over the whole system, and of any new or additional construction, together with such miscellaneous duties as will be assigned him by the P.M. He will have charge of all maintenance, transportation and communications equipment, and be responsible for its upkeep and repairs.

An *irrigation superintendent* will have full charge of all irrigation operations, including the diversion of the water from the Helmand River, and its conveyance, distribution and use on the land, to the end that all lands shall receive the water to which they are entitled in a prompt and orderly manner; that all waste or losses of any nature be reduced to a minimum; and that damage to lands from inefficient use of water or lack of adequate drainage be prevented.

A *chief clerk* will have charge of all office work, including accounting, purchasing, timekeeping, payrolls, cost keeping, stenographic work, etc. Through the warehouse and yard man, the chief clerk will be accountable for the whereabouts of all property, stores and supplies owned by the Boghra project, and will maintain a continuous inventory which will at all times be open to the examination of the P.M.

A *warehouse and yard man* will be in charge of all property, stores and supplies. He will report directly to the chief clerk.

An *hydrographer* will have charge of all canal and river

234

gauging stations, and of all regular and miscellaneous water measurements, to the end that accuracy and uniformity be obtained. He will have charge of all permanent water records, including their recording and filing. He will report directly to the irrigation superintendent.

A *watermaster* will be in full charge, under the irrigation superintendent, of the conveyance and distribution of water in his respective division throughout the main canal and from the main canal turnouts down to the individual water user on each field lateral. He will have supervision over the main canal, laterals, sub-laterals, field laterals, drains, wasteways and flood channels; and all structures and other facilities connected therewith, and rights-of-way.

A *ditchtender* will be in charge of the conveyance and distribution of water in each of the laterals, sub-laterals and field laterals assigned him. He will report directly to the watermaster.

Watchmen will be placed at strategic points, permanently or temporarily, as required, to prevent the occurrence of dangerous situations, or to maintain the flow of water as desired, or for any other purpose deemed necessary. Ordinarily watchmen will work under the immediate supervision of the watermaster or ditchtenders.

The *shop foreman* will have direct charge of the shop and be responsible for the upkeep and repairs to all maintenance, transportation and other equipment of like nature, reporting directly to the maintenance superintendent.

Each *maintenance crew* will consist of a foreman and laborers, or specialists and laborers. The specialists will be such as welders, masons, etc.; or tractor, dozer, grader, shovel, backhoe and dragline excavator operators, etc. Crews or individuals shall work in any division under the supervision of the maintenance superintendent, or his local representative, which in many instances may be the local watermaster, where special arrangements have been made. Maintenance work will be varied, such as repairs to banks, fixing breaks and clearing away debris; elimination or control of water vegetation; maintenance of structures; additions to structures or the construction of new ones; installation of additional facilities like turnouts, checks, or water measuring devices; elimination of rodents; etc.

Telephone Section:

Chief to be in charge of the operation and maintenance of all telephone lines, and of radio communication, if any, reporting directly to the maintenance superintendent.

Three *operators* will provide continuous twenty-four hours per day service to all telephones on the canal system, under direction of the chief.

Two *linemen* will work as directed by the chief.

Girishk Power Plant:

A *chief power plant operator* will be in full charge of the operation and maintenance of the plant, including the distribution of electric power therefrom. He will report direct to the P. M.

Three *assistant plant operators* will maintain electric power service continuously twenty-four hours per day.

Three *power linemen* will perform all operation and maintenance work on the distribution system, and will otherwise be of general assistance around the plant. Each will report to the assistant plant operator on duty for that particular shift, or to the plant operator himself, as may be arranged.

And then, folks, there were *General Rules for the Use and Delivery of Water*. Briefly, a few of these follow:

Water Conservation:

Save water! Make every acre-foot irrigate a maximum acreage of growing crops consistent with satisfactory yields. Water saved will make productive hundreds of square kilometers of desert land that would otherwise remain forever barren.

How is water lost? By breaks in banks of canals and laterals. By irrigating large areas with a stream too small, causing unrecoverable percolation below the root zones. By irrigating with a stream too large, causing pondage at the lower end of lands and large run-off into the drains with erosion and loss of soil. By not irrigating at night, by not irrigating continuously until your whole field is finished. By not arranging with your neighbor to take the water when you have finished with it. By not notifying the ditchtender well in advance of the aproximate time you will be through with the water.

Results of Wasting Water:

Large areas remain barren that would produce crops if such lands could be irrigated with the water lost. Large areas become waterlogged by deep percolation. Alkaline salts appear on the surface, and no plants can grow. Large areas become inundated with standing water that drowns out growing plants. Soil is lost by erosion, fields are ruined; the lost soil can not be replaced. It is your loss. You get low crop yields per acre.

"Bakh-sheesh":

The demanding of, or the receiving of, *"bakh-sheesh,"* or the like, from any water user for providing water, or services, or for any reason whatsoever on the part of the project offical or employee, will be sufficient reason for his immediate discharge.

Lines of Authority:

All O.&M. work will be handled through official channels only, with but rare exceptions, which in such cases shall then be with the entire knowledge of the officials concerned. This will avoid confusion and maintain the proper *esprit de corps*.

*   *   *

237

AFGHANISTAN VENTURE

It was early afternoon along the Jalowar canal . . . the day, December 19th. Perplexed over the significance of a new experience, I was approaching the village of Soz-na-i. Back there in the wide sandy bed of an arroyo some four hours ago, a precipitous climb out to the desert mesa above had forced an abandonment of the car until my return on foot in the late afternoon. The parked Chevrolet was two miles from a main three-way road junction. Here access roads constructed and maintained by M-K-A, Inc., were denoted by bright yellow sign boards with black figures and arrows: "Kandahar 80 kms." — "Kajakai Dam 136 kms." — "Arghandab Dam 40 kms."

Along a caravan trail skirting the desert, I had hiked to the Salizar canal, followed it for an hour, then cut across rice fields to the Arghandab River and then along its north bank to the *bund* of cobblestones and brush projecting obliquely several hundred feet into the stream. This diverted water into the Jalowar. I had made notes on the weir's state of repair. I had jotted down data relative to the kind and percentage of the irrigated areas devoted to the crops grown under the Salizar, like rice 80%, wheat 15%, wild pasture 5%. The condition of the Salizar, and very roughly its estimated capacity — all had been noted. Data so observed had been written down on my maps. These were arranged as a portfolio and carried in a neat roll. One long map in small scale showed the Arghandab project from the dam to junction of the Arghandab and Tarnak rivers, a distance of about ninety-six kilometers, or sixty miles. Main features indicated were the some thirty ancient canals; the precipitous mountain masses rising singly or in ranges from the surrounding plains; the Dori, Tarnak and Arghandab rivers; Kandahar and various towns. Then a series of single maps showed these features in more detail on a larger scale, all very useful to a civil engineer on a reconnaissance of this nature.

238

Habitations had been few and far between. The few people contacted had been friendly. My approach and progress down the canals and river, I discovered, was being heralded in advance. Had not a shepherd who was pasturing his fat-tailed sheep on a knoll a mile away, upon spying me, burst forth into a shrill wild song? At this same instant had I not observed in another direction, a lone traveler stop, listen intently, and in an instant turn his gaze toward me? There he stood motionless for a time and in silence observing my onward movements. And again, some distance along, faintly and from afar would come another and yet another of those eerie high-pitched chants.

This Jalowar canal, a main source of water for several thousand acres, was running at full capacity, even though in winter. I determined to follow it through, noting the crops irrigated, the manner of distributing water to the lands, the condition of the channel and banks. A trail traveled by animals and people would continue on the canal bank for a ways. Where the going was rough it would take to the desert a little distance away.

This valley lay verdant in the warm sunshine of this early afternoon one week before Christmas with growing wheat, alfalfa, clover. Almond, apricots, grape vines, fig trees — all were bare except for a mere scattering of bright yellow leaves. The stubble of rice paddies, now colorless, furnished pasture for those little black, hump-shouldered cattle. Conspicuously red and large, a few beautiful pomegranates remained on the thickly planted, low shrubby trees. Now brownish-green and light yellow from the frosts, Bermuda grass throughout the orchards gave the appearance of picnic grounds. Low ridges had been thrown up by shovels to contain the flooding irrigation water within single checks about each tree, or in contour border checks. No oxen were at work, but in a few orchards you would see a single man spading and overturning the sod deeply throughout the whole of a five- or ten-acre, area.

Water was being turned from the canal to field ditches by the simplest contrivances of sticks, water grass, brush, or cobblestones.

Unused water from the lower ends of fields passed readily into the next canal down the slope, the Manar canal, without ponding. Also there were ditches at intervals carrying water directly from the Jalowar to the Manar. There was no evidence anywhere of lavish use of water or waterlogging.

There were groves of immense mulberry trees, also a scattering of these fruitful trees along the canals.

Approaching the outskirts of a village, I overtook a nicely dressed young man, clean-cut, erect, strikingly handsome, perhaps twenty-six to twenty-eight years of age. His curly jet black whiskers were smartly trimmed. His turban was clean and pure white in contrast to his dark brown skin. His white pantaloons, although with the customary bagginess, the tailored dark blue jacket, and the brightly polished black oxfords — all lent to this intelligent looking young fellow the decided appearance of spruceness.

In answer to his look of interest, I explained that I was an American civil engineer *(mo-han-des)* making a field study of the canals for M-K-A. Would he like to look at my fleece-lined leather jacket which I carried, or my gloves? And I handed him a pair of light leather-canvas gloves with gauntlets, on each of which was pictured a Missouri mule. These I had procured of Penney's in Sacramento. As we briskly walked along, he courteously examined this gear and talked in a friendly manner, then suddenly turned off to a mosque, rather small but of better architectural appearance than many.

I walked on a short distance and, turning about, raised my arm high in a gesture of friendly parting. The young mullah (Moslem priest) — for such by now I had decided him to be — hesitated and did likewise.

Warmly pleased upon being the recipient, so it appeared, of this mark of friendliness in return, I quite forgot or else did not sense the gravity of the situation in which at this moment I was all but surrounded. For here was I, a foreigner, deep within a Moslem nation, surrounded by strange people in an out-of-the way back country unfrequented by foreigners in the manner I had now undertaken, alone and afoot, and the sun was now lowering!

Relaxing, I leaned forward resting both hands on my walking stick. With keen interest I watched the approach and entrance of the mullah to the mosque.

In strict military form, the mullah, standing at attention and most erect, executed a series of snappy salutes and animated gestures to the front toward the mosque entrance, to the left, then to the front again. Then suddenly making a "right face" toward Mecca he gave a right hand salute, held it for a moment, then shot his uplifted and extended right arm and hand directly into the sun following it with an upward glance — and then with precision as promptly withdrew it, passing the tips of extended thumb and fingers left to right from ear to ear across his bare throat, the while flashing my way a significant glance!

For the briefest instant the eyes of the mullah reflected into my own the light of the sun! This I will not soon forget! At that moment a long lanky fellow, whom I had noticed lounging on his haunches nearby, arose with alacrity. Promptly he disappeared behind some bushes in the direction of the trail I had just now taken. He wore a pale blue turban. The mullah, making a snappy rightabout face, stepped briskly into the mosque.

Nonplussed, I proceeded along the north bank, the desert side, of the Jalowar canal which skirted the northern limits

241

of the town of Soz-na-i. Walking slowly I subconsciously mused about the incident at the mosque.

Could it be that the lanky chap had been instructed by the mullah to follow me as a protector? A protector from what? That throat-cutting gesture: did it signify the penalty to be imposed on anyone in the vicinity who attempted to molest me, an American *mo-han-des* engaged, as I was, on engineering reconnaissance?

Then again as I noted the heavy fleece-lined jacket carried over my left arm, a good felt sombrero, a pair of good gloves, a pair of heavy field boots, good warm shirt and slacks, socks and warm underwear — say, those articles of good clothing — why hadn't I thought of it before — all worth a good 2,000 afghanis — oh, and the ring (Norman's ring) with the beautiful alexandrite stone. Say, is that lanky character an outlaw, an assassin (you'll be surprised; look it up in your own dictionary, folks)? Could he be "one of a Mohammedan secret order which fanatically practices secret murder committed under the influence of ha-sheesh (marijuana)?"

But there was yet another possibility — for it is written in the Koran: "O true believers, wage war against such infidels who are near you!" Well, what infidels? Non-Moslems? According to the mullah's conception perhaps I was such a one.

Instinctively I tightened my grip on the tough but light hardwood club I carried, the lower half of a discarded surveyor's level rod. Shod with brass, about eight feet long, invariably I had carried it on long hikes over rough terrain, through brush, used it as a pole in vaulting wide ditches, as a defense against charging dogs.

Soon I came to a broad caravan trail, a main route between the city of Kandahar and points in the northern part of Kandahar Province and the upper Helmand River valley 150 miles away, or to Ghaz-ni and Kabul off to the northeast. It followed the dry bed of an immense arroyo. At in-frequent intervals storm run-off from the far mountains and desert must have swept away at will the several main canal crossings. These had to be restored by many men with shovels after the waters receded. When included under the new project, such canal crossings would be replaced by inverted siphons to carry the canal water under and across the arroyo. This would avoid much inconvenience and interruption to water service.

Beyond this the north bank of the canal was almost as high as the tops of the mulberry trees where it fringed the town of Soz-na-i. This I followed on top in order to better size up the situation bordering the village. However, it was too narrow and rough to be used as a trail by people or ani-mals. Up here one could look over the tops of the adobe dwellings and bazaars to the wide expanse of the Arghandab River beyond, now glistening in the afternoon sunshine, and to the rugged mountains. The caravan trail could be seen winding up their precipitous slopes toward a high pass leading to Kandahar in the valley beyond. At the river two long camel trains were fording the stream obliquely along the shoals of the shallower water. Proceeding in opposite directions, they were meeting in midstream.

Glancing downward through the branches of the mul-berry trees to my right, I caught just a glimpse of the blue-turbaned fellow slinking along behind some old adobe walls. Pretending not to have seen him, I wrote down some notes. The village was admirably protected from desert sandstorms and "shamals" (north winds), because of this long high bank of earth flanked by high mulberry trees. Planning to ditch this unwanted follower, I walked swiftly forward in plain sight for a few minutes. Then casually disappearing down the steep bank to the water's edge, I proceeded in the op-posite direction. There was no bank on the other side of the canal — just a fine sandy, grassy beach sloping gently down

243

to the water from nearby adobe dwellings and a scattering of low shrubs. The water was perhaps thirty feet wide and three to five feet deep.

Pausing for just a moment to observe this attractive setting, I was startled by low voices and soft laughter!

Quite inconspicuously they had all the while been observing this strange foreigner. Who had? A little maid, the friendliest and prettiest I had yet been privileged thus to meet in Afghanistan. Maybe around sixteen; I wouldn't know. Nearby was someone in an olive green purdah, with unseen face turned partly away, washing some pottery in the waters of the canal. Well, folks, her whole appearance reflected immaculate cleanliness. Freshly and smoothly combed was her shiny black hair. There was no indication of her being about to run away. Sunshine and warm friendliness fairly beamed from her brown oval face. The merriest of smiles flashed a glimpse of dainty white teeth. Black eyes under long dark eyelashes twinkled with delight. She met my eyes steadily for one minute, then in high glee leaned toward her companion and in low tones reported on this strange fellow; and these maneuvers she repeated again and again, her sparkling eyes never once leaving mine, her countenance the while radiating gaiety.

Too confused to speak intelligently, I could only call out, "O-Oh hello-o-o, over there!" She responded with an outburst of merry laughter and a parting wave of the hand (open palm and fingers extended) as I turned to leave.

Well, this was an astonishingly unexpected but happy event. Whether it was in conjunction with another one equally unique and delightful soon to occur, I have been inclined to decide affirmatively. For not 200 feet further along, around a sharp bend, was another secluded spot set off by shade trees and a small beach and several dwellings spread about in semi-circle.

Belles of Shamalon! Wow! As though actually planned

244

in advance and now being staged, so it appeared, nonchalantly and unabashed in nymph-like beauty, out strolled a number of lovely girls, beauteous in figure, coloring, countenance, and dignity of carriage — and adorned only as endowed by nature — nothing more, nothing less! To be regarded with wonder and delight, that they expected, and with an elevated feeling of pleasure to be looked upon; that was evident. And in these matters I, an American, could not let them be disappointed.

And as I surveyed this delightful scene, my thoughts returned to an image of the youngster by whom I had been so impressed but a few moments before; her frank and open countenance, the merriment of her smile, her expression of utmost trust in me, an American, a complete stranger in her village! And I knew that the recollection of her and these other enchanting maidens would forever be endeared in my memories of the Kingdom of Afghanistan!

*   *   *

The sharp crack of a rifle!

Turning, I spotted two horsemen not more than one-half mile back along the Manar canal. They were crossing the narrow bridge over which I had passed but minutes before.

My route had taken me along the main caravan trail to the river opposite Soz-na-i. There I had paused to observe a long string of camels, perhaps fifty, fording the river on their way north. Each carried freight compactly loaded and carefully balanced in a saddle arrangement on either side of the single hump — goods from the city to the back country in the Province of Kandahar and upper Helmand River valley.

Another caravan, of even many more animals, had just arrived from the north. Some of these kneeled patiently in the loose sand of the river beach, their burdens remaining intact. Others, free to roam, rolled in the deep dust beside the trail under some poplar trees.

Cameleers of sober mien, weather-beaten, rough looking fellows with ragged beards and well worn clothing, strolled about among the animals, or sat on their heels or haunches in groups, just resting.

I likewise sauntered about, attempting an outward expression equally stolid and noncommittal. This must have gone over big, for I attracted no attention.

After that I had followed across some beautiful fields and well-kept orchards under the Ne-ga-hon canal, jotting down notes on what I saw having to do with crops, use of water, drainage, condition of laterals and main canals, capacities, etc., and anything else that would possibly be of interest to us in planning the modernization, operation and maintenance and tying-in of these ancient canal systems to the coming new irrigation facilities of the Arghandab valley project.

I was planning to arrive back at the lone Chevrolet in the arroyo well before sundown.

Here was a narrow trail closely paralleling the base of a sharp incline bordering bottom lands of the river valley. Ahead could be seen riffles obliquely offshore in the stream's placid waters. Here was the diversion *bund*. Here also abounded tall wild grass and willows sufficient to screen a man.

A second report, followed by the low whine of a bullet! I chose to halt. The meaning of this? I'd soon discover.

The horsemen, weapons held high, waited.

A man came running forward on foot. Breathlessly he approached shouitng. Excitedly he pointed toward a gray clad figure near the *bund,* slightly concealed by the vegetation, his rifle — a weapon of ancient vintage — at the ready.

"Am-ree-kan, Am-ree-kan, een rah kha-tar-nak ast! Jad-de, jad-de!" Strangely enough, between his gesticulations and

246

the few Persian words I understood; the messenger's admonition was perfectly clear: "American, American, get over on that main trail quick! Here is much danger! See that robber over there? He may kill you!"

Frankly, I couldn't see too much to get excited about. However, I altered my course to the higher ground and a narrow well-worn trail on top of the canal bank, and waited.

Now on a gallop the horsemen were drawing near. Reining close, for minutes both eyed me steadily and intently. Both carried bandoliers on each shoulder heavily laden with ammunition. Neither spoke — to each other or to me. Boldly, but respectfully, I returned the penetrating gaze of each. One, because of his dignity and carriage, good clothes and intelligent appearance, I took to be a *khan*. In England he would have passed for a lord. His beautiful black mare was sleek, clean limbed, and appeared capable of speed. She was equipped with a beautiful saddle well ornamented and polished. The other man rode in the rear and may have been a servant or attendant. The bay was equally well groomed, and tossed her head impatiently to move on.

Satisfied, the *khan* wheeled his mount and sped obliquely toward the river, halted and turned about, his rifle at the ready. The bandit, if such he was, remained at the *khan's* rear by several hundred feet.

The second horseman followed a short distance, stopped, waited.

I proceeded forward along this narrow trail, but rounding a bend in the canal was astounded to note some 500 feet ahead, three riflemen advancing on the double with fixed bayonets! I knew not what to make of this. But seeing no point in turning aside — friends or foes — at a brisk walk, I advanced along the trail directly toward these oncoming men. A quick glance to my right showed the *khan* on horse not 300 feet away, his gaze fixed on me and on the advancing riflemen, his own rifle at the ready.

247

Without hesitation, sweating and breathing hard, eyes fixed straight to the front as though focused on an enemy directly ahead, these three soldiers — if such they were — brushed swiftly past me as, with promptitude, I sidestepped the narrow trail!

Well, folks, directly I paused to wash my countenance in the clear cool waters of the Jalowar canal and sat down on the smooth rounded surface of a projecting black rock — to relax and think things over. Allah must be around here close and on my side!

Suddenly the stillness of this lovely sunny afternoon, one week before Christmas, was broken by a single rifle report. Then a hushed silence! Now three shots in biting succession!

I saw the *khan* cautiously ford the Arghandab and on the far bank turn abruptly about to await his companion. In midstream the bay neighed shrilly, inquiringly. The black in kind answered softly. The *khan* was seen to rein up beside several men at work in a field; then both horsemen took off at a gallop in the direction of Khwa-ja Mulk.

And then as though to assuage the mental and physical tension so lately experienced, an enchanting aroma of the essence of flowers pervaded the air. Strangely familiar, reminiscent of early youth on a southeastern Nebraska farmstead, of summer twilight, parents, sisters, brothers, and a path bordered with — that's it — petunias! For here, just a stone's throw from this Jalowar canal, was a cozy adobe dwelling almost hidden behind an immense yard abloom in gloriously rich profusion with every color of this simple yet majestic flower. So absorbed was the owner in irrigating his wonderful garden that moments passed before he noticed a stranger admiring this beautiful display. At once he directed a man, who was helping, to hand me a spray from a choice plant — blooms of deepest scarlet — sweet scented beyond comparison.

248

A kindly looking, straight, elderly man irrigating a wheat field further along left his work to join me. We walked on in silence to a rice processing yard overlooking the rice fields below. Noting our approach, a young man at this place shouted to men some half-mile away busily engaged in threshing and winnowing rice at a group of stacks. After each sentence he would turn, again eye me sharply, and then make a further report to those men. They began shouting back and asking questions excitedly. Directly they left their oxen standing and hurried over. After plying me with many questions, which to me were unintelligible, discouraged they gave up and instead showed me around the place.

Here were long low mounds of hulled rice, or just a widespread covering of rice a couple of inches deep, over the clean, dry, hard ground. These lots were in the several stages of drying, or curing, it seemed. Nearby was a large iron kettle supported by adobe bricks and with a high flue made of the same material. Here the grain was soaked and otherwise treated in boiling water during the process of removing the hulls, it seemed. Rice straw was used for fuel. Not being especially conversant with the Persian language, let alone Pakhtu, I could not grasp the fine technique expounded by these men for rendering this grain a readily edible article of food. Near the kettle was a hopper and arrangement into which the grain was fed for removing the hulls.

Pointing to the lowering sun, and with a wave of the hand, I bid the old man and these seemingly happy-go-lucky fellows good day.

And here was an arroyo fully a mile wide where it entered the river. Could this be the dry wash in which was parked the car? Again I glanced at the sun with a new feeling of alarm.

In the late afternoon shadows could be seen the intermittent glow of a scattering of dim lights in a patio on the bank well above the flat sandy bed of the arroyo. Here was gathered in silence a dozen or more men of this small isolated community — just a group of huts whose source of water is *kareese,* a ditch leading down to their nearby fields from the subterranean waters of the adjacent wide surface of a dry stream bed. What could this foreigner be wanting of them at this late hour of the day? Solemnly they puffed water pipes from relaxed positions on heels or haunches. Rising, an old man pointed in the direction of the mountains to the north, and to some dwellings upstream and across the channel.

Proceeding in this direction, I noted a teen-age boy coming from his adobe home followed by the admonitions in kindly tone from a man, evidently his father, on the bank. Yes, the road junction was up ahead to the right over the hill, the car straight up this stream bed. The boy would accompany me directly to the car; his father had carefully instructed him to do this. So much I gathered from the few words spoken and the gestures of man and son.

As we walked along, here was a picturesque and extraordinary scene. That is, to an American, and I'll wager it dated back to and far beyond Biblical times. Singly, in pairs, in small groups, women and girls in green purdahs sauntered over the loose sand upstream toward the *kareese.* The older girls and women each balanced upon their heads a three- or four-gallon water jug of tile. We met others returning, walking most erect, with these containers full of water. At the water hole, others lounged or sat about in small groups in quiet conversation. With one eye some peered through a narrow slit in their head coverings held that way by one hand. Others less cautious, or less modest (which was it? — I didn't know!) glanced out with both eyes. Others, openly inviting attention, wore head covering draped loosely over shoulders. So in the gathering twilight appeared oval, finely-shaped, patrician features surmounted and enriched by sleekly groomed black hair, lustrous metallic head bands, glossy nostril and ear ornaments. This not unnatural display of Afghan feminine adornment and excellence, so unaffectedly presented, occasioned a second glance on my part of honest approval and gratification.

Sighting the Chevrolet a mile away, I told the lad he needn't go farther. But no, as instructed by his father, he made no pretense of leaving my side until I had turned the machine about in the treacherous sand and was safely headed toward the road junction.

With a profusion of thanks, *"Mo-ta-shak-ker, besyar, bes-yar!"* and *"balkh-sheesh"* of four five-*afghani* bills, which he accepted without a glance at them, I waved good-bye — *"Khoda hafez-e-shoma!* (may God keep you),"* and left him standing motionless beside the road as the car laboriously climbed the grade to the main thoroughfare.

*   *   *

Time: Next forenoon.

Place: Khwaja Mulk, residential area surrounded by high adobe walls.

Foreground: Patow canal bordered by narrow rocky road and steep rocky slopes at base of rugged mountains, an area with thousands of cobblestone-covered mounds, a burial ground.

Scene: Large group of turbaned men.

I was returning from a reconnaissance of roads and trails on the southerly side of the Arghandab River below the dam. Attracted by so large a gathering, I paused to investigate. Approaching my car parked on the road was a burly, fierce looking fellow, a bandolier over each shoulder with a rifle, a pair of revolvers. Could he ride with me to Kandahar and on to Manzel Bagh? A schoolboy nearby who knew some English identified him as a constable. O.K., he could ride.

This other man with the warm and friendly greeting?

251

I should know him. I extended my right hand. This he grasped in both of his for a moment, then bowed slightly placing right hand over heart. Suddenly I remembered but could hardly find words to express my surprise. *"Shuma, gool ghashang — khob,"* as I pointed toward his home across the river and complimented him fervently again on his beautiful garden. The "petunia man" was overwehlmed with pleasure and walked with me and the constable over to the gathering of solemn men sitting crosslegged on the ground. What was the occasion?

On a smooth patch of hard ground awaiting burial before sunset of this day, two figures lay prone.

On the head of one — the familiar blue turban! The other — clad in gray!!!. . . .The outlaws of yesterday!

*　　　*　　　*

"Ak-ak-ak! Aya-aya-aya! Heh-heh-heh!" So in an hysteria of unearthly yaps the hyenas joined in the nocturnal chorus with wolves and jackals beyond the walls of the M-K-A headquarters compound at Manzel Bagh. Dogs from within took up the challenge.

Leaving the mess hall that evening, I had lain down on my cot in the barracks in spells of chills and coughing. At 9 p.m., wrapping myself in an army blanket, I stumbled over to the old King's Palace and into the hospital, fell into the first cot available — exhausted.

The only other patient, an Italian mechanic, lay sound asleep. No doctor, no nurse, no Afghan attendant at this hour of the evening on this day of the week. It was the weekend of the Juma before Christmas. This foreign colony was already entering into the spirit of Yuletide.

At least here with the big oil heater, the temperature would be warm and even. I could better get my breath. All night the howl of wild animals!

For five days they gave me double shots of penicillin and

had me breathe soothing fumes and steam from an improvised copper kettle.

Dimly do I remember Christmas Eve — trying to open and read twenty letters — weak beyond comprehension; in Spanish mumbling a few words to Leo from Venice, Italy — how beautiful his Venicia must look this evening with the canals lighted for Christmas. The Italian's face beamed. He could not talk because his jaw had been broken when the boom of a Northwest No. 95 dragline excavator had collapsed with Leo aboard.

And now, folks, it is New Year's Eve. All is well. I'll be back on the job January 2nd, so Dr. Randall says; and Mrs. Ward, our excellent nurse, confirms.

And again — has Allah been with me!

"And speak unto the believing women that they
restrain their eyes and preserve their modesty,
and discover not their ornaments except what
necessarily appeareth thereof; and let them
throw their veils over their bosoms, and not
show their ornaments unless to their husbands. . . .
And let them not make a noise with their feet,
that their ornaments which they hide may thereby
be discovered."

The Koran

253

XIV
Tales of The Arghandab

CHAPTER XIV

Tales of The Arghandab

A DAY OF GREAT import, this 22nd day of January the "topping off" party at Arghandab Dam! Afternoon and evening set aside for festivities marking a noteworthy event: the completion of this huge embankment rising to grade 177 feet above the old river bed. It extends 1,775 feet along its crest between rocky, precipitous canyon walls, of earth and rock fill with impervious clay core — truly an impressive creation.

In June, 1950, the first layer of silt overburden four feet thick had been stripped from the dam site. During the first stage of construction, work had been confined to the area between the rock-studded right abutment and the river. There had been excavation for the core trench to within fifty feet of the river's edge. This extended thirty-five feet below the original ground surface to bedrock. As fast as exposed, the bedrock was cleaned and pressure grouted. Clay material had then been placed and compacted to form a watertight barrier. A gradual gradation of coarser materials extended outward to the embankment slopes. Bottom-dump Euclid trucks in continuous procession had hauled this especially selected material from pits along the river.

Came then the second stage: Begun in December, 1950, holed through in February, 1951, an eighteen-foot diameter tunnel 900 feet long bypassed the entire flow of the river during the following summer by means of an upstream cofferdam. Midway of the tunnel a vertical shaft was driven to accommodate the gates and operating mechanism which will control the outflow of the water for irrigation purposes and electric power development.

In a rocky gap along the rim of the reservoir was being constructed the spillway. Here surplus water will flow into a ravine and be led directly back to the river about one mile below the dam. Several saddle dams close dips in the topography and are auxiliary in purpose to the main dam.

So here will be impounded 394,000 acre-feet of water for irrigation and electric power production. Thus will be tamed a wild river wont to expend quickly its energy and flood waters in the spring and then dwindle away in summer when so badly needed for use on some 150,000 acres of fertile valley land along the main channel, around the city of Kandahar, and out on the plains surrounding the precipitous mountain masses to the southwest. Soon the thirty existing canals, now only partially irrigating this area, will have at their command a year around source of supply.

So then, on this mild hazy afternoon of late January, the presence of hundreds of Afghan workmen proudly strolling along the crest of the huge dam occasioned no surprise. Dressed in their best — pride and dignity was manifest in their dark faces — in their demeanor. Laborers, truck drivers, jackhammer men, grade foreman, mechanics, Caterpillar tractor operators, shop men, machinists, Northwest dragline runners, surveymen, bulldozer operators, concrete men, drillers, grout men, garage workers, hard rock men, warehouse clerks, office workers, powder men — all and more were represented.

For special skills, many had been trained under the capable direction of a small nucleus of M-K-A supervisors. Each had helped complete this job — a monument to the enterprise and foresight of his own government — the highest authority of a free nation — and to cooperative Yankee ingenuity!

Ed Seepe, Sidney Thornton, and I spent the afternoon just looking over the works. Confined much to the office at Manzel Bagh, the accounting and engineering departments, my two congenial companions were intrigued by faint objects on the hazy landscape far up the river, as viewed from the crest of a saddle dam.

Driving several miles along a camel trail, we drew up near a small community of mud huts with thatched roofs. The advance of barking dogs was retarded by our light fusillade of stones which the animals paused to sniff. Strange people stared questioningly from dooryards as we climbed high on the crumbling remains of the massive adobe walls of an ancient fort. Its secrets would soon pass further into oblivion under the rising waters of a man-created lake.

Lost in reverie in the lonely silence of these unbounded open spaces, we retraced our way to the construction camp. Here abounded warm companionship; a cocktail party, buffet dinner, music and dancing. Everybody had been invited; Americans, Filipinos, Italians, wives and children. Mrs. Dawdy and her several assistants, wives of American and Italian supervisors, were charming hostesses. More power to Construction Superintendent Marshall Dawdy, his able assistant William S. Stott, and their staff of specialists, each in his own field, for a crowning achievement!

*　　　*　　　*

Well, folks, I visualized the work ahead; the integration

259

of these new water storage facilities, now nearing completion, and the downstream system of ancient canals. This was to be the first stage in the development of a modern irrigation project here in the Arghandab Valley. General Manager Ted V. Johnston, a few days ago had gone over with me the salient features of an agreement between M-K-A and the Afghan government to handle the immediate situation. I was to supervise the execution of this agreement, in addition to one of a similar nature on the Boghra Project. Important terms of the Arghandab contract or agreement were as follows:

Operation to include the operation and control of the discharge valves and gates, and the storage and release of water required for irrigation.

M-K-A to make necessary surveys and studies to determine quantity of water required for proper and economical irrigation of lands and crops under irrigation.

Maintenance to include work necessary to maintain dam and structures in safe and effective operable condition, maintenance of camp buildings in use by operating staff, and dressing of premises in vicinity of dam as mutually agreed upon in writing.

As part of the O & M program, to train an Afghan operating organization which will ultimately take over and be responsible for the operation and maintenance of the dam and reservoir and later of the canal system.

Operation to extend to canals and cultivated lands below dam which are under existing irrigation systems, and which receive water from surface flow of river.

M-K-A not to be responsible for maintenance, repair and improvements of canals, except of emergency nature agreed to in writing.

M-K-A to set up an organization to supervise control and

distribution of water and to train Afghan crews to take over ultimately.

M-K-A to have complete control over distribution of water, to set up schedules for delivery, to establish rules and regulations for use. The Government to co-operate in making such effective, and to furnish the necessary police power to enforce the rules and regulations if requested to do so by M-K-A.

There being no control devices on any of the existing canals, it is impossible to measure and allocate water with exactness. However, M-K-A will use its best judgment, and employ such means as necessary to make a proper and equitable distribution. It is understood that a completely effective program of water control is not feasible until the present canal systems are modernized, and adequate control structures and measuring devices are installed.

And so, folks, that was it; an outline of my job for months to come in the back country of the Arghandab and Helmand River Valleys of Afghanistan. There were to be interesting situations and experiences, some not without danger, many most difficult to depict to friends on the opposite face of the earth. Involved were Afghans in many stations of life, from lowly plowmen to ranking agriculturists, from laborers to graduate engineers, to generals of the army, to commissioners, from school teachers to governors. And so, then, on with the narrative — a tale of events in near-chronological order!

*   *   *

Our delightful winter season is passing, as mild as the Sacramento Valley. No fog, no wind, much sunshine, but with scarcity of rain; just enough to green up the desert with a light scattering of short grass. Progressively the days are getting warmer. Only yesterday appeared an almond tree clothed in masses of large pinkish white blossoms of queenly splendor. Near the King's Palace is a large tree full of red buds. Flocks of birds that act like robins, but which are grayish black, gather in the trees and drop down to hop over the freshly plowed or spaded soil behind our gardeners. These men take great pride in the preparation of flower beds along the drives at Manzel Bagh, of vegetable gardens near the mess hall. Out on the desert are enormous birds; eagles they are, with wide spreading wings and stocky yellow legs far apart, and big talons. They have wintered here.

Lately I have been on reconnaissance all day alone without guide or interpreter; just park the car at a strategic point and hike long distances to otherwise inaccessible places. In the interest of safety, upon leaving the office one leaves a note with Jane, (Mrs. Donald Schomp), our most business-like secretary in the engineering department, covering his itinerary. Like this one recently:

"Leave Manzel Bagh 8 a.m.; destination: Doost Mohammed; purpose: reconnaissance of Takatu and Takhi Canals and others upstream; return 5 p.m."

Well, this had to do with irrigated lands on the left flank of the river from Arghandab Dam downstream some thirty miles to the bridge crossing on main road. From the bridge I was able to follow a main camel trail remarkably well with the car. It took a zig-zag course around massive granite blocks, across narrow ravines, up and down steep rocky inclines, and finally atop a rounded mound. This overlooked the narrow ribbon-like valley and irrigated lands on both sides of the river below; the green wheatfields, ricefields not yet planted, and on the higher lands bordering orchards of mulberry *(toot)*, apricots *(azr-da-loo)*, almonds *(ba-dam)*, figs *(an-joor)*, grapes *(angoor)*, pomegranates *(anar)*, alfalfa *(alaf)* — all of the trees and vines were yet bare of leaves. Roughly the lands were devoted to 45% rice, 45% wheat and 10% orchards and forage. Eating my lunch, I noted representations of animals carved on some of the granite blocks, evidently ibexes, those goat-like animals with long horns curving far backward. Some had locked horns in fighting. Also were carved circles and eight-pointed stars, and pairs of hands with thumb and five fingers. Now what race of people left these traces? And how long ago?

And then down a steep rocky decline to the water's edge, here a narrow shelf barely allowed the Chevrolet to squeeze by. Again these strange pictographs. What idea was being expressed? And a long horizontal groove on the vertical face of this huge granite block; did this depict the highest flood level ages ago? And further along two miles, the absolute end of this road, a rice mill, a *bund,* a sharp bend in the river, a high rocky bluff. I walked up the canal to the diversion weir, a rock and brush obstruction projecting obliquely upstream; a crude affair but effectively turning a full supply of water into this canal, and then back through a pomegranate orchard surprising a lone man laboriously turning over the Bermuda grass sod with a primitive looking spade. Recovering his composure this dark fellow smiled and as I stood noting the progress of his work — two acres completed, three more to go — he nonchalantly burst forth into a high-pitched, wild song. It was then I observed, partly hidden through some mulberry trees and on a higher level space overlooking the river, an imposing adobe residence of pleasing proportions.

An hour later I had reached the top of the bluff. My maps of this country, unrolled, lay oriented on the ground. Here below lay a narrow winding valley and river flanked by rugged mountains alternating with vast expanses of open desert, all practically uninhabited. Far to the north stretched snow-clad heights, the source of our reservoir's water supply.

Upstream on the right some three kilometers, where a desert valley descended gently to the river, a small village with large trees nested cozily just beyond a low ridge. This I believed to be my destination — Doost Mohammed (Friend of Mohammed). I would have to go forward on foot. From this prominence I carefully selected the route I would follow, even to getting down to the river's edge. It was then I observed the handsome abode some 600 feet below; a large neat courtyard bounded on two sides by shapely one-story buildings, the whole within a compound surrounded by high adobe walls and shrubbery, the river just beyond and below. Downright homelike and attractive, this Moslem domicile, thought I, as with folded arms I peered unobtrusively downward. Just then some women in blue purdahs, who evidently had been sunning in the warm courtyard, made a dash for cover through as many open gateways or doors. Immediately at intervals of twenty seconds a voice from below distinctly sounded out: "Bad boy! Bad boy! Bad boy!" Examining more closely this situation, it was discovered the voice came from an indolent looking individual squatted on his haunches in the sunshine just outside the compound walls. And I chuckled softly at the feigned air of surprise and modesty exhibited by this blue-veiled femininity. An hour before, the chant from below in the pomegranate orchard had carried sufficient warning of the approach of an *Amree-kan.* Later chagrined, I learned "badbu" means "evil smelling" and not "bad boy" as it sounded!

Doost Mohammed, a sleepy village; it was mid-afternoon. Broken suddenly was the tranquillity; the dull strokes on a gong, the high pitched chant of a mullah from somewhere, reminded the people to pray:

"Allah is One. There is no God but Him.
Mohammed is the apostle of Allah!"

Along a narrow alley, the canal on one side, a high wall on the other, I traveled through the little town scarcely observed by anyone to a fig and apricot orchard beyond. Scenes of peace were these, far from the crowded city of

Kandahar. But the hour was late. Further examinations of valley conditions upstream could await another trip on foot tomorrow, or a journey by boat downstream from the dam later.

* * *

Halfway up this mountain road to the summit and off to one side was a spring. As I slowed down, from it came a camel driver well armed with bandolier and ammunition, and a rifle. Casually he looked me over and glanced inside the car, then sauntered toward an open flat nearby. A strange sight! Some thirty or more camels were kneeling in tight circular formation, head to tail. Their burdens lay on the ground within the ring where a campfire gave cheeriness to the gathering dusk. About the fire on their heels sat in silence a dozen turbaned men. The evening meal was being prepared and served. Soldiers? An attitude of quiet alertness prevailed.

Beyond in a mountain corridor flanked by serrated ranges as fantastic, seemingly, as those on the moon, whom should I overtake but Kelsey! His radio maintenance truck, a big yellow closed vehicle, had broken down. The rear wheels were resting against some stones at the side of the dusty road. Kelsey was preparing a camp for the night. With him were three men. Upon reaching Manzel Bagh I would send back help from the shops.

Suggesting I take along the two camel drivers, Kelsey on second thought asked his helper were these two fellows safe. To this Moos-ta-fah replied noncommitally.

Giving each a critical look, I said, "Well, Kelsey, with these two I'd feel safer than with just any pair of a more sophisticated looking breed which one might casually pick up on a dark night along Highway No. 99 in California."

Grinning understandingly, Kelsey continued, "Outlaws have given trouble along this road through the mountains, but the Army has the situation under control now, I hear."

At the summit the cameleers thanked me profusely for the lift and disappeared with their packs into the darkness.

Beyond the pass the road followed a dry stream bed, broad and gravelly. Profiled against the night sky, the black rugged turrets, the lofty spires and pinnacles of the nearby saw-toothed ranges, lent an air of mystery and enchantment unknown to this world.

Entering the gate to the compound at Manzel Bagh, I told a young Afghan on duty there with the transportation department of Kelsey's plight.

Said he, "Mees-tah Kho-shal, we will find the superintendent of transportation. But first, please, excuse me for two minutes. I pray." This lad could not have been more than eighteen, and I knew he was beseeching Allah for the safety of Kelsey and Moos-ta-fa.

Directly we found Mr. Fahey, who said within an hour two trucks from the dam would be along; one would tow Kelsey's truck to the shops.

Pleased and relieved, the young Afghan pressed into my hand some parched peas and raisins.

*   *   *

Another important day was this. At 4 p.m. the outlet valves had been closed; storage of water in the Arghandab Reservoir was in progress. The date, February 24, 1952. Now for a brief period the entire flow downstream had ceased. In this interim a new rating station with footbridge crossing had been installed just below the dam; another with cableway across the river had been erected just below where the water from the spillway would enter the river.

And now, three days later, Al Stanley and his hydrographic party, Shir Ahmad and several assistants, were rating the upper river station. In increments of about 200 c.f.s., the gauge height in feet, tenths and hundredths at the new rating station was being determined for each amount of measured flow from 200 c.f.s. to 3,000 c.f.s., as a beginning, and a corresponding rating curve formulated.

At the same time Chris Brown, now in charge of engineering, construction and operations at the dam and reservoir, was procuring data for discharge graphs of each of the two needle valves regulating flow from the reservoir. For a given elevation of the water surface above the dam the setting of each needle valve in percentage of the full opening was plotted against the discharge from the valve as measured by current meter.

Stanley's hydrographic party had measured diversions into each of the valley canals at periodic intervals, together with return surface flows to the river, and flows from one canal to another. Flows had likewise been measured past the cable-way station at head of the reservoir site, at the two river bridge crossings, and at Qala Bist, junction of the Arghandab and Helmand.

So it was gratifying to know that there was already being made a systematic accounting of the storage and distribution or disposal of the waters of the Arghandab River.

Likewise we were becoming familiar with the operation of each canal as practiced by local authorities. On-the-spot crop surveys were revealing as to the probable amounts of flow required during each of the weeks or months ahead.

I explained to the people that no more need they fear water shortage in late summer and fall. Without fanfare on this February 24th, 1952, the centuries-old habits of the Arghandab River were submitting to the control of men — men determined to harness these natural resources for the benefit of the common people of Afghanistan. Now they could grow more and better crops of wheat, corn, rice, cotton, tobacco, melons, sugar beets, vegetables, berries, grapes, orchard fruits; almonds, apricots, plums, figs, pomegranates; and livestock — cattle, sheep, goats; and forage — alfalfa, clover, sorghums.

New lands would now go under irrigation. Surplus raisins, dried tree fruits, grains, cotton, tobacco, sugar— all could be exported to Pakistan and India in exchange for rupees.

But there was yet much in the back country to study before one could discuss with intelligence the problems of this project with Afghan officials.

*   *   *

It was in the vicinity of Deh Sabz (Village Green); here the canals Nahree Row-zah, Ghulam Mah-deen, Sang-a-ree, all irrigated a beautiful land of vineyards and alfalfa fields. That the soil was deep, loamy, productive, was noticed by the sight, feel, and the wonderful scent of freshly overturned earth. Here a dozen perspiring men were busily engaged in spring work incident to the care of a vineyard. Anticipating an ample water supply, already the vineyard was being expanded. Vines being planted in perfect rows at exact intervals? No. Without wire, without redwood stakes, the vines must trail on the north bank of a slope, the fruit to ripen amidst the dense shaded foliage protected from the burning rays of the Afghan summer sun. The vines must be planted in the bottom of a two-foot deep trench, the excavated earth from which forms the south bank. Other men were engaged in pruning the vines, as we do in California, cutting off the long runners so as to leave two or three of the swelling buds from each of which will shoot forth a new runner to bear the season's bunches of luscious grapes.

Seeing me crossing the vineyard and taking an interest in their work, several friendly fellows paused to chat. Not that I could understand all their words, nor they mine, but I somehow sensed their meaning: How were vineyards cared for in *Am-ree-ka?* No ditches, no banks, vines in rows each way; with smiles and nods they understood that. The posts and wire arrangement upon which to trail the vines was

268

a little more difficult to explain and for them to understand, but soon that too seemed intelligible.

"*Kho-da ha-fez! Yek sa'at.*" "Goodbye, I'll be back in an hour," said I, pointing to the river. How close to the river did the vineyards extend? That's what I wanted to know.

And then a flock of fat-tailed sheep grazing on the Bermuda grass of a riverside meadow; a shepherd, his sudden shrill song.

Wending my way along narrow lanes between high walls, some right angled turns, soon I was again approaching the men of the vineyard. Now they were relaxing along the trail.

"*Boo-ro-boo-ro!* Zud!" said one in a low tone motioning behind me; go, go quickly! And I turned to observe two characters following. Upon seeing so many men, they hesitated undecidedly. About the waists of each were cartridge belts with side arms.

I bid them sit down. I would show them the maps. "Kandahar, rud Arghandab, Deh Sabz," as I pointed to these places on the maps of my portfolio. Yes, they understood, all right. One bent over me rather amused, I thought; the other in grim silence remained aloof.

I slowly surveyed the faces of the vineyardists, honest workmen all; silent, stern. For a fleeting instant their *jam-a-dar* caught my attention. With the faintest lift of his eyebrows and slight jerk of head, I caught his warning!

So with nonchalance I tucked the map roll under one arm; with firmness I gripped my club, the one-half of a surveyor's level rod.

"*Zande bash!* (May you live long)," I bid my friends in parting salute, and with a "*Khalafam chie?* (Something wrong?)" to the two brigands, I was again on my way.

* * *

More beautiful countryside, a warm spring day in the

last week of February, the Sang-i-zar Canal, a man running excitedly toward me across an alfalfa field.

Pointing in the direction I was about to travel: "Don't go that way! Go north through the village of Salim!" He ran to meet me admonishing further and excitedly in words I could not grasp. Not knowing the man's true intentions, I expressed thanks and continued my course west along the Sang-i-zar. For two hours I would alternately walk, pause and jot down notes concerning these "Gardens of Kandahar."

And here was a grizzled old man and a small boy loading two burros with bundles of green wheat.

But that distant droning — no, it couldn't be, flights were prohibited in Afghanistan—none had been seen for thirteen months! The old man and boy and I searched the horizon, puzzled, amazed. And then from the direction of Kandahar, over that black, saw-toothed mountain — no mistake about it — there roared forth a two-motored plane glistening white against the azure up yonder. Moments later this unusual visitor passed over us disappearing far to the west toward Iran. But for a moment it left within my breast a strange sense of loneliness, only to be followed by an uncommon feeling of exultation. This I could not account for.

It was then I caught the notes of a wild song in the distance, answered by another similar in the area I had just traversed.

"Koo-ja mee-rrii?" Turning, I observed in a nearby field two men plowing with oxen; a third man was running toward a brush hut inclosing a grist mill not far beyond. This runner did not slacken his pace as one plowman had demanded of him, "Where are you going?"

I marveled at this coincidence of the passing airplane, coincident with what I was soon to know. The sun was lowering to the west over the green fields. It was yet four miles to the Chevy parked along the desert; I had best hurry.

It was then the black-turbaned fellow emerged from the

gristmill; on the double he approached me across the wheat, dragging a large rifle? No, a large club bigger and heavier than mine; upon closer observation a post five inches in diameter, five feet long, blunt on one end, the other a sharp point ten inches long.

No fooling, this fellow is up to something!

"Khob, shoma che kar darid? (Now, what is your business?)" I shouted as on the canal bank I stood poised to meet him with blows from my longer, lighter, hardwood club. He pointed to a gem on my left hand.

Would he hurl the weapon, charge with the pointed end, ram? Weapon poised, he hesitated. In a split second a blow from my club would stun him; fatally, mayhap. He drew back perplexed. Came on again. A violent thrust to his neck, face, that would block him.

So 'twas the ring he wanted, my son's ring, the large alexandrite stone from Hong Kong, with brilliance unequaled it refracted the blue of a cloudless sky, the emerald green of the fields, the deep cardinal in the brilliant rays of the sun. How my Afghan friends had admired it; on the desert jobs had conversed quietly aside, then imitated the movement and roar of an airplane tail-spinning to a crash in China. Pointing toward the east, *"Cheena-Cheena,"* they would exclaim. I had smiled appreciatively, yet grievously. It had occurred fifteen minutes out of *Mengtsz,* Yunnan Province. The flight was routine from Kunming to Haiphong over rough mountainous country, tiger-infested jungles. Communist sabotage? A target for communist gunfire? Yes! No doubt about it. Days later Nationalist infantry and batteries of field artillery battled their way through to the site of the disaster.

So this outlaw with the black turban, club poised to strike, wanted Norman's ring!

"Pedar sag! Choob pa-een! You father of a dog, drop

that club! *Sarbaz, sarbaz, besyar,* many soldiers coming from Kandahar will kill you!"

That did it. With a thud his club flattened the wheat. *"Sarbaz — na — na!"* in unexpected alarm.

An accomplice (I wasn't sure) observing the scene from the mill, rushed over. "Soldiers! No! No! *Doo-roost. Burro!*" You're unharmed, be on your way!

Continuing on my course, shrill calls sounded from roof tops. Friends or foes? I would keep to the open fields. There under some trees two teen-agers, perhaps sixteen to eighteen smiled invitingly. They wanted to talk; unusual, I thought.

Beyond a mile, behind some crumbling walls, the slinking figure in black turban following again. Hid, thinking himself unseen.

Engaging a nearby shepherd in conversation, I kept the walls in view and pretended to jot down field notes. After all, those two girls back there had displayed friendly gestures of warning.

* * *

A concrete building at Manzel Bagh is occupied by the Royal Afghan Commission for M-K-A Projects; here I was ushered into the office of Morid Khan, President, a large well built man; tall, dark, smooth shaven, and pleasant.

Others entering bowed low placing hand to breast; some in addition kissed the back of the Commissioner's hand in morning salutation.

Jalaluddeen (Light of the Religion), the interpreter, ushered in an Army Major.

I would talk awhile, stop; Jalaluddeen would interpret.

At one juncture all gazed sharply at my ring; quite dramatically and effectively, Jalaluddeen described the pointed post, how used.

Afterwards at the guardhouse the Major said to me in Persian: "These soldiers will bring in anyone you point out," as two neat looking men in uniform appeared. "Bait the outlaws. Stun them if necessary. But don't kill them. Don't be afraid!"

*   *   *

"Your rifles, revolvers; what, *too-fang — tapanche — na!*" Arriving near the scenes of the previous day's experiences these soldiers appeared strangely empty-handed.

It was then I produced the "better idea" weapon prepared for me that morning in the welding shop supervised by Manuel Roberts (of Dixon, California). Just a ½" diameter steel bar three feet long embedded securely in a pick handle, and to the end of which was welded a gig, such as is used for spearing salmon. The *sarbaz* looked relieved with this in his hands. The other soldier had a two-lash whip with stocky handle. Manuel had reinforced my half-of-a surveyor's rod with a 2"x2½" steel slug welded to the shoe.

To the village of Deh Sabz we hiked first. Through a series of lanes and alleys crooked and narrow, between high walls, we wended our way. I led straight to the abode of a suspiciously acting character. A couple of days before at the suggestion of a black-turbaned fellow following not far behind me, this chap had emerged from a vineyard, passed me along a lane on the double. Minutes later he had reappeared from the doorway of this abode brandishing an ancient looking gun, while over the doorway on the roof barked a vicious dog. In passing I had almost laughed at what appeared to me as juvenile comedy. Beyond him I could see a young woman in the compound who also appeared amused as I casually made a gesture with my walking stick both at this fellow and his dog.

This morning we found this door partly ajar, the soldier pulled it shut, then hammered on it vigorously. Finally an eighteen-year-old *zan* appeared and stated that the man was away at work.

273

AFGHANISTAN VENTURE

We walked on for many kilometers. Oddly enough no one was in sight anywhere, except a scattering of hardworking men in the vineyard and fields. In the villages not a person was visible except occasionally one did get a glimpse through a gate ajar of men sitting on their haunches in groups smoking water pipes. Occasionally a dog, barking and vicious, charged forth from somewhere, only to retreat precipitously when counter-charged with salmon gig, whip and steel-shod club. One animal all but flattened a young almond tree in his hasty withdrawal.

In the late afternoon we grabbed a fellow who looked like the one who near that mill a few days ago had insolently demanded, *"Cher te zeh?"* (Where are you going?) Then he had attempted to wrest from me the walking stick. After a swift kick on his shins from my heavy boot he had retreated. Accompanying this rascal had been three teen-agers carrying between them a knotted root partly concealed in a turban. This fellow now offered some resistance as Becan seized his turban and with it tightly bound the man's arms behind him. The prisoner walked ahead of us a long distance to the car. In Manzel Bagh the Major had him held under arrest.

During the next two days we combed the countryside north of the Arghandab for traces of the outlaws that seemed to have been roaming at will. We entered villages in the back country, a half dozen or more, that stood out prominently above the valley on high, isolated hills. I had been curious about these anyway . . . from a distance like pictures you've seen in Biblical histories; the soldiers likewise were intrigued. We would follow up and along the zig-zag alleys, and peer over mud walls unceremoniously, just like we belonged there.

Curiosity was satisfied. Each village consisted of just one compound after another surrounded by eight-foot mud walls; mud huts with thatched roofs; stables with animals; scarcely

274

a man in sight. Women quietly cooking over open fires, children sparsely clothed, or not at all, in the warm sunshine. Chickens, maybe a camel or two or a couple of oxen, piles of camel or ox chips drying on the roofs for fuel, groups of women just visiting or gossiping maybe.

Then we would go over the immediate surroundings. There were men at work in the vineyards pruning and irrigating; all a very peaceful area except that one man left three women in a village and started following us everywhere, into the fields along the trails, and he'd walk close up behind me. At trail forks we'd start to go one way, he'd follow; we'd turn back and start to go the other way, he'd follow. Finally, "What's wrong? Where are you going anyway? *Burro!*" And without hesitation he walked obediently back toward his village (and his three wives?).

Approaching another town on a hill not far away we heard a shrill chant. Immediately children scurried for cover into compounds; not a person was visible in the alleys.

And then a horseman kept close behind us. He kept his turban pulled up over his mouth. I motioned him to uncover his face, and "what's the matter with your head? You keep pointing to it. Take off your turban."

But he was no one I'd ever seen before; just a simple and curious fellow returning from the mill with a sack of flour. Claimed he had a headache.

Finally we approached the flour mill where the man with the sharp pointed weapon had emerged; we grabbed two loiterers there. Also two plowmen in the nearby field where the assailant had lingered. With but little show of resistance, all submitted to having their arms bound behind them by the soldiers, who used the turban of each for this purpose. And with willow switches the soldiers induced the four men to walk along peacefully to the car some six kms. away.

That same afternoon, before Commissioner Morid Khan, the four men confirmed the information given by the prisoner of the first day: the whereabouts and identity of the outlaws who had dared operate in an otherwise peaceful countryside.

With that Morid's eyes twinkled; the major expressed pleasure. The Army would handle the situation. And they did, as evidenced by photographs that Iqbal, our Company photographer, exhibited around the engineering office. Here were two brigands hanging by the neck. A public execution had taken place in Kandahar. In the final stages of the round-up the Army Commandant had personally risked his life to apprehend the marauders.

*   *   *

Quite an undertaking this, planning the organization for managing, operating and maintaining a tremendous Afghan irrigation project under conditions of full completion, total development.

True, construction will not be completed for many years; full development will require generations. Nevertheless, like a structure of earth, wood, concrete, steel — whose design and construction must be planned in advance — just so must the organization be designed and planned that is to handle the project development in all of its stages.

Here would be 4,350,000 acre-feet of water in storage. 1,250,000 acres of land, roughly, awaited irrigation between the two dams and the Iranian border 300 miles away. A distribution system with many hundreds of miles of canals would be involved; electric power production and distribution; scores of agricultural experiment stations; innumerable demonstration farms.

A Commission, a Helmand Valley Authority, would have overall charge.

The visualization of such a project, the man-power, the equipment required in every department, the costs in dollars, *afghanis,* Pakistan *rupees,* all of this on my part had required many days and some nights of concentration. The

276

report and chart embodying this was wanted by the Chief Engineer in San Francisco at an early date.

But I had it about licked when one morning "Holly" walked in with a stranger, a Mr. Franklin representing the British Embassy at Kabul. Would you, Paul, explain to Mr. Franklin the Project and show him around the two dams, the Boghra system? His driver with the jeep was waiting to meet Franklin at Girishk. They would proceed from there to Farah, Herat and back to Kabul north of the Hindu Kush Mountains.

Well, it was midnight when we arrived at Kajakai Dam. We ate a meal with the night crew; coffee, doughnuts, ham and eggs. Under the brilliant electric lights, the whole job shone as bright as day. We were given comfortable quarters reserved for guests in a cottage made of stone at the site. There were many such for families of the foreigners employed on the job, with lawns and flowers, all on a bluff overlooking the Helmand River, the office, shops, equipment yards, borrow pit areas, bridge across the river, and the rising dam.

I found Franklin excellent company; of broad experience in the British consular service, most practical. Wanted to be in touch with the progress of the country, its people and all phases of the agricultural development. He had hunted quail, he said, with General Claire Lee Chennault around Kunming and Chungking, China; had lived in China many years, had never been to the States. "Jones, if you ever get into any difficulty in Afghanistan," said he, "let me know. We at the British Emabssy in Kabul might be in a position to help you out."

During the forenoon Mr. Donald C. Huss, field engineer, showed us over the work.

The dam fill was rising at the rate of one meter a day. Begun in 1947, a year had been spent in obtaining and shipping the equipment half way around the earth. By 1950, scaling and cleaning of the canyon walls for the abutments were well along. Two thirty-five foot diameter tunnels were being driven, of horseshoe shape and about one-half mile long. One would carry the release of irrigation water, the other flow for the production of 80,400 horsepower at a hydroelectric plant. Both would by-pass the flow of the Helmand around the dam under construction.

The sides of the canyon were marked with white lines delineating the axis of the dam and dividing lines between the various classes of fill materials from fines for the impervious core, through the several gradations to coarsest at the outer slopes, and the boulder riprap on the slopes.

The clay core had been set in a trench excavated to bedrock. The earth and rock fill will rise to a height of about 300 feet above stream bed. To seal a geologic fault, a shaft fifty feet in diameter and over 100 feet deep was being driven on the axis below the core trench. One day a Euclid truck went wild, plunging motor first into this shaft. However, Allah had been by the side of the dozen or more workmen in the bottom of the shaft. The accident had occurred while they were out for a mid-forenoon break.

Franklin and I were accompanied over the job throughout the afternoon by Construction Superintendent James L. Dunn, and his affable wife, a most gracious lady. At the site of the spillway a continuous column of trucks arrived, loaded, and departed with large pieces of granite which were hauled to the dam fill and dumped on the outer slopes for riprap. At dusk a huge blast of dynamite shattered more of the granite material to be removed for the spillway. The capacity of the spillway will be many times that of the flow of the highest flood of the Helmand on record. The overflow will be conducted through a rock cut to a nearby ravine, and discharged into the Helmand well downstream from the toe of the dam.

After a sumptuous supper — it was Juma — in a most

splendidly equipped and operated modern construction mess hall, Franklin said, "Well, Paul, shall we go for a wee bit of a walk?" For hours we walked about everywhere on this huge job where men and equipment worked at full force under the bright electric lights produced by diesel power; the machine and blacksmith shops, garage, tire-repair shops. Here were casings of monster proportions, the borrow pits of selected materials, a continuous line of Euclids hauled earth to the dam, the dumping of materials at the fill, the bulldozing into even layers, the compacting by sheeps-foot rollers, the hydraulic jet sprinkling fill, the huge rocks being rolled into place on the slopes, the compaction testing laboratory — the service station — and finally a midnight snack of waffles, sausage and coffee.

On this job were about 100 American, Filipino and Italian supervisors; several thousand operators, mechanics and laborers.

"Jones, how long have M-K's operations in Afghanistan been underway?" said Franklin.

"Since 1946, I understand. They built the road from Spin Baldak, on the Pakistan border, to Kandahar first. After that the Helmand River Diversion Weir at Girishk," I rejoined.

"What about the finances? Where is the money coming from?" continued Franklin.

"The Company entered into a contract with this progressive kingdom, this 'Star of Asia.' We think it deserving of this epithet," said I. "The country used its own dollars obtained mostly from the export of karakul furs, for which it is famed, as you know. $17,000,000 was spent by the Afghans, hard-won money. This took courage. It also attracted the attention of the United States Government which, in recognition of this sincere effort to fulfill a national aspiration, through the U.S. Export-Import Bank

279

of Washington, D.C., granted them a loan of $21,000,000," I concluded.

"Well, your statement is surely enlightening, Paul. The rest of the world knows so little about land-locked Afghanistan, so handicapped by isolation. My country, for one, is awaking to its possibilities of national advancement through determination, enterprise and courage. One sure thing, the King and Prime Minister and the whole government, shall we say, are bent on raising the economy of its people to that of the Western nations," concluded Franklin, stretching and yawning, and then suddenly as an afterthought, "I say, old man, do you know what's the toime?"

"2 a.m. Best hit the sack!" I exclaimed in surprise.

*   *   *

It's fifty-fifty now, this third week in April, the division of my time between the Arghandab and the Boghra. Around Ft. Nad-i-ali smiling people wave greetings from their new homes. Between villages lie green wheatfields by the hundreds of acres. In a series of dry lake beds far out on the desert, nomads have taken advantage of a stream that runs forty kms. southward with seemingly little loss in transit but evaporation. Here grow other hundreds of acres of wheat, corn, and melons. Out on East Marja, people are building their own ditches from our main canal turnouts to their fields. It may be years yet before the Government will have money to build laterals. Large camps are being established and the land occupied with the knowledge of the Agricultural Department at Nad-i-ali. People may crop it during the present season, 1952. Beyond that is questionable.

An independent people, these. Failing to make local agreements, Chiefs go to Kabul and the Prime Minister. They return with glowing concessions for their people, it is claimed. So regardless of unofficial opposition, and barring misuse of the water, my policy has been to provide an ample supply to all comers bent on growing their own food.

*   *   *

With Aziz-ullah (Dear to God) and Gool Mohammed (Rose of Mohammed), I waited one morning at Nad-i-ali for the arrival of Ab-dool Jab-bar (Creature of God). My two companions discussed something in low tones. Then:

"Polygens, where do you get all your strength, energy? Gool wants to know. If you take *da-wa* (medicine) for it, we want some of it from you."

On the impulse, impromptu-like, pointing to the clear blue zenith overhead, I replied, "Allah; Allah is my strength!"

As they slapped me vigorously on the shoulder, their faces registered smiling approval. A good answer.

Abdul Jabbar climbed in as good-natured and smiling as usual, his black eyes twinkling. A small man about twenty-seven, intelligent, for three years *tageman* (interpreter) for the Commission at Kandahar, employed now by the Department of Agriculture. Studied law in the University at Kabul, taught classes in law, lives with and supports his mother at Nad-i-ali. Would go to the States taking mother with him to finish law course; wants to marry an American girl. In Kabul had worked for Mr. Ludeen, Minister of Public Works. Mr. Ludeen had wanted Abdul to marry his daughter, but Abdul wanted to finish his education first. Besides "she's too brown!" said he.

"Well, Abdul," I had said, "Ludeen is a graduate in engineering from Cornell University. He stands in high favor with your King. Maybe you turned down a wonderful opportunity!"

By now we were approaching a camp of eighty large black tents. Huskies tore out barking viciously and described huge arcs as they misjudged the speed and direction of our car. Children followed; girls in neat-fitting, colorful pantaloons, heads surmounted by glittering little caps from under which projected numerous little pig-tails; boys in black gowns with skirts about to the ground. We circled the camp and came to a stop within the ring of tents.

A tightly packed audience mostly of men gathered, many with handsome features; patrician in fact. Could these be the remnants of a higher civilization? Most of the women unveiled, gathered in groups in front of the tents close by. They wore bronze or brass ornaments about their foreheads and over smoothly combed black hair; flat silver discs on one or both sides of the nose resting against the hollow of the nostrils. Some had blue or hazel eyes, but dark brown and black predominated. Many of the women, like the men, had straight slender noses, finely cut features, and were genuinely aristocratic in bearing.

An oldish-like man with mustache and black whiskers, green turban, loose garments and sandals, appeared from a tent. The crowd parted respectfully.

I said to him, "Is that your wheat over there (1,000 acres or more in the dry lake bed)? A good crop and you'll have plenty to eat."

"That is not ours. The Chakhansur people over in that camp own that. We are from Baluchistan. We have about 300 families, 1,000 people," said the Chief.

"What do you eat?" said I.

"We are hungry most of the time!" said the Chief talking vociferously. Two others joined excitedly and simultaneously.

There were a few camels about the camp, and droves of sheep and goats not far away, indicating that these Baluchis were mainly occupied in grazing herds.

The Chief at this point pulled out of his pocket a neatly written letter, saying it was from a Mazari Chieftain in Baluchistan to the Government of Afghanistan, asking that his people be helped to establish themselves on irrigated land.

282

Suddenly reaching for Abdul's shirt collar, the Chief twisted it with choking effect.

"What's that for? What's he want?" said I, alarmed.

"He is exacting a promise from me; that I will help put his people on irrigated land," said Abdul with difficulty.

At this the Chief released his strangle hold. Pulling Abdul's head to one side, he removed the young man's gray karakul cap and kissed the top of his head. And so was sealed the understanding!

As this mystic encampment receded on the shimmering desert horizon, Abdul explained that the Mazaris are a race of gallant fighters; have never tolerated foreign encroachment on their soil.

* * *

On the long drive to Kandahar, whom should I meet along the road near Abpashak but our Chief Engineer Hohlweg and another man, a broad-shouldered, distinguished appearing individual wearing a handsome gray karakul cap; Mr. Ludeen, the former Minister of Public Works and a mainstay in the Afghan Government.

Mr. Ludeen smiled broadly and looked pleased as I extended my hand in greeting and remarked spontaneously, "Oh, I've heard a great deal about you, Mr. Ludeen, and everything has been highly complimentary."

* * *

"Where are you going? I want to go to the Arghandab Dam."

It was while waiting for my pass to get through the main gate at Manzel Bagh. I don't usually tell strangers exactly where I'm going so I said beyond Kandahar on the Rhoor-a-bad Canal.

Here, surrounded by Afghans, was a man of copper-hued complexion, of perhaps 165 pounds weight, five feet, eight inches height, and with a bush of gray-tinged hair. His manner was compelling but friendly, as he asked, "Where are you from?"

"California," said I, "and you're from Italy? You say your name is Durrani?"

"Oh, I've worked in California, too — Hollywood. I'm an Afghan. But I'm from Arkansas; Stuttgart, Arkansas. I can read Persian. I learned it in the University, although I can't talk it."

Mystified I rejoined, "Well I thought I'd heard about everything. However, 'an Afghan from Arkansas,' now that's a new one. Would you mind telling me in what business you are engaged, Mr. Durrani? And how is it you're from Arkansas?"

Said he, "Rice; *Minute Rice.* Went to the States when quite young with my parents. Just now came back. I like the Afghans."

"You mean you grow rice in Arkansas? Oh, you process it for food, is that it?" I continued in ignorance.

"Yes. Now I am traveling through Afghanistan and the other south Asian countries; my company is trying to perfect a better, cheaper rice food for the low-income people of the earth."

That evening at mess in the dining hall with Mr. C. Brennon, American advisory accountant to the Afghan Government, and his vivacious wife, I recounted my experience of the afternoon.

"Why Durrani is worth millions," said Brennon. "He has perfected a nationally known food product, *'Minute Rice.'*

And then I listened intently to Brennon's account of some facts regarding Ataullah Durrani, once a member of a reigning royal family. Durrani, while working with Americans in the Persian oil fields, had been impressed by the confident ease with which they attacked engineering problems. He expressed his desire to become a research chemist.

284

The Americans urged him to pursue such a career in the States. In New York City he became successful in an import business; in Hollywood as a Middle East expert on "King of the Khyber Rifles." But his leisure time throughout was devoted to experiments on perfecting rice as a food. To prepare rice for eating, it ordinarily requires rinsing, several pans must be used, and the mixture must be constantly watched as it cooks. Finally Durrani persuaded the Arkansas Rice Growers Association to set him up a laboratory where he could continue his experiments. Within two months he had developed a process whereby the rice was cooked to a certain point, cooled rapidly with water, then dried and packaged. This product would keep for months and required only one minute of cooking before serving on the table — light, white, fluffy; each grain plump and separate. The Army began using it in canned rations. A huge processing plant was erected in the rice country near Houston, Texas. The General Foods Company turns out the product by the hundreds of million packages.

So it had been to me an education to meet this "Afghan from Arkansas," and to be told about him by Brennon. In his undertaking in south Asia I humbly wish him success.

*   *   *

"Abdul, those little black seeds of the American watermelons — why do you throw them away? They're like gold, very valuable."

Our most efficient chef of long-standing at Chah-i-anjir only smiled deprecatingly.

On this day the heat by mid-afternoon had reached 119° F., outside in the shade.

Deliciously sweet, cold, juicy, refreshing, were these striped melons grown from seed brought from the U.S. In the Company truck gardens at Fort Nad-i-ali, under the competent supervision of Ricardo from Genoa, they had been carefully nurtured.

"*Anha kharab* ast, they're no good," returned Abdul. "Now those *khabooz* at Kabul you should see. Four of them make a load too big for camel," and his eyes gleamed with pride as with arms held full length he brought finger tips of both hands together illustrating the enormity of these products of that magic land.

*   *   *

The season is here when the turnover of American personnel is heavy. It's partly because of the intense heat. From California are most of the newcomers; Marysville, Santa Barbara, San Luis Obispo, Los Banos, Modesto, Santa Rosa, Watsonville; and from that last had come Glenn Foster. Already his *yen* for collecting weapons of self-defense had asserted itself. Quite an interesting hobby this, in a land of antiquity where ancient arms are still of practical use, as deadly as ever; swords, daggers, pistols, muskets. I had accompanied Foster to bazaars in Kandahar. But for my purpose a bandolier and dependable automatic would be most desirable.

Glenn said to me one day, "Jones, you remind me of a certain type."

"Couldn't imagine."

"An old army colonel out in our early West. You should be in the movies." said he.

"Really?" chuckling with amusement. "I'm astounded," said I.

*   *   *

And then Whitey Leaders, American, Argentine-born, Chief Steward for M-K-A, had this to say, "What's this about the bandits — or something — I hear you're meeting? These Afghans are peaceful, they don't hurt anybody, do they?"

"Says you, Whitey, secure here in the Manzel Bagh compound, on the streets of Kandahar. Hey, take a day off tomorrow. Why don't you? Let's go to Moo-shan beyond to the end of the road; then follow the Du-ow Canal into the out-back." This I said with an objective.

"Where's that?" said Whitey more soberly, now suspicious.

"Fifty kilometers down the Arghandab near junction with the Tarnak. We'll take along two soldiers armed with rifles. You will walk ahead, a sort of decoy. I'll follow you afoot at 500 meters. Behind me will trail the soldiers at 500 meters. What you and I can't handle, the soldiers will take over. O.K.?" I challenged.

"Say, you sound too anxious. No; I've got work here!" said Whitey, somewhat disconcerted, but coming up smiling.

By now the dining hall was partially filled with men in for a snack of coffee, doughnuts, cookies, cereals, milk, before retiring; Americans, Italians, Filipinos, a rugged, multifarious looking lot.

"So you see, Whitey, that's why the .38 automatic — my trusty companion in the back country. But after all, conditions are no worse in some places here than I've met up with 'South of Market Street,' " I continued, branching out into territory closer home.

"What do you mean 'south of Market,' where?"

I might have expected it. Ray Dillon had left his coffee at a far table. A burly Irishman from San Francisco, his eyes gleamed fire.

"In San Francisco," said I. Dillon's facial expression intensified. "Between the Embarcadero and 3rd Street. Once I started across there at night from the Ferry Building to the Examiner Publishing Plant; I worked there Friday and Saturday nights when at 'Cal.' in Berkeley. A cop advanced on me from a black alley. 'Do you want to get slugged, Mister?' he asked. 'No,' said I. 'Then go up Market Street and down 2nd.' said the policeman."

At this Dillon regained his composure and grinned with

understanding. "You see, I was raised 'south of Market' in the Mission District," said he.

*   *   *

The direction of aim was perfect, elevation slightly high, for the 5 lb. stone missed the windshield by inches, striking with a thud on the car top immediately over my head. It was along the main road from the dam; there I had spent a couple of hours with Chris Brown concerning the reservoir water releases. At the crest of a hill, and a sharp bend in the road, this fellow had suddenly emerged from between two boulders, paused, raised both arms over his head, and with all his might hurled the rock directly at me in the oncoming car.

Slamming on the brakes, reversing at top speed, I grabbed the steel-shod club, and was after him afoot. Surprised, he hesitated, then broke into a fleet run, zig-zagging between granite blocks up and over a ridge. Reaching the top, I called to a man tending his sheep nearby. The shepherd had witnessed everything.

"*Kuja?*"

"Down toward that village!" he pointed excitedly.

Below, along the silvery ribbon marking the course of the Arghandab River, lay the village of Haji Qala basking sleepily in the summery sunshine.

*   *   *

This summer I had been bunking in two places, 100 miles apart; Manzel Bagh and Chah-i-Anjir. That's how as a roommate I chanced to fall in with Lee Brown. Tough and rugged was this "grade boss"; neither slope nor alignment stakes set by engineers' instruments had he needed for guidance on fifteen miles of heavy duty road construction. Over boulder-strewn mountain slopes, across tortuous ravines, this road was to extend from Pomazai to Arghandab

288

Dam, so located easterly of the river as to avoid crossing the spillway channel.

On this job were only little Afghan Johnny the self-made interpreter, the bulldozer and "cat" crews, and Brown. This was not a difficult job for Lee, fresh from the jungles of Brazil. There, claiming his attention, had been the location and clearing of right-of-way for a pipe line under construction. He had been hampered by unfriendly Indians. Boa constrictors had dropped from trees. These snakes had coiled around the driver's cage atop the RD-8 caterpillar tractors in all-embracing attempts to crush the operators. Lead from a .45 had no effect on them; only the crushing weight of the RD-8's.

No; from the haunts of tropical reptiles to the lonely deserts of Afghanistan, nothing fazed Brown.

*　　*　　*

My companion on this 100-mile drive of the afternoon had been one of unusual experience. He was now faced with a crisis, a dilemma. Mostafa (moos-ta-fa) had returned from the States, and there lingered with him a taste for American life. A construction foreman of long standing on this MKA Project, he was now considering a trucking business of his own between Herat, Farah and Kandahar, to make more *afghanis* the better to enable him to take Zeenat to America or Canada, if the Government would allow it.

His experiences in our West had been interesting; carpentering on an eastern Oregon housing project, finally becoming a foreman; boarded with a family one member of which was a schoolteacher who treated Mostafa like a son. And he had visited M-K projects in twenty-two States; almost took a job with the Company in Canada, when Zeenat in distress had called him home. She was alarmed. Her father was predicting Mostafa's wedding to an American girl — her mother had died — the stepmother was most unkind to Zeenat in their home at Dilaram. But that was not all, even though Zeenat knew in her heart Mostafa had proven his love for her by returning to Afghanistan.

Mostafa's three sisters in Kabul were now disapproving of Zeenat; she couldn't sew, she couldn't cook, she was much below the social level of their family whose forebears stemmed from royalty. In short, Zeenat was no compeer to Nargees, who was lovely, beautiful, intellectual, refined, had everything. Could accomplish all housewifely duties, and unless he wed Nargees, the sisters — the family — would have no more of Mostafa. What now? The young man was troubled.

"Poligens, what should I do? How would you settle this?" Mostafa had asked me, a non-Moslem, point-blank.

"What is Zeenat's idea, what does she say?" I parried.

"Take us both, only marry me! Gladly will I be Nargees' servant!"

> "A decent provision for the poor
> is the true test of civilization."
>
> Samuel Johnson
> 1709 — 1784

XV

Enter . . .
The Governor-General

CHAPTER XV

Enter . . . The Governor-General

SAID GENERAL MANAGER Johnston, "Jones, I have just come from the office of the Governor-General. In contacting the mirabs, he insists that you be accompanied by a soldier. Don't ever go into those areas again alone. And by the way, tomorrow at 10 you will see him and explain what we propose to do about the release of reservoir water this summer to the canals of the Arghandab Valley."

So yesterday in the early forenoon found me and Abdool Ra-oof, one of our interpreters, picking our way in a battered Ford through the crowded streets of this ancient city of Kandahar toward the seat of provincial government. Most interesting, this.

There were folks in strange garb; brown people all over the sidewalks and out into the streets moving in all directions; burros in droves carrying wood, gravel in canvas bags, long, conical wicker baskets of fruits or vegetables; women and children; horses laden with stones from the mountain quarry; there were lumbering camels similarly laden. There were colorful carts drawn by one horse on the trot, with passengers facing to the front and rear. There were four-wheeled drays loaded high with goods to be distributed to merchants about the city. These were toilsomely pushed and pulled by barefoot, perspiring men. Lorries with vigorously sounding horns and loaded high with freight and passengers at a precarious altitude, forced their courses through the traffic, as did out-dated buses jammed with people and baggage on both decks, all bound for distant places. There were men delivering slabs of snow-shoe shaped bread stacked high upon their heads, or trays of flowers similarly borne. One merchant was washing nice looking vegetables; turnips, lettuce, celery, in the *jui* of running water along the crowded street.

Women were out making early morning purchases in purdahs of gray, blue, green, black, with white lattice work over their faces. (They could see you but not you them.) Others parted veils to peer forth with one eye.

Bordering the sidewalks were bazaars by the thousands; inclosed cubbyhole spaces open clear across the front, perhaps twenty feet by twenty feet in area, with wares of every odd description. Vegetables, meats, fruits, hardware, copper wares, bolts of vari-colored cloth, gorgeous rugs, sewing machines, trinkets, jewelry, firearms, tailor shops, grocery goods in large flat bowls. In a big open space surrounded by alcoves were displayed piles of staple articles of food; rice, corn, wheat, flour, raisins, rock salt, sugar, tea; being sold wholesale.

Long narrow dark alleys led off the main streets; some crooked and deserted and dubious in appearance, others crowded with both animals and pedestrians. Through these in the distance one caught glimpses of the high massive walls which surrounded the older part of the city. That large adobe building over there is the post office; nearby is

294

the beautifully domed mosque. There is the plaza. Close by is the capitol building, a large square affair with court-yard of attractive shrubbery and flower gardens. Here is the seat of government for the Province of Kandahar which includes most of southern Afghanistan, an area the size of North Dakota.

"Over there is the Governor's downtown office," said Rauf, "but we will go out to his residence." We traveled another mile to the military headquarters in the suburbs, the "presidio" we would call it in our West.

We drove through a gate guarded by soldiers, stated our business, and were allowed to pass. Here were cool lawns, shade trees and flowers, and a large white one-story building with wide verandas.

Waiting in the reception hall, I studied the surroundings; white walls, archways covered with portieres, vaulted ceilings, large bay windows, beautiful rugs.

"The rugs are from the north over the mountains near Mazar-i-Sharif," said Rauf. Opposite us in easy chairs sat two elderly men, also a younger one. From his attire I judged one to be a tribal chieftain.

The Governor-General entered shortly. "How do you do?" said he in perfect English, and shook hands warmly as Rauf said, "this is Paul Jones."

He was a strikingly handsome man, between forty-five and fifty; stocky, athletic, wearing heavy cork sun helmet, blouse belted and loose fitting of bluish gray, slacks of a creamy sun-tan of beautiful material perfectly tailored, white socks and well polished tan oxfords.

One glance at this man would convince anyone of his being an aggressive leader, competent executive and business person, and a fearless soldier. Pleasant spoken and direct in conversation was this Ab-dool Gha-nee Khan, the Governor-General of the Province of Kandahar, Kingdom of Afghanistan.

AFGHANISTAN VENTURE

Soon a general officer entered and sat down beside me, the Commandant of all military and police forces of the province, unassuming in appearance but of the dignity and bearing befitting an officer of high rank; derring-do personified. He is the Acting Governor-General in the Governor's absence, the Governor himself being a General of the Army.

As we talked the General sat on a sofa before the bay windows. In one hand he dangled a string of beautiful pearly white beads with white silk tassles. Each bead dropped at intervals from between his fingers representative of a prayer. The chief opposite me did likewise. (Or could he have been a body-guard?)

The conversation concerned the use of stored water released for irrigation in the Arghandab Valley during the coming summer and fall, a steady supply, this being an unprecedented situation.

Through Rauf, the General asked about and discussed many details. Inwardly I rejoiced and felt deep satisfaction for having gone out among his people in the back country acquiring grass-root knowledge of conditions which I was now able to discuss with authority and confidence. At one juncture a telephone call interrupted. The Governor's response was a curt *"ba-lee, ba-lee"* (yes), accompanied by an emphatic nod of his head of jet black hair with the military cut. He apparently had the idea new canals were under construction and would be completed in time to distribute water to blocks of heretofore lands yet unirrigated this season. What is the area and location of these lands? He wanted to know.

"Field surveys and studies are now underway covering these lands. No construction will begin until the situation is thoroughly investigated and until authorized by the Government," I said. "In general, however, a diversion weir is contemplated by which water may be diverted from the Arghandab River into a Highline Canal to facilitate distribution into existing canals on the northerly side of the river without the use of existing temporary brush dams. Likewise, for the same reason, use may be made of existing canals on the southerly side of the river enlarged to divert an ample supply of water at the diversion weir for lands in the vicinity of Kandahar and to the south to or beyond the Tarnak River. Just how much new land is to be taken in, and where, will not be known until later."

The General expressed concern that all lands brought under irrigation be listed for taxes.

I said, of course, but that M-K-A., Inc., had nothing to do with this matter.

His Excellency asked regarding the proposed enlargement of the Patow Canal, and was informed no determination of this had yet been made.

Our plan of operations for this season was then explained to the Governor-General as follows: A steady flow of water will be released from Arghandab Reservoir for summer and fall irrigation. Each canal will divert this water from the river just as has been done in the past with the natural flow, and distribute water to the users just as heretofore. No attempt will be made by the Company to distribute the water between the canals, or between the water-users on any canal. We expect each *mirab* (ditchtender) to make full use of the water for growing summer and fall crops.

I expressed a desire to meet each of the some thirty *mirabs* (canal supervisors) out on the job. At once I was requested to be at the General's office the following *say-sham-bee* (Tuesday) at 10 a.m., May 27, 1952. The mirabs would all be there together with the District Governors.

The Governor- General finally asked about acreages; how much land is actually being irrigated in the Arghandab Project now under existing canals? Answer: Probably 90,-000 to 100,000, and with steady supply of water beginning now most likely about 120,000 without extending canal

297

system, eventually with total development probably 150,000.

As to the Boghra Project, how much is being irrigated? Answer: Probably 8,000 on project proper and 3,000 beyond limits by nomads awaiting assignment of lands. The General expressed disappointment at this and stated he would like to see at least a total of 30,000 acres under irrigation this fall. I explained that water for this would have to be diverted from a low flow in the Helmand River, but that in early 1953 we expected to begin storing water at Kajakai Reservoir.

Walking with the General out to his car, a brand new green Chrysler, he said he would be glad if I'd come to see him any time; forenoons at his residence, afternoons at his office in the capitol. Only let him know a couple of days previously. Again shaking hands warmly and with a pat on my shoulder, the General drove away with other military men who had been waiting. Here was a real friend, I decided. Than I was abashed by the recollection that not once had I used the term "Your Excellency" in addressing him. This oversight had been unintended, the courtesy ordinarily used by Americans, unthinkingly being omitted by me.

Leaving the grounds, Rauf said, "A lieutenant back there asked were you an Afghan."

"Well, Rauf," I said, "my brown desert complexion topped by the karakul cap apparently cast doubt in his mind as to my nationality."

As to the cap: At the engneering office I had been showing Jan, our blueprint man, a *National Geographic Magazine* which contained pictures of the royal family in their gardens at Kabul. Admiring the King's attire, I had exclaimed spontaneously and half-seriously, "Jan, that's the kind of cap I'd like, just like the King's!"

Jan said, "We get you one, Polygens. This evening we go to bazaar; tailor take your measure. *Ba-lee?*"

"O.K., *ba-lee*, we'll do that, Jan:" And thus it was I had

acquired a fair imitation, I suppose, of royal headgear, a silvery golden shade intermingled with black.

And again Rauf and I wended our way through the mixing miscellaneous traffic of the city streets. The piles of apricots, spring apples and several varieties of plums were appetizingly displayed in the bazaars. By now the black peaks and mountain masses round about were shimmering in the gathering heat of midday. Manzel Bagh was an oasis. In Persian this name means "garden of flowers." Now to Rauf and me it was exactly that.

*   *   *

June 3rd finds me again at headquarters in Manzel Bagh. I alternate between the Arghandab Project here and the Boghra 100 miles to the west on the Helmand River. Yesterday I got word from the Governor-General's office to come in today to talk about water distribution problems. So, soon after 1 p.m., Mah-ta-bood-een (Moon of the Religion) and I were approaching the capitol through the courtyard, a beautiful garden area of semi-tropical shrubs and trees; loquat, orange, pomegranate, pine trees among which were blooming what looked to be Spanish broom in dazzling yellow glory, as in the Sierras at home.

We walked along wide verandas where men sprawled in siesta relaxation, it being scorchingly hot. The surroundings of adobe buildings, the plaza, the air of abandonment, reminded one of Mexico. We found the Commandant in his office, an army colonel, first assistant to the Governor, and he led us into the Governor-General's office, a large assembly hall, in the far corner of which was seated at a desk the chief executive of Kandahar Province.

"I'm sorry to have troubled you," he said. "Be seated." All in the Pakhtu language as he shook hands quite friendly.

He continued dictating for some little time in a low, even tone to a nicely dressed young man who sat rather stiffly opposite across the huge table, and then discussed something at length.

After that, through the *tageman,* Mahtabudin, we con-versed briefly about the water delivery situation from the new Arghandab Reservoir; how a delegation from the lower valley had been in to see him the day before because they were desperately in need of water. A large increase of flow was already coming down the Arghandab River, I assured him, because of increase in amounts released from the res-ervoir during the last couple of days.

I said I was headed down that way right then.

So the General said if I would wait a little while there would be a man in to ride down the valley with me.

At that he put on his sun-helmet and left alone by the front entrance. I could see the Chrysler outside in the drive-way. Immediately the Colonel took over, rapped loudly, rang a bell, and six soldiers from as many doorways rushed out to join the Governor-General.

Then turning to me, the Colonel said in Pakhtu "You appear to be fasting also." Mahtabudin relayed this in English.

"No, it's just too hot to eat much," I returned, "and I've lost weight."

Then the Colonel, Mahtabudin and I relaxed into a sort of siesta, this being during Ramazon, a whole month in which the Moslem people eat no food and drink no water from well before daylight until evening darkness. And, as if this were possible, during this season they are even more meticulous in religious devotions.

Shortly Mahtabudin roused to say, "This Governor-General Abdul Ghani Khan is well liked; he is doing many fine things for the people. Anybody can see him by appoint-ment. That's the way he wants it. Any soldier can come to him and state his grievances. He is a military governor sent down from Kabul eighteen months ago. He is very firm with his civilian subordinates. The last Governor-General wouldn't see anybody, besides was too easy going. This man is different; He works twelve hours per day."

"I thought he looked tired as he went out," I said. "But the fasting during Ramazon, 3 a.m. to 7:30 p.m., must get everyone down."

Then the Colonel rapped and a man appeared with a small rug, spreading it on the floor. For about twenty minutes both he and Mahtabudin faced Mecca and rendered devotions to Allah.

Then we relaxed some more; in fact I dozed off a couple of times but was quickly alert when Haw-jee Sool-tan Mohammed joined us. *(Haji* means one who has traveled to Mecca.) This man was elderly but in spite of his age exceedingly active. He walked rapidly into the room clad in turban, loose fitting shirt, pantaloons and sandals; a very brown man with heavy black whiskers. But on top of all this wore a heavy overcoat buttoned up to keep out the heat.

"He has more money than you and I will ever see." said Mahtabudin. "Owns a great deal of land around Panjwai."

As the Commandant, Sultan Haji, Mahtabudin and I walked through the courtyard on the way out, a young man escorting his elderly father by the arm approached from among the trees. The old man was crying hysterically as he addressed the Commandant. In fact, he seized the Commandant's shirt collar with a slight twist, the gesture for exacting a promise. The Commandant talked to him quietly and gently, got him quieted down; then took a paper from his own pocket, signed it and handed it to him. Whereupon the old man became profuse in his thanks. He started to remove his turban and to bow low, but was stopped by the Commandant who apparently was saying "none of that, it's not necessary." It seems this man was sick

301

and wanted approval of an application for a passport into Pakistan, there to see a physician.

Mahtabudin, Sultan and I drove twenty-five miles to near Panjwai where at the river we found bone dry the Spirwan Canal that irrigated Sultan's land and that of others in the vicinity. The wind was picking up small whirlwinds of dust over the mile-wide dry river bed. So I assured Sultan that upon our return to Manzel Bagh we would continue building up the flow of the river by additional releases from the reservoir until there was a substantial flow as far as its junction with the Tarnak, some twenty miles below Panjwai. In fact I had an idea we already had released during the last two days the necessary additional water to provide sufficient flow to all canals heading out of the river at their respective diversion *bunds* between Arghandab Dam and the junction with the Tarnak. Beyond that point no reservoir storage would be released for the irrigation of lands, as it was the lower limit of our project. This I explained to Sultan. Within forty-eight hours I expected all project canals to be amply supplied. We would be out to his lands tomorrow to check on the situation.

Sultan was delighted. He would return to Kandahar with us this evening, and come out to Panjwai and down the river with us tomorrow.

It was dusk as we entered the city again. The streets swarmed with people out in the cool of the evening following the day's fasting. They were shopping in the bazaars for food. Large plates of freshly picked, purplish white mulberries were much in evidence; a delightfully sweet fruit, and plentiful. There were piles of ripe apricots, creamy in color, fine flavored and sweet with a slight taste of peach. There were early apples, and grapes almost too sour yet to eat (picked too green). The plums were rich in color but so tart that my teeth were set on edge for days. Cucumbers were in season, piles of immense ones everywhere, a boon

302

to the traveler on foot in the heat of the day away from water.

"Mahtabudin, perchance is that fruit washed in the *jui* — the ditch of running water along the street?"

"Oh, no," said the *tageman,* this interesting and intelligent young man who so expertly, it seemed to me, had been my helper over the language barrier throughout the day. "People want to see the dust on the fresh fruit before they buy it, for in this way they know it has not been dipped in the foul water."

"What is that group of men doing up there on the roof?" I inquired.

"They are setting out food and drink."

Just then the dull boom of cannon reverberated over the city. Mahtabudin and Sultan smiled broadly, and in a manner that indicated relief.

"The fast is now over for the day." said the *tageman.*

And I added, "Yes, and until the white thread becomes distinct to you from the black thread at the dawn; so states the Koran. Is that not so, Mahtabudin?"

Then I left them along the crowded street, they having agreed to meet me the following morning at the public square by the cannon.

These two had entered the city refreshed. Sultan had requested that I leave the road and follow along a *kareese* that led from out of a long narrow valley between two massive black mountains. This is a typical source of water supply where dependable surface flow is not available. Here were shafts dug by generations of long ago extending vertically perhaps fifty feet into the ground on a straight line at intervals of 100 ft. or more. They were connected by tunnels. Extending down the slope of the land, the intercepted water flowed by gravity into an open surface ditch, after flowing perhaps for miles through the tunnels.

It was into one of these shallower shafts that Sultan and

Mahtabudin had descended about 5 p.m. to take cool baths following the intense heat of the afternoon.

While they bathed I absorbed the fantastic scenery all about. Rising steeply from the surrounding plains to heights of 2,000 or 3,000 feet were black mountains, serrated with pinnacles and spires. Between were corridors with fields of ripened wheat. Beyond were wide irrigated plains. Far in the distance to the south was unbroken desert. A turbulent yellow ocean it appeared to be, with the slanting rays of the lowering sun upon it and bringing into relief the shades and shadows of innumerable sand dunes. A slight breeze lifted fine yellow sand like the spray of the sea.

*   *   *

Sure enough at the appointed time, Sultan awaited us at the public square, where a number of cannons were mounted around a platform. He was alert and agile, "rarin' " to go. The Commandant had reminded me, "Haji Sultan can handle any situation; there's no need to take along soldiers."

Haji drove a new Chevrolet sedan, a rarity in Kandahar, but got in with us along with a companion who resembled characters you all may have seen depicted in Biblical literature. Sultan shouted to the two men left in the Chevrolet to follow us.

We found the Spirwan and Zangawat Canals full to overflowing; the water had arrived early in the morning. Probably never before in a thousand years had there been in June an irrigation supply such as this. The M-K-A project right now had begun to yield immense benefit to Afghanistan. People were wreathed in smiles and jubilant.

We drove on to Panjwai. Here already was the Afghan version of a boom town; residences of stone, a large school building and many new bazaars were under construction. Here we picked up a young Afghan engineer who appeared

304

to be in charge of this development, Panj Gool (Five Roses).

Over a road, only in name, we wended our way, fording ditches and canals, crossing precarious culverts of poplar poles and brush covered with loose earth, for ten miles to the home and land holdings of Haji Sultan Mohammed. We turned through a double swinging gate of poles set into a ten feet high adobe wall topped with camels thorn. This wall extended for many kilometers undoubtedly around the entire property of 1,500 acres.

"Mahtabudin, in California or Texas we would call this a ranch; in our South a plantation. What is it called in Afghanistan?"

"*Qa-la,* meaning fort," he replied, and soon I was to see that this term was most applicable.

Down a long lane we drove in the old black Ford; alfalfa fields on the right, a solid row of huge mulberry trees on the left and beyond them a large newly planted vineyard. Then we entered a large orchard of pears, almonds, pomegranates, apricots, plums. These trees had never been pruned, and formed a high canopy overhead. Around each tree was a basin to receive irrigation water.

Mahtabudin said, "Sultan tells me he has 250 farmers on this place; his vineyard consists of 80,000 vines. He is planting 20,000 more this year, because of the new reservoir at Arghandab."

We at last came to a stop in a grove of exceptionally large mulberry trees, and under these had gathered at least fifty children of all ages standing or running about in play. They were awaiting Sultan's return in joyful expectancy.

Proudly he said, "These are my grandchildren and great-grandchildren." as various ones smiled happily at the old gentleman, or ran forward for attention.

I congratulated Haji upon this display of affectionate welcome. In reciprocation he said, "Every time you are

305

down this way stop in. Stay with us. Live with us as long as you want. Anything we have is yours."

Beaming Sultan led us around to the far side and the only gateway to the fort. My immediate family lives inside the *qala*," he said. "All of the dwellings outside are the homes of my relatives. We are all one family."

And in wonder I surveyed this Afghan settlement and stronghold surrounded by fertile irrigated lands, at the edge of the Dasht-i-Poghdar, the "turbulent yellow ocean" of waste lands as seen from the north, and stretching southward 100 miles into Pakistan.

I said, "This reminds me of how our people lived among the Indians in the frontier years; a stockade of logs within which to live, or to flee for refuge to, and withstand attacks of savage people." And then I waved an arm toward the desert horizon. "You haven't always known what to expect from out there; foes, their character or number, raiders?"

Sultan said, "When we are attacked all the people can go within these walls. From on top of the walls, from the turrets, 100 of our men can withstand the attacks of 1,000 from the outside."

Again I surveyed in wonderment these surroundings of mud huts — these homes of peace loving people. And within the compound I studied the fifty feet high adobe walls, some 400 feet long on a side with projecting towers at the corners. A walkway and parapet topped these walls. Here riflemen over the top of these breastworks, or through downward slanting holes, could cover approaching enemy tribesmen. From the towers, machine gunners, or riflemen, could cover the entire front of any wall. There were a well of water, storehouses, gardens and several homes inside the compound.

"Sultan has four wives," said Mahtabudin. "He has just married another, to replace the one he lost. He always has four wives."

306

"When one dies she is replaced maybe by a sixteen- or eighteen-year-old girl?" I suggested.

"Well not necessarily. He would probably marry a widow with children," said Mahtabudin.

We were conducted to a large adobe platform on one side of which was a grape arbor, and overhead a thatched covering. Immediately several older boys brought out from somewhere a very large rug, twenty feet by twenty-five feet, of beautiful design and soft shade of a dark red.

"Sultan is inviting us to sit down and be comfortable," said Mahtabudin removing his shoes, as I did likewise. Then someone brought a number of pillows, or rather bolts, probably of cotton about eighteen inches in diameter and three feet long. These you lounge against when tired of sitting cross-legged or on your heels.

Soon they began to bring out food and drink. About twenty-five persons sat to my left and right, cross-legged on the rug, and Sultan sat opposite facing me and Mahtabudin.

"These are all for you," said Sultan, as Mahtabudin and I drank mulberry juice and hot tea; ate bread, cookies, a large roll, English walnut kernels, parched corn, sugared almonds, pine nuts, kurd (deliciously tart and sour like lemon), whey liberally seasoned with powdered dried mint leaves, and a couple of kinds of hard candies.

"The women are preparing meat for you to eat when we return," said Sultan.

"Some of these men are your sons, maybe?" said I.

Sultan pointed out the four nearest him, and said, "These are my sons; all the others are relatives."

At this juncture a child of four or five came across the courtyard and sat down very close to the old man. He put his arms about her, the cutest dark-haired, brown-eyed little thing, and so clean; the only evidence of feminity I had observed within the fort. By rapid mental calculation I concluded there were at least thirty women and girls inside the

307

compound, besides many outside the fort likewise invisible.

"When you go home to your country we want you to remember us," said Sultan, as I gazed in admiration at a bed of petunias beyond the grape arbor, radiantly multi-colored in the noonday sunlight.

"Well, when I see hollyhocks like those growing wild in your vineyard, and lovely petunias like these around your homes (pointing), then I'll think of this Qala; this abode of friendly Afghan people, your wonderful hospitality, your co-operation in making a success of this great irrigation undertaking." And as I talked and Mahtabudin translated, Haji Sultan's face beamed with understanding.

"You can have anything you want here, just anything. From any of these men you can take by force what you want," said Sultan. These were his exact words as repeated to me in English by the *tageman.*

"*Mota-shak-ker besyar, besyar* . . . many thanks, but I wouldn't think of doing such a thing." said I.

Turning to Mahtabudin I said, "Now we had best go further on to inspect the canals and river as far as its junction with the Tarnak; about twenty-five kms. is it not?"

"The road is very poor," said Sultan. "We will go with you," as he climbed into the back seat of our car flanked by a Mul-lah (Moslem priest) on one side and Panj Gol on the other. A young boy handed Sultan a rifle.

As we headed west I remained silent for a time in meditation, and analyzed the situation. The Qala offered protection from any enemies up the valley on the south side. A boundless uninhabited desert of sand dunes guarded approaches from the south, or did it? Along the river, dry bed a mile wide, were camps at intervals; groups of open black tents of nomads with flocks of sheep, camels, goats, burros — a semi-wild people. They apparently mind their own business and are generally thought peaceful. Their flocks graze on wild vegetation, mostly Bermuda grass, along the river.

This road parallels a border line between two types of civilization, agricultural and nomadic. Sultan had said in answer to my question, do wars take place here, "Yes we have water wars when there is a shortage of water." And Mahtabudin had suggested, "There is much gold stored inside the Qala." And then I had been told of frequent raids by tribesmen. So I concluded anything could happen to these peaceful argicultural people if ever they were caught off guard.

We stopped at least fifteen times for shovel work to make culvert crossing and fords passable. Beyond a little village, Moo-shan, the desert sand dunes jutted out into the valley. Here large areas were being planted to grapes in expectation of an abundant water supply. The soil conditions appeared ideal here for grapes. The release of additional water at the Arghandab Reservoir two days ago had not yet affected the Mushon Canal, and it was almost dry.

We walked further for a couple of kilometers and out into the dry overflow channels of the river. A light wind stirred up the fine sand, making vision beyond a hundred feet impossible. Yet at intervals there was a lull in the storm and one could then glimpse a camp of the nomads.

Suddenly a shrill chant or song was audible above the wind and flying sand from the direction we had just come. Of this the others took no notice but to me its meaning was ominous.

We found but a trickling stream in the river; obviously but local return flow of about six c.f.s. I explained that lands below here were not entitled to stored water, but that nevertheless I would not be satisfied until ten to fifteen c.f.s. above return flow was passing this point. In that way we would know for sure that all canals upstream were diverting water to the limits of their demands or capacities. "We will continue releasing 100 c.f.s. additional each day at the dam until this condition obtains," I told Mahtabudin for relay to the other men. They understood and smiled in gratitude.

Returning, we had not driven more than a mile when I observed two well-armed men ahead; one carried several stout clubs. The other a rifle, revolver, and cross bandoliers of ammunition.

One signaled to stop. Believing them to be local farmers wanting to know about the water situation, I brought the Ford to a cautious halt.

Approaching closer, the fellow with the clubs said, "We *want* to ride!"

"Nay." said I.

With leveled rifle the other advanced. "We *will* ride!" this fellow demanded.

"You *shall not* ride!" This from Sultan in low measured tones, as both outlaws upon closer approach gazed surprisedly enough into the bore of Sultan's aimed rifle and that of the .38 automatic held in menacing firing position by the Mullah.

"*Zood — zud* (hurry-hurry!)" and in haste I stepped on the gas as the Afghan engineer in the back seat uttered these words in *Pakhtu*.

"Mahtabudin, at first I took them to be friendly rural police!" I said, recovering from my surprise.

"No peace officers are out in places like this. Those were brigands!" said Mahtabudin.

"Would they have robbed us all of money and valuables and left us unharmed?" I asked, well knowing the answer. Mahtabudin said, "No, sir! They would not just injure you. You would be killed outright. Even just for your cap, your clothes, shoes."

Arriving again at the Qala, all disembarked in the shade of huge mulberry trees. Now the ditches were full of water. Both Sultan and Mahtabudin plunged in for refreshing baths. Examining maps spread out over the hood of the car, I appeared occupied as the Mullah, Sultan, Mahtabudin, and the others engaged in mid-afternoon religious devotions facing Mecca on a nearby prayer platform. This consisted of a raised place about thirty feet by thirty feet of hard earth surrounded by a low wall. Shaken somewhat by our recent encounter, so it appeared to me, the Mullah and Sultan had laid within easy reach the automatic revolver and rifle.

It was pleasant as we all relaxed for a time here in this wondrous shade. The heat of the day was approaching its greatest intensity.

Dozing, I studied the layout of the nearby massive walls, the relative values of their military defensive and offensive features.

Were one commanding the 100 men inside the fort, what were the tactics to which he would resort in withstanding a foe of 1,000 from the outside?

Or with 1,000 under one's command, just how would one approach and overcome such an impregnable bastion? Oh no, not with modern weapons. And in the throes of the solution of this weighty problem I must have fallen fast asleep only to awake with a lurch. An arrow in my side; oh no, not that. Yes, just that! Mahtabudin with a stick had poked me in the ribs as a reminder to make ready to join the others at lunch; a spread of tea, bread, barbecued mutton, rice, vegetables and kurd.

This the women of Sultan's household had prepared, delicious in the extreme.

*   *   *

"Agha, I have married a widow. She owes money; 5,000 *afghani*, a debt contracted by her former husband. Am I obligated to pay this?"

In answer to this supplicant before the Police Court, the Commandant, acting as judge, peremptorily arose from behind the table, shoved back his chair, eyed sharply the man with no turban and with the long hair down over his

311

shoulders, and had this to say, "Why certainly you shall pay the 5,000 *afghani!*" Whereupon, with a disparaging look he tore up a piece of paper, throwing it disgustedly into a waste box. "Next!" and sat down.

A captain picked up the top paper from a large pile on the Colonel's desk. He stepped to the edge of the platform. This overlooked the military compound where had gathered a small crowd to be present at this early forenoon session of the Court. "Raman Tallak!"

"Agha, I am Private Raman Tallak; my unit is at Herat. My leave of absence expires tomorrow. There is no transportation to Herat for four days. Will you extend my leave and write explanation on it to my company commander?"

The Commandant nodded affirmatively. "Next!"

Selecting another paper, the Captain called out, "Fatima Parveen!"

Half sobbing, a middle-aged woman in black purdah, unveiled, entreated the court: "I have two sons. We all live in Kandahar. The older one was arrested; put in jail. He did no wrong. But he has escaped jail and gone to Kabul. Now the soldiers are holding my younger son under arrest in place of Ba-ran who escaped." With this the mother broke down into uncontrollable grief.

The Colonel quickly leaned over the woman with both hands on her shoulders consolingly. "There, there, *madar* (mother); everything's going to be all right. I'll attend to it at once!"

Mahtabudin and I had only come in, as instructed, to see about getting a soldier to go with us all day, but somehow had been sidetracked into the Commandant's office. Here we had been given, oddly enough and conspicuously, seats slightly to the left and rear of the Commandant as he conducted court. Scores of cases were before it.

*   *   *

Beside the Kandahar-Girishk road near Hauz-i-Madat

stood a brand new Chevrolet Fleetmaster station wagon equipped with radio receiving and sending set. Accompanied by Mahtabudin and the soldier, I brought the old Ford to a standstill. The *tageman* conversed with the driver, and turned to me. "They are out of petrol. En route from Herat to Kandahar. Both Russians. Say they don't understand or talk English. Are wanting to buy wool from the Kandahar Woolen Mills."

The driver was a man from Russian Turkestan dressed like any Afghan. He did the talking. The other in spruce Western dress, including a Panama straw hat, sat looking straight ahead; unmoved, silent, in one of the rear seats.

"Mahtabudin, tell them our road crew may be along at any time. They carry gasoline for emergency use. Are we sure these fellows are out of petrol?"

Private Ramadon seemed amused; tossed his rifle lightly across his knees, eyes twinkling merrily. Perhaps the conversation had not been translated entirely and I had missed some of the pertinent facts.

As we started forward, Mahtabudin said, "They are afraid of us. They know you are an American."

* * *

Near noon we entered the office of the District Governor at Khugiani. A military assistant had two soldiers round up any about town dependent upon the project for water. Soon a small crowd congregated. Would the District Governor be favorable to putting a few pole bridges over the canals at key points to render them more readily patrollable? Also furnish more effective police control in the areas covered by project canals? We named seven canals: Sangizar, Merihud, Dakhabad, Kala Shamir, Salim Katza, Duow, Charshika. Were the people all getting sufficient water? At this last a lively discussion ensued. The chairman and every man present talked vociferously and simultaneously without cessation. This lasted fifteen minutes. As the tumult subsided the acting District Governor without qualification announced, "Yes, everyone on those canals is getting irrigation water in abundance." As to the road and culvert work, "The people are busy in their fields. But we will have the army take care of this. Also give police protection as far as the District boundaries."

At this juncture a man introduced himself to me as being from Sa-leem Kat-za; a wiry, agile sort of fellow, rather oldish. Would we go with him up the Kushk-i-Nakhud Valley; to look at a prospective water supply? A *kareese*, he called it; the company might be interested. O.K., we'd go.

But this was not a *kareese* in the valley. It was three-fourths way to top of a 3,000 ft. mountain, up a precipitous narrow ravine. The "man from Salim Katza" climbed like a mountain goat. He was extending a tunnel started by other men who had abandoned it because of the opposition of a spirit they thought inhabited the mountain. Salim had gone to the Mullah about the matter, had been assured he need have no fear in continuing the excavation. He expected eventually to intercept a good flow of water. In the tunnel it did seem that one could slightly detect the sound of running water through crevices leading forward from the excavation. Salim would just have to keep driving to find out for sure.

Before starting down over the steep and rocky decline we paused to rest. Glancing about, I noted with surprise a lone tree growing from a seam between granite rocks. A scrub oak it looked to be. But no, it had fruit, both green and ripe; figs!

"Over there was fought the Battle of Miawand." announced Mahtabudin. "The British forces were destroyed."

"What happened, Mahtabudin? Did you study about it in school? Tell me."

Piecing events together, this is what occured: Miawand

314

Pass is fifty miles northwest of Kandahar, on a secondary caravan route to Girishk and upper Helmand River points. Here on the plains to the west, plainly discernable to us on this hot June afternoon seventy-two years later, defeat was inflicted on a British brigade under General Burrows by Ayub Khan; to be exact July 27, 1880, during the Second Afghan War.

Ayub Khan, Shir Ali's younger son, who had been holding Herat during the British operations at Kabul and Kandahar, set out towards Kandahar with a small army. A brigade under Burrows was dispatched from Kandahar to oppose him. Upon arrival at the east bank of the Helmand opposite Girishk, Shir Ali-Wali of Kandahar-deserted Burrows. This necessitated a withdrawal of the British to Khugiani.

However, to prevent Ayub's forces from passing to Ghazni, Burrows advanced on Maiwand, already seized by Ayub. The Afghans numbering 25,000 outflanked the British. The artillery having expended their ammunition, the native portion of the brigade got out of hand, pressed back on the British battalion.

The brigade was routed, well-nigh annihilated. Of the 2,476 British troops engaged, 934 were killed, 175 wounded or missing. This necessitated Sir Robert's famous march from Kabul to Kandahar.

* * *

Later that afternoon in the car parked under mulberry trees surrounding a public lawn, or plaza, I marveled about this terrible battle fought so near here. We had stopped at Khugiani that Mahtabudin and Salim might enjoy a dip in the nearby canal after our strenuous excursion up the mountainside. Evidently Salim considered this trip quite unusual, for in crossing the park to the ditch I noticed him arouse several sleepers from their siestas. Each in turn half

315

arose on an elbow to look interestedly in my direction. After that I must have relaxed and fallen asleep in an upright position behind the wheel. Thus for thirty minutes, time meant nothing, until startled, I awoke to sense the unusual, a surprise. For all about, some ten-deep, had gathered citizenry of Khugiani; standing motionless, solemn-eyed, turbaned, respectful, intent upon one object — me. (Had I passed into another world? Indeed their disconsolate looks indicated such!) With all the nonchalance at my command, I yawned, stretched, replaced my sun helmet, and noticed the feeling of relief on the faces of my audience.

Tageman Mahtabudin and Rifleman Ramadan climbed aboard.

Taking my hand in both of his, Salim exclaimed, "Praise be to God for your kindness!"

"Zande bash! Salamati! May you live long and with good health!" said I.

And we were off towards Kandahar in a cloud of dust.

* * *

Engineers will be interested in how we proposed to distribute water this first season from the Arghandab Reservoir, thus ushering in a new era of prosperity for this garden valley of Afghanistan.

At this conference arranged by the Governor-General in his office on May 27th, there were present District Governors or their representatives, from the Districts of Dand, Pangwai, Khugiani, and Arghandab, seventeen *mirabs* or canal supervisors, and the Commandant. Mahtabudin again acted as interpreter.

The water situation I explained to these people substantially as follows:

Location and construction to bring water to new lands and to distribute water more directly to existing canals, is now under survey and study. No construction will be started this season.

A steady release of water from Arghandab Reservoir will obtain during this summer and fall, sufficient to allow diversion from the river to the full capacity of each existing canal between the Dam and junction of Tarnak and Arghandab Rivers. Water will not be available for diversion beyond that point. We will reduce releases accordingly when we see that all water above junction is not being diverted. We expect you to run your canals all summer and fall to the extent that you can make full and efficient use of the water.

The Company will make no attempt to divide the water between the some thirty-two existing canals.

The Company will not interfere with the distribution of water to the many individual water users along each existing canal.

The Company will do no maintenance work along the river, at any of the existing diversion *bunds* or along any of the canals. We expect you to so maintain and improve your existing canals this summer and fall as to make the best use of reservoir water.

We suggest:

That you apply summer and fall irrigation to your vineyards and orchards in ample quantity so that the vines and trees will be the more hardy than heretofore for the increased production of fruit next year and in the future.

That you plant a larger acreage to summer crops this summer than heretofore has been advisable; and increase the production of melons, corn and fall vegetables during this and the following years.

That you take advantage of the new, all-year around water supply by increasing your acreage and production of alfalfa and clover; that the acreage of wheat and barley planted this fall be expanded to the limit.

Whereas heretofore the summer and fall water deficiency has kept your productive irrigated acreage down to around

317

90,000 to 100,000 acres, it now appears that all of the some 120,000 acres covered by your existing canals can be made to produce abundant crops with the steady water supply now available by reason of the Arghandab Dam.

With the addition of the power system now contemplated for the Arghandab Project, and the accompanying development of the underground water supply by wells and electric power, it is estimated 30,000 acres additional can be provided with water in the Arghandab Project, or a total of 150,000 acres.

The District Governors said that, at any time, I could make arrangements through them to contact each *mirab* on the ground; all seemed pleased at the prospects of ample summer and fall water, the first in history.

The foregoing was included in a regular report on operations to General Manager Ted Johnston. To this it seemed advisable to add the following:

This narrative of operations has been presented purposely in a detailed manner. Otherwise much of the background and basis for present and future actions would have remained obscured. For purposes of record, mention should be made of actual instances experienced by the undersigned that impressed upon him the prime necessity of law enforcement in the areas covered by the Arghandab Project, if water diversion, distribution and delivery — that is, project operations — and, later on, maintenance of the completed project, are to be carried out successfully by the officials concerned.

On the face of it, the reason these agricultural people live in small communities in compounds, or within towns surrounded by walls, is for mutual protection from outlaws who roam at will on or off the beaten trails in those areas between communities, and unmolested by peace officers or the military, in any noticeable way. Peaceful people live in fear of robbery, assault and death. "These brigands kill their

318

victims outright for any article of small value," I have been informed by ones who know.

The only safe way to travel through isolated areas off the beaten trails is to carry a stout club and better still an automatic, or be accompanied by an armed soldier, or go in the company of others. The average American newcomer is skeptical of the necessity of these precautions, as I was myself for a long time. To such skeptics I would challenge any, if he dares, to travel as a decoy alone, unarmed and afoot at one kilometer ahead of me over any route on the project to be selected by me.

During last December and February in making reconnaissance and crop surveys in isolated areas of the project, alone and on foot, this writer had experiences which bear out the foregoing statements, and are noted below for purposes of record:

Arghandab Dam Road: Attacked by man with large rock.
Jalowar Canal: Warned of death in passing mosque, followed by one man.
Nagahon Canal: Accosted by two armed bandits.
Deh Sobs Canal: Warned not to follow this canal — nevertheless continued — and soon was followed. In town near end of canal was threatened by man with rifle.
Zanjiri Canal: In vicinity of village of Deh Sabz was attacked by ruffian with club near a grist mill.
Sangizar Canal: In vicinity of village of Deh Sobs was attacked by man near a grist mill with long heavy club sharpened to a point. In returning to parked car along desert road was followed.
Nakwadak Canal: Warned not to proceed alone.
Panjwai Canal: Followed near river by suspicious character.
Boghra Canal, third turnout above Lui Manda: Followed by two suspicious characters when following out private ditch about two kms., from turnout.

AFGHANISTAN VENTURE

Mushon Canal: On June 4, 1952, while returning from
vicinity of Charshika Canal diversion in company with
three local men and interpreter, group was accosted by
two armed bandits who made demands. Same were repelled by rifle and automatic.

> "Experience joined to common sense
> To mortals is a providence."
>
>   *   *   *
>
>   Matthew Green

> "He who would benefit mankind, must
> reach them thru their work."
>
>   *   *   *
>
>   Henry Ford

XVI
The Lion of Mohammed

CHAPTER XVI

The Lion of Mohammed

O H, PLEASE DON'T do this!" admonished Abdul Jabbar. "These men are servants. Let them salute you, or us first." These words came from the young man in the back seat. Seated beside him was Gul Mohammed, to whose home we had been invited for a noontime repast, and Abdullah Rahim, both of the Agricultural Department at the Fort Nad-i-Ali Experiment Station, the latter being head of Colonization.

Since it had constantly been my practice to wave a friendly gesture to our Hazara road crews, a salute, as it were, to the dignity of hard labor, I was somewhat abashed to be informed that my method of doing this was undignified, a violation of social etiquette.

From their features it is quite evident these Hazares are of Mongolian descent, and originating, as claimed, with the westward sweep of the barbarians under Genghis Khan. This Mongol warlord had sacked and ravaged Asia and led his barbaric hordes to forge the greatest empire the world has yet seen; had made the name "Tartar" a cry of terror down through the centuries. This had all begun early in the thirteenth century, some 750 years ago.

Nevertheless, these descendants of a barbaric past whom we were now passing along the road, I had found unsurpassed as good workmen; intelligent, faithful, dependable, friendly. So, following Abdul's well-meant reproof, I would merely flip my hand over the wheel unnoticed by my passengers, and seeing this gesture these groups of Hazares would respond to a man.

Beside me sat Haji Hasheem, whose interest at this moment concerned improvement to his source of water supply for his rather extensive lands west of Girishk. Construction of the Boghra Canal had caused some disruption. Haji had taken up this matter with the head of state, the Prime Minister himself at Kabul, if you please; and today we were out to determine in what way the situation could be quickly corrected. To me the remedy appeared simple: A controlled outlet from the Boghra Canal to which Haji was entitled, and the digging of a deep ditch through a low ridge to his fields. This would assure him ample water for delivery during the times it was unobtainable from the original source which had suffered molestation from our construction operations. Haji would furnish and pay for all labor and materials used. Just permission to do the job was all he wanted. My answer was "yes." So was settled here in the field for all time a matter which had been buffeted around for months among several far-removed commissions and individuals of the higher brackets.

Gul (Rose) led us into his gardens to rest in the heat of midday and be served refreshments. Surrounded by high adobe walls topped with camels thorn, here was an area of fruit trees and flowers; beautiful big mulberry trees with ripening fruit, purplish white; trees of apple, quince, pomegranate, fig, almond, apricot, English walnuts, and grapevines. And there were "poplar" trees so-called, that looked more like sycamore or oriental plane. And small roses in large loose bunches, a deep scarlet. Rose petals in trays were drying in the sunshine. Spanish or Scotch broom in dazzling yellow profusion, reminded me of the Sierra foothills in California. In sunken basins, easily irrigated, bloomed flowers of multi-colored assortments.

At the gate we were greeted most formally by the cutest little fellow, about four. From his shoulders hung what we would consider a girl's dress; black, and loosely draped to the ankles. Cropped short was his black hair. Snappy brown eyes matched the brown of his skin and his pink cheeks. Ahsam soberly extended his hand and in Persian said, "Welcome to our home."

On the dried mud platform in this oasis, we sat or lounged on rugs and pillows. Soon two menservants brought out platters of food and placed them on a long, narrow, white cloth over the rugs.

There were barbecued beef, chicken, rice, potatoes sliced and fried in batter, cakes, water cress, bread the look of waffles and the shape of snowshoes, curd as sour as though flavored with lemon, but tasty.

Large plates of mulberries were eaten with a relish.

Said Abdul Jabbar, "Our king, the fourth one back, died from eating six plates of mulberries. He had 300 wives."

"Are you sure it was the mulberries, Abdul?" I asked.

Later we were served warm milk, tea, and finally candy.

A son about nineteen was home from college at Kabul; nice looking, rather lordly, a student of economics. An older son is the City Clerk of Kandahar, Gul told me.

Three daughters and several grandchildren appeared through a low opening in the east wall, but no mother, or mothers. A young girl, I think a maid whom I mistook to be the mother of one of the grandsons much to the amusement of all, released the small boy to the care of Gul, and then stole glances from behind the trunk of a tree nearby.

The college boy said he played in the softball and soccer teams, also some tennis.

"In *Amreeka* our girls and boys play tennis together, go to classes together. Girls serve in the armed forces of the United States," I said.

"Do they sit together in the same seats?" translated Jabbar.

"It all depends; if they want to do so, they may," I rejoined.

After this there were brief glances my way, with subdued conversation, the gist of which I could not comprehend.

Later turning to me, Jabbar asked, "Was it not Shakespeare who said it's better to converse with a wise man than to read a good book?"

During the afternoon there arrived from Nad-i-Ali in a jeep Aslam Khan and Archtur Mohammed. The former is acting head of the Agricultural Exploitation Department, the latter chief of the Kharoti. As they ate mulberries and drank tea, talk centered on colonization of lands under the Boghra. Achtur was well pleased with the treatment accorded the Kharoti, comfortable homes, wheat and vegetables from their own fields, no more of this wandering from place to place. They occupied lands under completed laterals.

Abdullah Rahim and I, together with Achtur, had been lately to the camp of Sarda Khan Jan far out on the East Marja Dasht. Already 100 families had several hundred acres under irrigation with growing crops of corn, melons, sorghums, vegetables, quinjet. From far away Baluchistan 500 more families were en route by caravan under Chef Hakeem Dad.

At the camp of Shah Nazar Khan, twenty families from Chakhansur were living in a group of *choperie*, dwellings made of brush and grass. Already from the Boghra Canal they had excavated a long lateral on a contour, thus providing a large area with water. This was green with growing crops. Invited to sample bread freshly baked on preheated cobblestones, we had eaten sparingly knowing full well that the camp's supply of flour was limited.

An encampment of the Dilaram people with well laid out ditches and newly irrigated land, was making a good showing.

I had cautioned these people — their chiefs — to keep in touch with Aslam Khan and Abdullah Rahim at Nad-i-Ali, inasmuch as the Agricultural Exploitation Department had charge of the colonization, and had given these people permission to grow crops on the land only this year pending possible contracts with M-K-A for the construction of a planned lateral system later. Beyond the end of the year to crop the land — well, that was up to the Government. No boundaries had been fixed between camps. On these wide open, smooth fertile lands of East Marja, with an ample supply of water available within a couple of miles from turnouts along the main canal, no boundaries were necessary. Each camp would provide its own ditches. Presumably the Government would tax the lands a small percentage of the crops produced.

Under the spreading shade trees of Gul's garden, in the sweet scented atmosphere of luxuriant flowers, during the intense heat of this June afternoon, we had discussed these matters pertaining to land settlement; at least in so far as I had been informed through the translations of Abdul Jabbar.

Finally, leaning toward Abdul and looking me squarely in the eyes Aslam Khan said "Since the day you first took this job, we have all been very happy."

"It has been to me a great pleasure and satisfaction to work with you men and your Government in the interest of your people," I rejoined.

*　　　*　　　*

AFGHANISTAN VENTURE

Project Manager Ted Johnston said, "Jones, at the end of Ramazon we'd better see the Governor-General again; I can't understand what people are doing with all this water. With soldiers, — well maybe we ought to exercise more control over the diversions."

"You have a point there, Ted, perhaps. Shir Ahmad suspects also that water is being wasted. But before taking drastic action, let's follow the water through, you know; from measurement at points of diversion to places of actual use in the fields," I cautioned.

And hence for many days, in the Dodge Power Wagon with the four-wheel drive, I had accompanied Shir's hydrographic party everywhere. Flows from the river into each of some thirty-two canals had been carefully measured. By boat we had reached otherwise inaccessible diversions. At Qala Shahmir every few days we had hiked two miles across swamp cedar bottom lands to measure the flow at the Tarnak junction. This marked the lower end of the project. Flows of no more than ten to fifteen c.f.s. here would be satisfactory, a criterion by which we knew all canals were being satisfactorily supplied. Were the flow little or nothing, we would order Chris Brown at the reservoir to increase the release in increments daily of fifty or one hundred c.f.s. until satisfactory flow was restored.

We had followed along each canal to the end of passable roads. From there we had gone afoot to the point of last delivery on field, orchard or vineyard. Southward from Kandahar, unfavorable topography was causing the continuation of a semi-swampy condition in a large grassy area, or *chaman*. Other than that nowhere was water being wasted. The slope of the valley is such that water unused in one canal, or area, finds its way to the next canal below, and so on. Here was the answer; all was well. For, true to the instincts of water-hungry people, surrounded by vast deserts, not one acre-foot of the precious water was being lost un-

328

necessarily; either by deep percolation, by surface runoff, or ponding. People assured us they were making full use of water on vineyard and in the production of summer crops which never before had received any irrigation water at this season of the year. They were expressing their gratitude through us to M.K.A., by saying in Pakhtu: "We are praying God to be good to the Americans."

The points regarding beneficial use and conservation of water were again emphasized, as in our talks with the District Governors. These men assured us of 100% co-operation. They mentioned the Patow Canal people as having in times past diverted an excessive portion of low river flow to the disadvantage of all canals further downstream. We stated that from here on out such trouble should not occur. There is ample water for all the canals if beneficially used without waste.

In connection with the distribution of water to these some thirty-two canals covering upwards of 120,000 acres of irrigable lands during this first summer of operations, we drew attention to what was in reality a lack of physical control by M.K.A. over the facilities for distributing the released reservoir water to the canals in the desired and proper amounts. We only diplomatically could consult and advise with each *mirab* about control of water. The Governor-General of Kandahar Province, and each of his District Governors immediately concerned, did, however, express to me a willingness to help out in any difficult situation such as this could develop into should it be necessary for M.K.A. to enforce an equitable distribution of water among the canals. But at no time did this appear necessary, however.

The group of water-users under each canal, independent of all other such groups maintains diversion weirs placed obliquely to the direction of flow in the river. They are made of limbs of trees and brush held in place by the pressure of the water, by anchors, by weighting down with rock, and being made partially watertight by grass, moss or Bermuda sod carefully placed. No metal or manufactured timbers of any kind are used. The materials are transported out into the stream on the backs of men; one group loading, one carrying, one unloading and placing, all to the continuous admonitions of the *jamidors* to speed up operations: *"Yallah, yallah, yallah!"* These men are water-users from down along the canal — or men provided by the water-users — who perform their share of maintenance work in accordance with the number of *jeribes* (half acres) they have under ditch.

It is the practice to provide an overpour wasteway in the lower bank of the canal not far downstream from the diversion barrier. This may be over natural rock surface, or made of the same kind of materials similarly placed as in the river barrier, so as to allow any unneeded amount of water to overpour into a channel leading back into the river. The amount of back flow to the river, or of flow past the diversion barrier, may be governed by the addition or removal of materials in these crude weirs. We are attempting to maintain a regular and steady flow in the river of released reservoir water, whether up or down, by increments of fifty cfs. when changes are necessary. This results in the least damage being done to the barriers, or *bunds* as they are called.

Such are the diversions works on the Arghandab River, the type of which must date back to the beginning of recorded history. At intervals when crops can stand being without water for a few days, certain canals are dried up for cleaning; the removal of weeds, water vegetation, sand deposits and unwanted obstructions. Again this work is performed by large groups of water-users with spades or shovels typical of Afghanistan and universally used, which look like our shovels that could have been worn or ground down to about one-half the original size, with homemade wooden handles upon whch is fitted a sliding smooth block of wood for a barefoot rest in pressing the tool into the earth.

During the summer the two forty-eight-inch discharge valves at the dam were being calibrated to determine, for the existing elevation of water surface in the reservoir, the amount of water being released from each valve for settings of 10, 20, 30, 40, 50, 60, 70, 80, 90, and 100% of the full opening, as indicated by actual current meter measurement, or the curve for the rating station just downstream from the dam. It was found that for any setting of the valves with slight changes of head even up to about 1.5 meters, the change in flow as plotted on the discharge curve for the valve was inappreciable for the purposes intended. So these calibrations were discontinued until a change of perhaps as much as five meters difference in water surface elevation had occurred.

And the foregoing gives an indication of activities upon which we were engaged during the first season in the operation of the Arghandab Reservoir.

But to continue.

*   *   *

It was Edes, the several holidays immediately following Ramazon, a season of gladness, in a way like Easter. Everywhere we traveled about Kandahar and outlying villages and communities, people were picnicking and celebrating, dressed in their best.

Not overly concerned with holidays, Shir, I had noticed, was inclined to prevail upon his helpers, Bharat and Kareem, to work on those days as usual.

So it happened that in mid-afternoon far out beyond a lone mountain along the dry Tarnak, in a land of drifting sands, we had been beset by three ruffians. They were poised just fifty feet ahead to let fly with a barrage of rocks. As one, Shir and I hit the sand; he charging forward with fists clenched, I with the steel-shod club. Frightened, two fled ahead around the mountain. The third, a teen-ager, fixed in place, grinned broadly unafraid — offered me an English walnut!

As we rolled forward, an unexpected scene unfolded along the banks of the Rhorabad Canal. Howling, jeering, angry, a mob of 600 people on a holiday outing threatened retaliation.

Like an enraged bull, the Dodge Power Wagon roared forward into the midst of the astounded crowd. It suddenly halted. Shouting words to me unintelligible, hoodlums in the forefront closed in with a vengeance. A crisp order from Shir, and Kareem and Bharat were over the tailgate preparing to set up the Price current meter measuring equipment, unmindful of the milling confusion. I climbed out and with extended rod attempted a shoving movement with no progress, until given assistance by a wiry elderly man in a pure white turban. He had masterfully elbowed his way to my side. With arms extended and with no words uttered, he and I slowly moved abreast around the truck, created a narrow but clear opening. Suddenly from somewhere, brandishing two-lash whips, five rural police charged through to our aid. Striking with well aimed blows, these fellows promptly restored order.

Jostling our way to the water's edge, Shir began measuring the canal's flow, Bharat and Kareem holding the tape on either bank, I writing down notes. Hundreds were clamoring now for vantage points to view what to them was an unusual proceeding, some of them even climbing trees.

Something under water must have bitten one of Shir's bare feet. He suddenly jumped and kicked violently as I shouted, *"Mahi* (fish)!'' not meaning to be funny. Three hundred Moslems roared with delight. Three hundred to their rear pressed forward to obtain a better view.

High above in the tree, something was shouted down in stentorian tones. "Bharat, what does he say?"

"Don't shut off the water!" replied Bharat.

With an O.K. sign I waved upward to my friend and yelled in English, "We won't!" — producing another round of merriment. At once this was increased in volume and finally by loud shouts of approval as Shir added something plainly both informative and amusing.

* * *

Shir brought the Dodge to a sudden stop. The man beside this lone desert trail wanted a ride. Lean, sunburned, wearing light weight sandals, arms and legs bare, draped loosely in faded green garments, slightly hidden from view and suspended from his neck was a — "Well, Shir, I hope you see what I see; exactly like mine. An English Webley .38 automatic! A highwayman?" and I may have chuckled — just a little.

Shir — to me, "That's not funny!"

Shir — to H.W.M., "Why do you carry that gun?"

H.W.M. — "Just because I want to!"

Shir — "Where do you work?"

H.W.M. — "I have no job."

Shir — "Where do you live?"

H.W.M. — A shrug of shoulders.

Shir continues in tones becoming increasingly shrill — staccato! — to me, "See, he walks away. No longer wants to ride with us!"

* * *

"Some nice residences in this part of Kandahar, Shir, wealthy people? But over the windows there are no screens to keep out the flies, no glass to keep out the wind and dust; you have to brick the windows shut in winter to keep out the cold. How come? But say, who lives in that comfortable home there (pointing)?"

"Jane. You don't know Jane? She's a good friend of mine. At one time I would have married her. But I married Hamina instead. She is in Kabul now with my sisters; expecting a baby next month. Jane is engaged to an Afghan in Switzerland. Wants to still be my friend, but I have a good wife. Hamina teaches school here in Kandahar, in a girl's college."

Just then a friend pulled up alongside in a Chevrolet; got out, shook hands warmly. Chidingly Shir said, "Now just look at me — all day long up to my neck measuring water. But Khosro here, look at him, a City official, just goes to the office to sign papers. Pretty soft, what!"

*   *   *

Shir had given me bits of information about his family starting with twenty-two-year-old Hamina to whom he was most devoted. He was proud of his nine sisters and one brother, of his ancestry. He wouldn't talk about them though unless one asked, and I was learning how serious it could be with a once prominent political family should a major change in government occur. His father had once been Commandant of the Province of Kandahar, had received his military training and education in Turkey. With a change in the regime of Kings, he had been cast into prison there to remain seven years, followed by five years at home under arrest; wasn't allowed to leave the premises. Shir told me that he himself, as a boy, for three years likewise was not allowed to leave the confines of his home even to attend school. All this took place in Kabul. The King and the Prime Minister had given all of his family a bad time, including his sisters, brother and a cousin.

"Tell me about your sisters, Shir," I had suggested.

He said, "Well, Ghadise is about to graduate from the University in Kabul. Then she will continue her studies for three years to become a doctor of medicine. Zinat is principal of a girls' college in Kabul. Lateefa is married, lives near Herat, makes lots of money in the sheep and karakul lamb business; exports hides and has much land. My other

334

sisters are younger, still in school. And there's Moostafa, my brother in charge of the Kabul Radio Station."

*   *   *

"See what I have," said Shir, holding up sheets of a letter meticulously written in Persian script. "These women!" and he indicated with pride the lip-sticked impression of a woman's lips.

"Lucky fellow, you. She sends you a kiss!" I said encouragingly.

"Yes, on seven letters a week, one every day!" He smiled, started to read.

"Don't they come through the postoffice?" I questioned.

We had just rounded the public square in Kandahar. Today had been a scorcher. People were coming out into the cool of late afternoon. Three men had hailed us. Khosro and the Army Major I recognized. The Major has charge of 200 soldier trainees, drafted men in the service for two years. Assigned to our Company, these especially chosen few were learning to do everything from keeping time and making up payrolls, to being auto mechanics, to driving Euclid dump trucks on the dam embankments. The Major had handed Shir the unstamped envelope.

"Yes, I get Hamina's letters by both mail and through friends," finally replied Shir, having skimmed through her missive.

And then we had driven ninety miles — Shir, Bharat, Kareem and I — in this tough, rugged Dodge Power Wagon with the four-wheel drive, to and beyond Qala-i-Asad on the road toward Kajakai Dam. Over all this rolling desert, sparsely covered with low bush, signs of human habitation or of animal life were few. Now we were at a road junction, site of a Hazara road camp.

Here the men had spread their rugs on a hard level space. The some thirty gathering around looked freshly

335

bathed, and with change of clothes already appeared refreshed from a hot day of work on road maintenance. These descendants of Genghis Khan with Mongolian features were friendly: Would we stop for *chay* (tea) — camp overnight? No, we were going over the mountains to Derakhud and the Teereen River country above the head of Kajakai Reservoir. Wanted to check road conditions, to inspect two river gauging stations, to look over the agricultural situation along the rivers, for there shortly the rising waters of the reservoir would force people to move out to other lands provided for them by the Government. Did these Hazares know about this road over the three passes? Yes; three days ago thieves had waylaid the caravan from Kandahar, taken all their money, killed two men!

Then we had driven on a little way to a fork in the road. Here a decision had to be made.

Shir: "Well it's up to you, boss. You heard what the road *jamador* said — 'the camels peepuls had troubles up there.' " And Shir pointed along the road to the right, to a range of high mountains, rugged, mysteriously blue in the gathering twilight.

I: "Shir, you've been over Paj Pass. What happened?"

Shir: "Sixteen outlaws attacked. Eight on left of truck, eight on right; carried four-foot clubs with 'soft metal' (what you call?) tied to ends with wire!"

I: "Soft metal? That was lead, Shir!"

Shir: "Our truck climbed over big piles of rocks laid in road. Was hard to fight and drive, too. What you think now, boss?"

I: "A road block, eh? Hamina and the new baby, you want to see them, no?"

Shir: "Sure!"

I: "Well then turn left towards Kajakai Dam. Tonight over Paj and the other two passes we wouldn't have a Red Chinaman's chance!"

Interior of King's ancient Palace occupies area of a city block.

An ancient fort becomes an island as waters of the Arghandab Reservoir rise.

Ruins of old army quarters. Adjacent to structures along river is a compound of some eighty acres surrounded by massive adobe walls.

— Photo by Rey Entienza

General Manager and Mrs. T. Y. (Ted) Johnston with Vice-President and Mrs. Richard Nixon, and other guests, at Manzel Bagh.

Karadeen and helpers assist in surveys, Boghra Project. Such men become very efficient under training of American and Filipino field engineers.

Jacinto ("Jack") Sabiniano, Filipino field engineer, and author at Manzel Bagh.

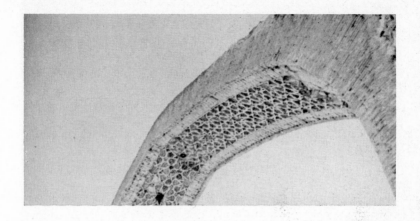

Geometrical designs in perfect symmetry against the azure blue of the sky. Note below the fine mosaic — an artist's delight.

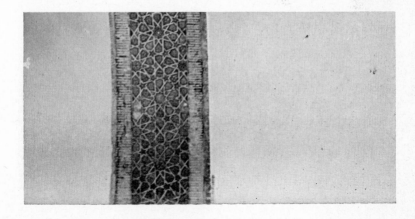

Caravansary along river at Ghazni, important trade and caravan center.

Camels kneel as burdens are removed.

Congregation of 10,000 assembles outside the walls of Kandahar for Eeds. Devotionals are led by Governor-General.

A group of husky desert men congregate for an inspection of the camera.

Qala Beest (Fort Twenty) at junction of Arghandab and Helmand rivers. These walls surround possibly 100 acres.

Fortress within walls surmounts hill, and can be seen from all directions for many miles. Auxiliary forts stagger both sides of river up and downstream.

In front of this public building the national colors of black, green and red are proudly displayed.

Arghandab Dam – stored waters rising for the first time crawl toward the granite rock-covered slopes. Overflow discharges into channel leading to Arghandab River.

Petunia field for seed purposes — a riot of color — at Nad-i-ali.

Horse-drawn artillery rolls over a parade field. Note the caissons.

Author poses beside two chunks of opium found in debris by archaeologists.

Sports pavillion on Chaman at sundown. From nearby parade grounds, thousands view fireworks on surrounding fortified ridges.

THE LION OF MOHAMMED

July 2nd: Rested and refreshed by good food and soft beds, a brief visit with friends at this huge construction camp. We crossed over the imposing embankment rising high above the Helmand River, soon to begin storing 4,000,-000 acre-feet of water. We emerged from Kajakai Canyon to face a rising sun. This lemon-yellow ball of fire cast a lemon-yellow haze over a river that appeared like a stream of quick silver in the early morning light. To the right and left loomed rugged desert mountains rising precipitously from the flat valley lands which were a veritable garden land of green production. Rice paddies, patches of cotton and tobacco, fields of corn, melons, alfalfa, clover, quinjet, ripened wheat or stubble; vineyards (the grapes of the Afghan valleys rival those of our Southwest), orchards of pomegranates now spotted with large red blossoms against a bright green foliage, almonds, apricots, plums, figs. In green pastures were flocks of fat-tailed sheep, goats, small black cows with some Jersey-colored (but they weren't Jerseys), camels.

Our road — if by that name it could be so described — had once been graded and widened from a caravan trail; maintenance had ceased. It hugged the base of steep mountain slopes. By time-consuming detours, we edged precariously down into washes, picked our way across beds of loose coarse sand between huge boulders, and climbed out over an all but vertical bank on the far side. Masses of debris that had been swept down steep ravines by mountain torrents completely obliterated the trail in places. Gully crossings partly washed away, we filled with rock. The road shelf we widened at washouts with sloping walls of stone!

I marveled at this rugged vehicle, its 100% adaptability. The heavy tires — not a cut or a puncture — Goodrich and Goodyear, they were.

At 3 p.m. we reached Darakhud, the Tirin River and the gauging station. Refreshing indeed was a swim in the

337

deep cool water in view of the shimmering mountains. Shir rounded up a crew to make repairs to the cableway. Not until dusk did we return to the headquarters of the estate where we were being made most welcome by the several brothers who owned and operated these large properties. Shir classified them as "millionaires." Abdul Kayum and Toor Agha were the two oldest. Toor awaited us; would we care to join them *"bala?"* Yes. So we ascended an outside stairway to a flat roof. A place had been reserved for us.

Rugs to sit upon, long round pillows to recline against, with these we were graciously provided. Twenty sat cross-legged round about. The dignified elderly man on my right owned much land soon to be submerged by the lake. With the money paid him by the Government, he would purchase good land elsewhere.

"Wouldn't you rather use a knife, fork, spoon? It's all right," he said.

"No. When in your country I conform to your customs," I assured him. The man's countenance beamed as Bharat translated this.

Here's a scene I've read about, never dreamed of experiencing, thought I: An *Amreekan* on the opposite face of the earth, close to the heart of Asia, soon to dine with strange people — friends — in the soft coolness of this July evening; peace and silence reign. Bathed in the bright moonlight, a spirit of serenity pervades the rugged mountains, the glistening river, the green fields and orchards. The friendly stars sparkle in brilliance. Faintly through the still night air, from a distant village, sounds the irregular staccato-like beating of kettle drums. A never-to-be-forgotten fairyland, is this.

Noting my reverie, someone said, "We wonder what you think of us. Perhaps dirty, unkempt, at a lower level than you?"

Quickly Shir interpreted into English.

"Decidedly not," I responded. "I have observed your homes, your valleys, inclosure of mountains, imagine myself one of you; an Afghan, a Moslem. In this isolation, passage of time means nothing. Here is peace, calmness. You are never hurried. In your ways is happiness. In my country also we find great happiness, we are free people. Yours is a free nation. In humility we likewise worship Allah, the one God, the Supreme Architect of the Universe. So may it ever be."

Shir promptly provided an interpretation into Persian. In this, to my plain remarks, I sincerely hoped he had added or injected something of beauty and eloquence. This I knew him to be perfectly capable of doing.

Deftly three men-servants rolled out a narrow white cloth over the long mat, and quickly placed thereon platters of chicken, rice, vegetables, slabs of bread. Unobserved, a dainty little miss appeared, seated herself directly opposite me by her grandfather. The men ate hungrily, healthily, Shir and I from the same bowl. Delicious *chay* was served in individual pots. Tea is a symbol of welcome.

Then there was general relaxation, subdued conversation; the little child snuggled happily in her grandfather's arms.

"Now they will have evening devotions," said Shir.

Quickly we put on our shoes, while all stood. Led by Bharat we slipped quietly out into the night, to our beds on the hard adobe platform, three in a row under the stars.

Clix-clax-clox. Rising on one elbow at dawn I beheld two horsemen crossing the Tirin River; shepherds driving flocks to pasture, men walking swiftly and silently bent on covering distance in the coolness of the morning. To me, the night had been cold.

Forthwith appeared a servant with three pots of tea and three slabs of bread, rolled up our bedding, disappeared with it.

During the ever increasing heat of the day we completed

339

repairs to the Tirin cableway and supports. By mid-afternoon relief was sought in the swift, cool, deep waters of the river.

July 4th: We early forded the Tirin on our way to Helmand River gauging station. Then on a contrivance of poplar poles and brush, uncertainly supporting a foot in depth of earth decking, narrow, plainly intended for camels in single file only, we crossed two large canals.

Then just beyond at the fort and District Governor's headquarters, we paused at a grist mill. Here were two five-feet diameter granite blocks a half-foot thick; the nether stationary, the upper revolving. Water falling down twelve feet in a chute — a half-log hollowed out — struck the wooden impeller blades of a vertical 6" wooden shaft fixed in the upper mill stone. Wheat, corn, or a mixture of both, was fed mechanically at any rate desired at the center between the two stones. Centrifugally, flour was thrown out around the periphery into adobe bins.

Shir was under the impression the District Governor was lax in providing protection for the gauging stations — Government property.

Curiosity overcame these isolated valley people. From an adobe hut rushed forth a barefoot girl clad in pink pantaloons, red waist and little round yellow canvas cap, from below which protruded twenty pig-tails. Reaching the lane, she clapped hands over her mouth as her black eyes gazed in wonderment at the passing yellow machine.

And there was roadside lunch under a spreading mulberry. Boys and girls, thirty-eight in number, grouped at respectful distances; a few smiled. Men left work in the nearby fields. A mother and teen-age daughter, when unobserved, by turns from behind flowering shrubs peered over the garden wall.

"Shir, what did you just say to that lad?" I asked.

"That it's whiskey!" sheepishly.

Sniffing suspiciously at some grapefruit juice handed him

340

in a paper cup, the boy had all but swallowed a slug of this delicious S & W brand product, then hastily thrown it to the ground.

For Kareem I had poured a cup of tomato juice. Distasteful to him, he hurriedly pressed it on another lad, who, accepting it, studied the large red tomato on the can wrapper. A sip, a wry face, this juice likewise returned to earth.

Dried beef, — *gow,* and Nabisco salted soda crackers; — *gandam,"* wheat, I explained. In minutes our supply would have been exhausted had not Shir summarily slammed shut the lid of the large tin box.

The steel cable at the gauging station we found too frayed and unsafe upon which to cross the wide Helmand by cable car. From the recordergraph, Shir removed the sheet upon which for some months past the flow of the river had been indicated by a wavy inked line; put on a new one. The station should be removed to a better location upstream, the cable replaced at an early date.

In pairs, six teen-agers hastened toward the road dropping head gear in excitement. Two in discomfiture squatted on a ditch bank alongside the lane, backs to the truck, giggled over their shoulders and motioned coquettishly to Shir. The other two pairs at various distances, hesitated, smiled modestly, waved with open hands.

Come 4 p.m. invariably a barefoot girl began herding three cows on Bermuda grass along a ditch, keeping them away from an adjoining field of corn. Red cap, numerous pig-tails, pantaloons drawn in at ankles, at dusk she returned to the orchard.

A shepherd lad by hand tossed water into his mouth from shallow cow hoof tracks where a trickling stream seeped slowly across a heavily pastured slope — this near the river of clean, flowing water.

At sunset, women and girls in numbers gathered along the sandy beach of the river, here to relax in feminine freedom; to fill earthenware jars with good water. Later, balancing these jars on their heads, they withdrew to secluded quarters in the orchard.

We were preparing to leave. Shir had purchased *"ghee"* (liquid butter fat) for domestic use. Heated to high temperature, it would be stored in earthen jars. Our tank was refilled with water. Several sacks of flour from the mill were loaded. Esah, a younger brother of Khayoum, and a manservant, Elyas, to look after him, would ride with us to Kandahar. Also Reza, to care for the flour. Kareem was being left behind to guard the gauging stations.

As the mountains still shimmered in heat waves, we all relaxed on the thirty by thirty-foot adobe platform in the shade of a thatched covering, indulged in *chay* and dozed. Subconsciously I watched a man making a lariat from black and white goat hair, periodically dipping it in water. It was a work of art. And hard candy was passed around on the occasion of a new-born child to a wife of Khayoum, a son, and that explained the drum beating of last evening. Passing men would remove shoes, spread out a prayer rug, and spend fifteen minutes facing Mecca in silent meditation.

Khayoum and Tool Agha — others also — warmly bid us goodbye; urged us to return when we didn't have so much work to do.

Rolling across the desert plains towards the mountains, water in the radiator boiled. A lone wolf paused undecidedly. But it was 5:30 p.m. The heat was breaking. Ahead lay three formidable mountain ranges crossed by a trail graded for passage of caravans primarily. At both ends we'd been told about "the camel's peepul's troubles" — waylaid, robbed, men killed, one week ago. But by what other route were we to get out of here?

At the entrance to the first canyon appeared one lone habitation, and some green rice paddies on a hillside.

On the mountain slopes grew a scattering of bright-leaved shrubs. As the radiator cooled I went off the road to examine one; it looked like a species of oak. Twenty-five yards away a lizard peered over a boulder. With my .38 Webley revolver (a British Army weapon), I aimed and fired — thought him blown to bits. I waited, cautiously he (or his pardner) appeared again. A second shot.

Coming on the run, the lad Esah exclaimed, "What are you shooting at?"

"Only a lizard," I replied. But should have said *"booz-maj-je,"* else Esah would not have run so excitedly back to Shir for further explanation.

A man appeared leading a camel. His wife and child followed on a burro. These were the only travelers met that night over the mountains.

Then a military outpost: three soldiers, a hut, mulberry trees, a dugout kept full by a trickle of water. We refilled our radiator. Shir smoked a few drafts from a water pipe. The soldiers were spreading out their rugs for evening devotions, rifles within reach against trees as we waved them goodbye. Shir drove. Bharat rode the running board on the left side. Now in the gathering dusk, every road-turn ahead I watched with fixed attention; apprehensively, .38 in readiness.

"Shir, do you think our passengers back there know the striking force of those tools?"

"Polygens — in their belts they carry daggers!" hastily explained Shir Ahmad.

"O.K., Good. Then tell them to pass forward to Bharat that steel-shod staff!" A high canopy inclosed the bed of the truck, closed in rear by a flap, or partly open, as desired.

The moon rose above the mountain — brightened was the whole rugged landscape. Over the saddleback we descended onto a gently sloping plain. Strewn about in wildest disorder lay huge blocks of granite, as large as houses.

Crossing the rocky, gravelly channel of a wide arroyo,

at a left turn in the trail and sharp ascent, we almost lost our road amid the moonlight shadow patterns of low shrubbery. Up a steep mountainside went the Power Wagon over a route plainly intended only for camel trains and jeeps. Eight zigzag ascents, eight hairpin turns — eight brinks of disaster — there was no turning back. Over the saddleback and down the descent: Exactly the same situation.

Each hairpin turn the truck surmounted by a series of edging movements, forward and backward, as Bharat each time planted large rocks between the edge of the precipice and the nearest front or rear wheels. A slip of the brakes, an instant of mis-judgment, and Shir and Power Wagon would plunge downward into space — and eternity!

Approaching the turns, Bharat and I preceded the truck, and the passengers brought up the rear. Until the turn was completed I prowled about, alert against surprise. During these movements no words were spoken. Shir at the wheel was calm, unperturbed.

And so we descended into a small valley which was here an irrigation ditch, a long row of shade trees and moonlight shadows, then crossed the hard gravelly bed of a creek where running water was pooled, and came to a halt for lunch. Ten boys out of nowhere grouped to watch; they had seen our lights on the mountainside. Elyas sprawled on the ground, sick.

"What's the name of this place, *baches?*"

"Neesh!" one spoke up. Quiet, sober boys these were — ate soda crackers with zest, eagerly caught empty tin can from the peaches tossed by Bharat. A peaceful place this — "beside the still waters."

Soon we left the lonely little settlement far behind, and were crossing a sage-covered desert, reminder of Arizona far away. In the overpowering serenity of this vast expanse, bathed in mystic Afghan moonlight, one sensed an Infinite

Presence, an unmeasurable feeling of security and well being; no fear.

Therefore in relief I had replaced the .38 in leather holster, cocked feet on dash, surveyed the distant range now closing in, and enjoyed travel over a straight smooth road again.

Of a sudden Shir took his eyes off the road; gave me a quick look, glanced at holster, said nothing, then, "You'd better be ready!" He stopped at the edge of a declivity; below lay an unusually wide arroyo.

Reza, Bharat and I scouted both ways for a passable descent and crossing, and motioned Shir ahead. We found old trail in bottom of dry wash, gained the far bank.

Shir cautioned, "The road ahead is very dangerous." But to me the mountain range seemed yet far away.

"You mean Paj Pass? We won't be there for a while," I rejoined.

But Shir continued calmly, "We are coming to what looks like a village. It's not a village. No huts. Just a grove of mulberry trees. Mud fences along lanes lead off to one side."

"Blind alleys! Say, Shir, its a trap for caravans, for lorries — and us! Can you keep on the main road?"

"Yes, if no big piles of rock; road blocks like you say. Bad peepuls lives here!" And with Shir's last word, a sharp bend in the road around a low hill brought us squarely into a grove of overhanging mulberry trees.

Two white-clad figures in the outer limbs to the left were prepared to drop down on the truck — five in the forks were undecided. Off to the left in the shadows, dimly visible in the gleam of the headlights, a green-clad figure followed by two in white rushed toward a point in road ahead to intercept us. On my right one attempted to flag us to a halt as two others emerged from a low opening in a wall and tried to leap on the running board. Just ahead three were closing in from the right; the one in lead with long pole, on the end of which dangled a green rag, charged the wind shield. I aimed at him point blank. "Don't hit any!" yelled Shir, and a split second saved this man. Instead I fired low over their heads.

Shir was stepping on the gas, dodging any road blocks, keeping both his head and the main road, and refused to be misled by the tricky lanes. Whatever ideas these outlaws had were promptly abandoned as the Dodge Power Wagon roared through the grove and up the grade toward the third range, the most precipitous and ragged looking of the three.

Again a long series of steep zigzag stretches overhanging deep canyons; hairpin turns sharper than any previous, where a camel train would almost double back on itself, and Shir made the three passengers walk behind, while Bharat and I hiked ahead or rode alternately. At one level place near the top we rested for the others to overtake the truck.

"There's gold under this road here!" said Shir.

"Let's look for it some other time," I rejoined.

"O.K., you mine it. I'll join the bandits back there at Haji Alam. We'll rob you!" admonished Shir, jovially.

And then we ascended the last section to the summit, Paj Pass, where we waited for our passengers, then began the descent.

And these grades were steeper; the courses shorter, the hairpin turns sharper, the ravines deeper. Ideal were the ambushes from which to be waylaid by outlaws. But all of this made little difference now.

Suddenly near the last hairpin the lights shone fully upon two men peering down into the road-cut just ahead. Without hesitation I fired — not to hit — and they were our passengers! They had gone on ahead while the truck was negotiating the last turn. In disgust, Shir's voice rose to a high pitch, blasting them with epithets of pointed Persian meaning. Why had they been so careless?

The truck now rolled over a narrow, winding road among rocks the size of a car, strewn about in wild confusion over a gently sloping plain. The scene appeared ominous enough, but more so as ahead and about twenty-five yards to left there loomed into view a tall figure atop the largest rock. Erect — motionless — black rifle with butt resting on rock, cross bandoleers, garb luminously white in the full moonlight from turban to sandaled feet; and in vivid contrast, tanned brown, indeed, were his face, hands and feet.

"Bharat, Shir? Over there, who's that?!"

Already I had him covered with the .38! Should he take aim I would fire this time for a hit.

But he remained motionless, alert, facing the power wagon.

Lowering the revolver: "Shir, he looks like a soldier."

"But he's not a soldier!" and the truck leaped forward.

"He's not a bandit, else he would not stand there like that. He carried an army rifle. A military outpost back among the rocks and brush, maybe out of sight. Probably a soldier out of uniform; much cooler on a hot night like this. He is guarding the road, the south approach to Paj Pass; heard the firing up there awhile ago," I half-way soliloquized.

"Could be," said Shir.

"Say, Shir, there's something strangely familiar about that fellow. I have a feeling he portrays to me happenings in history, American history. But in these solitudes how could an Afghan soldier do that? But I'll remember the way he looked there in the bright Afghan moonlight, all my life, I guess. A perfect target; serene, fearless, stern-faced, challenging or daring someone: But who? What?

"Could this be it: He stands for law and order as opposed to banditry, oppression, tyranny, in any form. He looked to me like a sort of civilian soldier; alert, ready for

347

action. Why, Shir, he'd fight in a minute, a minute-man!" I stopped speechless.

In mute surprise, both men glanced at me.

'Al-hamdo-lellah! (Praise be to Allah). Do you *hombres* know what day this is? Wow-ee-wow! Right now in the U.S. it's the Fourth of July, Independence Day!"

"All our *baches* learn in school about our Minute-Men, armed citizens who pledged themselves to take the field at a minute's notice. This was just prior to, and during our War for Independence. At Concord, where the first battle was fought, there stands a memorial, a tribute to these brave men. I've seen pictures of it. And Shir, Bharat, I'm amazed: That scene by the road back there, except for the clothing, was practically a duplicate of the statue of a 'Minute-Man' at Concord, Massachusetts!"

And now we were approaching the road camp of the Hazares. Shir said, "What's that crossing the road ahead?"

Looks like a hyena," I replied. "Say, you'll see Hamina and the baby, after all, Shir! Well, when I get to Manzel Bagh I'm writing to the States all about our Fourth of July weekend, to a special friend in North Dakota."

And so that's the way it was.

During our absence, heart-warming had been the message placed on my desk, circulated among all the Americans:

The Royal Afghan Commission for
Morrison-Knudsen Afghanistan Projects,
Kandahar, Afghanistan,
July 3, 1952

On behalf of the Royal Afghan Commission and the people of Afghanistan, I wish to extend congratulations on the celebration of your 176th year of Independence on July 4th.

We are most grateful for the diligent efforts and work

which you have put forth in helping us to build a strong
and progressive country, just as you have done in America.

We thank you from the bottom of our hearts.

(Signed)   M. MORID KHAN
President

"Beyond the dim unknown standeth
God within the shadow."
— James Russell Lowell
1819 — 1891

XVII
Kabul -- Wonder City

Royal Mail Stage?
Agonized Waiting
Parting Goodbyes
Clay City
Toward Mecca at Dawn
Kareezes — Ancient Engineering Art
The Wandering "Kooches"
Kalat-i-Ghilzai — breakfast
"Beyond the Northwest Frontier"
Caravansary
Ancient Ghazni
Fabulous Naiff — Rare Entertainment
Soccer Team
Hotel de Kabul
The Old City
National Colors
"Kabul Policeman? No, M-K-A."
Strategic Kabul
Historic Kabul
Constitutional Government
Royal Coronation Oath
The Cabinet
Clashes with British
Abdur Rahman Khan
Bacha-i-Saqao

CHAPTER XVII

Kabul -- Wonder City

A QUICK SHOWER, a box of lunch hastily supplied by Whitey Leader's Afghan mess hall force, and we were off for the downtown Kandahar stage depot. Once I had been here to view the situation as Mr. Berry, Chief Administrative Assistant, and Mrs. Berry were buying tickets to Kabul and traveling on to Ja-lal-a-bad, Khyber Pass, Pe-sha-war, and Karachi. Pointed out to me had been a Royal Mail stage. This had compared favorably to some discarded by the Greyhound Bus Lines about the time F.D.R. became President. O.K., I had ridden in more dilapidated, anti-quated vehicles, I could wager.

Upon Shir's insistence we took the two-gallon thermos jug; it was heavy and awkward but we would need fresh, cool water. Sandwiches, crackers, cookies were in a light box, change of clothing in a knapsack.

At 8:30 p.m. the bus took position in the station yard, cov-ered by the headlights of Truck No. 22 driven by our Man-

353

zel Bagh driver. Shir climbed aboard with the lunch and water to find seats. This coach was not the more to be desired Royal Mail earlier depicted. In the darkness I stumbled over the jinx of a jug and many feet; crawled through a narrow opening between back of seat and ceiling, and plummeted into an even narrower space among the five occupants already jammed into the seat extending wall to wall. Maneuvering with the help of other passengers in the rear, I awkwardly gained a simulated upright position; head bent forward sharply to clear ceiling, elbows thrust tightly into lap, knees wedged against back of seat, one foot trapped between, the other crushed on top of two or three large *kharbooz*, and these watermelons within a narrow range rolled uncertainly.

Eyes becoming accustomed to near pitch darkness, I sensed the situation: six men abreast, no aisle, second man from window — all jammed together like sardines in a can, all soaked with perspiration on this hot August night.

I was overwhelmed with a sense of forced immobility; claustrophobia, that's what it was, twice during this one and one-half hours of waiting. I squirmed in near panic. Only by imposing self discipline was I restrained from crawling out of there somehow; to ride with the baggage on the roof, or to give up this vacation trip after all.

But ah, now we're off. It's 10 p.m. The driver comes aboard, seats himself, starts the motor. All's well. But no; a helper enters with large open bucket of gasoline. Aided by light from a lantern, he fills the emergency fuel tank beside the driver's seat. Men of Afghanistan, is Allah's beneficient protection over you unbounded? By sheer force of willpower I focused on the irrelevant:

"Hey Shir, what's all the shouting about?"

"Mohammed, oh Mahmud!" the man beside me had of a sudden shouted.

"Woo-uf! Hosen?" a voice in the distance returned, fol-

lowed by a spirited conversation. Then broke loose a bed-
lam as some ten other passengers called to well-wishers evidently scattered among the large crowd outside, until there
was high pitched response from each. "Azizullah? — Khara-
din!" And there were private conversations and convulsions
of laughter simultaneously between the "outs" and the "ins,"
until I all but forgot the seating arrangement.

"Well, please, they are just saying goodbye," Shir at last
informed me.

Rolling and bumping out of Kandahar, we were soon in
the open desert, cool and bearable, and here was Shar-i-Safa
(Clay City). I had dozed off to sleep. It was then 12:25 a.m.
We walked about and ate melons, a firm variety of muskmelon; hard, but sweet and of white meat. And here was
our former radio man at Chah-i-anjir in a jeep with his
wife, a huddled figure in back seat under a black purdah and
with small child. Shivering in shirt sleeves, I wished for
dawn. Now I could readily trade my seat for the one next
to the window. Short of stature, my five seat-mates sat comfortably upright, as I dozed and occasionally slumped forward on the shoulder of a man in the seat ahead. Each time
he roused, straightened up, smiled patiently, and, half
asleep, my head each time hit the ceiling a resounding bump.
This stimulated subdued amusement from other passengers.

At 5:30 a.m. our conveyance halted beside the flowing
water of an irrigation ditch. To limber up, to get warm, I
jumped and trotted about. All washed in, and drank from
the clear cold water. Everyone like soldiers formed two ranks
for morning devotions — fifteen minutes — and I remained
standing respectfully just to the rear of the group, likewise
facing Mecca.

The many campfires appeared inviting in the early
morning light as, near and far, they marked the black tented
abodes of the nomads.

And then we continued on this almost due northeast

355

course up this mile-high valley of the Tarnak toward Ghazni and Kabul, from Kandahar 225 and 315 miles, respectively. To our right was the dry, wide, sandy channel of the Tarnak. Just beyond rose a 9,000-foot-high range of desert mountains, and on their farther side lay the valleys of the Arghastan, Lora and Ghazni. These are really one continuous valley which joins the Tarnak and Arghandab valleys below Kandahar.

Indicating mouths of canyons to the west, were groves of poplar trees. There, during rainy seasons, streams emerge on the valley. The water is mostly absorbed by the coarse sands and gravels. So along here was irrigation. Underground water found its way into *kareezes*. Of these we crossed many, a mile to two miles apart, extending on a zigzag course out into the valley plain. Each is a series of wells, or shafts 150 to 300 feet apart, dug to gravelly water-bearing strata, and connected by small tunnels through which the developing stream flows by gravity finally to emerge at ground surface into an irrigation ditch. Men descend occasionally to keep shafts and passageways clear of any obstructing debris. Many of such *kareezes* extend for miles, are the continuous work of many generations.

Except for small groups of mud huts, or little villages ten to fifteen miles apart,, the nomad camps contained the only inhabitants. About them were large flocks of fat-tailed sheep, goats, camels; happy, carefree seemed these people — Kooches — on this bright cool Juma forenoon. Over there the beating of drums and dancing girls signified a wedding. Each tribe wanders over a definite area where pasture is available; the high lands in the summer away from heat and insects, the lower levels in winter. Their only home is the *ghydee*, a black tent of wool felt supported by willow latticework. Tents are easily taken down, made into long rolls and supported and conveyed crosswise on the backs of camels. Young children, chickens, lambs are secured firmly to the backs of camels, or supported in baskets balanced on both sides of a burro. Baby camels are made secure on the backs of their mothers. No monotony of city life for these people; always a change of climate and a variety of scenery. But by the irrigation of new lands the government is offering them inducements to settle down. That's what we of M-K-A are endeavoring to help accomplish.

Kalat-i-Ghilzai 7:30 a.m. Green-fronted bazaars faced both sides of the thoroughfare, a good looking hotel loomed up across a small green field. Shir, Bharat, Sayed and I went into a dark-looking establishment of adobe; sat upon a dirty rug on the ground. The proprietor appeared with a metal jug, poured water over our hands, proffered a muchly used towel. Soon he returned, a pot of hot tea for each with sugar, and we furnished our own sandwiches. Then outside we walked along the sprinkled and well swept street eating grapes — nice looking and delicious — bought from nearby fruit stands. And around here were patches of good looking alfalfa; cottonwood, willow and poplar trees.

Farther along we noted every community had its fort (Qala) in good state of repair; thick walls thirty feet high inclosing an area of perhaps a city block. At each corner was a turret, a parapet along top of the wall from which riflemen, spearmen, or archers (according to the period in history) could project missiles at attackers. These strongholds reminded one of the stockades used by our own early settlers for protection against our American Indians. And now we were passing through that mystifying land known only to the British in India as "beyond the North West Frontier," entered via Peshawar and the Khyber Pass — fastnesses of forayers and raiders on the mountain and plains British military outposts of that Indian Province.

Then at Ghazni it was 11:30 a.m. as we pulled up for a break and lunch at a tea house seated on chairs. Here women walked with men, not especially careful to keep their faces covered. Sayed and I wandered down to the river, a wide gravelly bed with trees and flat lands. Here was a caravansary, a resting place for both men and animals. Caravans were in all stages of loading and unpacking; hundreds of drivers, perhaps a thousand camels, and this an American viewed with bewilderment. But in overwhelming wonder I mentally surveyed the gate to the ancient city of Ghazni, and was taken backwards in time 2,000 years as Sayed and I entered that strangest of cities, walked its narrow crooked streets, mingled with people indescribably different. It lies on an isolated ridge at the head of the Tarnak valley. It is of strategic importance commanding roads and passes in several directions, is surrounded by a massive wall just above level of the surrounding plain presenting a formidable appearance, and 150 feet above is the imposing citadel which completely dominates this city of 20,000 and surrounding country.

Near Ghazni, Shir explained, are four dams, constructed by Sultan Mahmud Ghaznawi (997-1030 A.D.). One known as Bund-i-Siraj has been reconstructed. They appear to have been built following the same engineering principles that govern modern earth and rock-fill dam construction.

Along the main road that passes through the newer city of Ghazni were many shops where shoes are made. As we viewed these, Sayed said suddenly, "There goes General Manager Ted Johnston and Jalaluddin in that car. Back at Kandahar a man told me they are taking pack horses into the Hindu Kush out of Paghman."

Shir exclaimed "One hears just anything. These crazy peepuls!"

Joking with and entertaining the passengers, Shir said to Baba, a dignified elderly gentleman with cane, "Ever know Naiff? He's a man can do anything. Hunts leopards, cooks, builds houses, makes rugs, is a merchant, has four wives, can fight with a gun. You don't know Naiff?" (To me aside: "Naiff is a fictitious, a fabulous character.")

Baba searched his memory, studied, came forth with an answer. "Why yes, I knew Naiff at Mazar-i-Sherif. Hunted gazelle together near Sar-i-Boom." And those within hearing convulsed in merriment, Baba joining, passed our thermos jug for another round of cold water.

"Baba is seventy-eight. When that age I'll be glad if I'm as active," said Shir. "And please, boss, please, no American in Afghanistan but you would dare take this journey, none can walk as far as you." And as this compliment was translated into Persian, I suddenly felt red-faced and conspicuous mid the good-natured glances of these strangers.

Ascending the valley plain north from Ghazni one beholds a range country. Near Shashgao is crossed a 9,000 foot pass which is surely blocked by snow in winter. Run-off to the south is into the Arghandab and Helmand River watersheds; to the north into the Kabul River, thence into the Indus River in Pakistan.

Now we descended the Shiniz River valley. Rearing skyward ten miles to the west loomed a peak rivaling in height Mt. Shasta and Mt. Whitney. In the Logar Valley near Shaikhabad were scenes of local prosperity; luscious green fields of tobacco, rice, corn, melons, all terraced in perfect rectangular regularity. Here unveiled women in groups displayed interest in these developing crops as they strolled in the freshness of the late afternoon.

Lively cheers and songs emanated from Kandahar's soccer team up front en route to play Kabul during Freedom Week. The leader chanted the first line of a verse, completed by all in loud unison and handclapping; the while others in perfect time supported with a wildly sweet refrain punctuated by deep gutteral notes and prolonged vibrations, like —— "huh! hu-u-ah-u-u-u-hu-ee! hu-ee!"

* * *

359

AFGHANISTAN VENTURE

I was awakened at daylight by the clatter of hoofs and the muffled rumbling of rolling wheels, a battery of horse-drawn field artillery.

In the dining room a flashy black-eyed French lady remonstrated in broken English, firmly demanded her rights from a confused waiter. A teen-age gal, who from features and peasant-like manner of dress, could have been adjudged Russian, impassively ate breakfast at next table. And a Yank sat down to boiled eggs, black bread, a pot of tea with nary a murmur.

Ghulam Hosain, the hotel proprietor, arrived early. He was a pleasant courteous young man wearing a tailor-made, neatly pressed blue suit with pin stripes, of beautiful materials, and a gray karakul cap. He was most apologetic for my difficulty of last evening in procuring accommodations.

I was extremely fortunate, however, to have been accompanied by Sayed. He had insisted of the desk clerk that Hosain be phoned at his home. And now I voiced appreciation to Hosain, himself.

Sayed, accompanied by his young son, called for me early at the hotel; we would see something of downtown Kabul. In the older portion the narrow streets were crowded with early forenoon shoppers and I proceeded to take 35 mm. black and white and color pictures of scenes strange to foreign eyes. Mixed with the crowds were droves of burros carrying goods. Strings of camels, heads held haughtily, disdainfully, with 500-lb. loads, were entering the city from faraway places, or leaving on similar missions. And there were droves of sheep from which butchers or anyone could select an animal to slaughter.

Then we walked out to the American Embassy, merely to make contact, and were greeted courteously by a young man in the front office. Frankly, the tattered, faded appearance of the Stars and Stripes, hanging listlessly from the Embassy staff, in this a free nation, was disappointing. Was not this a week of celebration commemorating Afghan independence? The national flag, the nation's colors of black, red and green were proudly on display along the main streets. Holiday crowds everywhere. Beside the Kabul River at the Soviet Embassy the Hammer and Sickle flew 'mid bright red newness.

And then we entered the city police station. One of the Commission on the trip north thought best I get a permit to take pictures. The police authority referred us to a federal officer in another building. From Sayed's explanation this officer got the idea my purpose was to secure permit to set up a photographer's studio in Kandahar. No, I merely wanted permission to take pictures, 35 mm. color, of the military on parade tomorrow. But the officer couldn't understand. Perhaps, thought I, Sayed does not talk his language — Pushtu. On our way back to Hotel de Kabul, we were joined by Naser, a friend of Sayed; a plain-clothes man, I assumed somehow. He would help me formulate a written application to police. Seated at a table in the hotel room, I wrote, and read the results to Sayed. Sayed interpreted in Persian to Naser. Then I reflected that with all this formality the task was hopeless.

"Naser, you are on the Kabul police force?" I inquired.

"Oh, no," volunteered Sayed, Naser works for M-K-A at Arghandab Dam!"

*   *   *

Kabul lies at the western extremity of a spacious plain, at the base of two barren rocky ranges. From out a narrow gorge, called Deh Mozang Pass, and at the angle formed by these mountains, the Kabul River emerges. Conspicuous fortifications extend along the top of these ranges; a massive adobe wall with round towers at short intervals, constructed at the time of the Moslem invasion.

Of great strategic importance, Kabul commands routes

361

to all passes northerly and westerly over the Hindu Kush, and to Herat. Also easterly into Pakistan, south and south-westerly into the provinces of Kandahar and Farah, into the Helmand Valley watershed. Hence this capital city's history has been stirring and eventful. Through it have passed successive invasions from the west into India.

Annexed by the Persians in 516 B.C., it fell to Alexander of Macedon in 326 B.C. The Moslem conquest followed in the 600's A.D. After the 1100's began a series of invasions — Genghis Khan, Tamerlane, Baber (took the city in 1504; held it for fifteen years). Modern Afghanistan dates from the mid-1700's under Ahmad Shah, whose empire extended as far east as Delhi, India. In 1835, under Dost Mohammed, Afghanistan became a buffer state between British and Russian rivalry.

British interference in Afghan internal affairs brought on the Afghan Wars (1839-42, 1878-81) and the fifty-days war of independence in 1919, won by Amaullah, a pro-Westerner. Because of his attempted radical reforms, however, he was deposed in 1929. He was succeeded by Nadir Shah who was assassinated in 1933, to be followed by Nadir's son, Mohammed Zahir Shah, who is continuing to carry out a program for the complete modernization of his country.

Afghanistan has been helped by its neutrality in World War II. Also by postwar loans from the United States.

Since 1931 the Government has functioned under a constitution which provides for a King and Cabinet, a Senate of sixty appointed members, and an Assembly of 120 elected representatives.

The Senators hold seats by right of past services or nomination by the King. Most have rendered great and meritorious service to their country.

The Representatives are elected by ballot from among the voters in every constituency.

362

Suffrage has been extended to all men over twenty possessing sound moral character.

The King is vested with great power. Only he can declare war or negotiate peace or enter into treaties. No law passed by the legislature can become operative until his sanction is obtained. In an emergency he can issue a proclamation overriding any existing law. He is sworn to preserve the independence of his country at all costs. The Royal Coronation Oath is:

"I swear by Allah and the Holy Quran that in all my acts and deeds, I shall defend the true religion of Islam and the Independence of the Fatherland. I will respect the rights of my nation and will work for the progress and prosperity of the country. I will rule according to the Mohammedan Law and the Fundamental Law of Afghanistan."

The practical work of the administration is conducted by the Prime Minister and his cabinet, the divisions of which are:

War	Public Works
State	Health
Foreign Affairs	Post & Telegraphs
Interior	President of the Senate
Justice	President of the Assembly
Finance	Director-General of Mines
Education	Director-General of Agriculture
Commerce	

Ministers who have no seats in the Cabinet are:

Minister of the Court
Chief Secretary to the King

* * *

Out of India had come the British, who captured Kabul in 1839. They capitulated in 1842 with guarantee of safe conduct to the frontier, but en route were brutally massacred, 16,000 of them. In retaliation for this treachery, the British once again occupied the city, and upon withdrawal partially destroyed it.

In 1879 the British resident and his entire staff were slain. Then followed the Second Afghan War in which was fought the Battle of Maiwand on the desert plains near Khugiani, a near-massacre of the British forces.

Since 1880 great improvements have been effected, beginning with the enlightened rule of Abdur Rahman Khan. Kabul and vicinity especially were benefited. There were established cotton and woolen mills, cement plant, electric power plant, sugar mill, food processing and canning factories, leather goods industries, match factory, furniture factories, stone works, government arsenal and mint.

At least one conqueror, Sultan Babar, has been publicly and substantially remembered, although his rule was but for fifteen years and that some 450 years ago. His tomb stands on a grassy slope west of the city, a charming spot.

Not so with another, Bacha-i-Saqao, a brigand chief. Release from his cruel clutches is commemorated in stone. The shaft is in a public square named the Column of Neejat, or Deliverance. The extensive commercial area nearby is called the Neejat Bazaar. Across the broad boulevard lies Chaman-i-Huzuri, the parade and playgrounds where each year Afghan Independence is celebrated.

And so now this was Freedom Week. Large crowds from the city and surrounding country had gathered on this Chaman in celebration of the nation's independence. There were games each afternoon and evening in the Sports Arena. Fireworks, military parade, picnics; much as we Yankees would celebrate, or used to commemorate, the anniversary of American Independence before the days of the automobile. On this bright afternoon in late August at this altitude of 5,900 feet, the cool refreshment of passing breezes, the shade of the trees beside the wide canal, the broad expanse of Bermuda grass meadow over this extensive Chaman-i-Huzuri — all was indeed delightful. And especially so to me was this experience after the many months of desert life. So I walked aimlessly about in relaxed enjoyment, little noticed, although among the people I saw no foreigners.

There seemed to be no planned entertainment in progress on the grounds, except that soldiers were keeping clear an area in anticipation of the parade of the morrow.

Boys with water pipes walked about offering men a few drafts of tobacco smoke for which a small fee was charged.

A dozen bowing, whirling dancers performed to the rhythmic but irregular beating of keg drums. These men hopped and spun as they tossed their heads to right and left, long hair flopping about like a mop; a wild-like tribal performance of patriotic flavor. One by one they dropped out from exhaustion, to be replaced by others. The people everywhere delight in this exhibition of skill.

And then I became pickpocket conscious, although I had most of my money consisting of 2,500 *afghanis* in a money belt under my shirt. But foolishly, I decided, I had allowed the green edge of my passport to be visible, although securely buttoned down by the flap over my left hip pocket. Twice two men approached simultaneously from front and rear; quickly walked away with stealthly glances backward as I casually faced them.

Then there was the lad who stood fifty feet in front of and facing a man sitting cross-legged on the grass in attitude of prayer; face uplifted toward sky, palms open upward on knees. He fired questions at the boy in staccato tones. The lad as promptly responded, part of the time in a high-pitched voice looking upward. This word portrayal of some religious theme or scene, or perhaps an exercise on the catechism, drew a large and appreciative audience.

Following sundown the sports pavillion across a thorough-

365

fare and facing the sports arena was beautifully illuminated in colors. This, combined with lavish use of flags and bunting of black, green and red, surmounted by a large bright star, presented a most pleasing appearance. I wandered across the Chaman to the lake. From across the field floated Indian music and the strangely wild and lovely voice of Soraya. The people love her singing. Along the distant mountain ridges, upwards from the fortifications, were hurled rockets which exploded high above in brilliant display. Symbolical of freedom was this, of Afghanistan's independence; of that of my own beloved land so far away!

*   *   *

Dense crowds surged against the ropes, threatened to break through police lines along the boulevard in front of Neejat Bazaar, and all the way into the city along this route soon to be traversed by crack units of Afghanistan's armed might. The tonga driver had let me off here in front of the ropes, just across the boulevard from a narrow footbridge leading to the Chaman. I headed for this bridge, a signal for fifty men to duck under the ropes and follow. Police with swinging two-lash whips met them (or us). Some turned back. I proceeded unmolested, made the bridge, joined the crowds lining the south side of the Chaman under the trees, and found a point of vantage from which to take color pictures.

Across the open grassland at this early morning hour the military forces already were in massed formation preparatory to march.

And then for two hours and longer, without cessation, the hundreds of units in division after division; everything in infantry, cavalry, artillery, with war planes above, passed in review before a hundred thousand and more Afghans. Lining the main streets of this wonder city, focus of Afghan and Pakhtun culture and economy, these people were enthusiastic with the spirit of patriotism.

But the color pictures taken by me, seventy-two of them, should tell the story.

In the forefront rode the Commanding General followed by his staff on beautiful spirited horses. Boldly I, a lone foreigner from a conspicuous position, took their pictures using a Bolsey 35 mm. camera, a General Electric Light Exposure Meter. And I was sharply conscious of being observed by the high officers. I had no permit to take pictures. Of course, any moment now film and picture taking equipment will be confiscated. I'll go to prison. But no, nothing happened to me. Don't ask why. All about people were interested, let me have an unobstructed view; one man even held the camera while I slipped in another roll. I continued capturing views of scenes unknown to folks at home.

These men marched proudly, gallantly they rode their splendid mounts, erect and stern-faced manned the caissons and artillery pieces; rigorous, disciplined, nothing less.

Mortar units, pack outfits, mountain artillery batteries. I was seized with a strange yearning, for here were familiar animals in largest, sleekest perfection — Missouri mules!

* * *

It was at the Hotel de Kabul. Said Shir, "Say, Paul, do you know what this joker wants me to do?"

I turned to note a rather mysterious smile on the face of Alam Terakee, my friend and fellow-worker from Chah-i-anjir.

"Please, Alam wants to engage for future marriage his two-months old son to my daughter, if Hamina has one," announced Shir. "I told him no, no."

Avoiding the issue for the present, Alam said to me, "I'll call for you tomorrow evening at six. Want you to eat *pelau* with me in my home. While I'm with M.K.A. my wife and baby are living with her mother in Kabul."

And then Sayed and I took a bus to the Parliament buildings out about ten miles southwest from the city. The ap-

367

proach was along a lane of tall poplar trees. En route was much surburban development; modern looking stone bungalows on nice-sized lots. At the capital grounds we walked up a curving road to the front of a building as large, it seemed, as the State Capitol of California. It stood on a broad knoll surrounded by fine old shade trees, spacious lawns and flower gardens. Many women and children were picnicking here. The Parliament was not in session, so we were not allowed to enter the building. Sayed told me that he had been employed in the Finance Department at the Capitol here for four years before going to work for the Commission at Manzel Bagh. His hours had been 8 a.m. to 4:30 p.m.

On the way back to town a twelve-year-old boy greeted me in perfect English with, "Good morning," and gave a snappy salute. This he had been taught at school.

*　　*　　*

People were filling the grandstands; a sea of brown faces, again not another foreigner in sight. This is an oval-shaped stadium open at one end, the roofed-over pavilion being on the easterly side. I found a seat about half way up on the west side; bricks covered with loose coarse sand.

First to enter the arena were seven units each composed of 100 to 200 academy or college boys and young men clad in white shorts and shoes, and shirts of green, deep blue and pale blue.

Then followed a soccer game played on the Bermuda grass turf. Toward the end of the ball game some ten runners started off on the marathon race, which seemed to be ten kms. in length. In this one man held the lead far in advance for eight kms., then fell back to second place. Three runners finished the ten laps, not far apart; a splendid race.

In the school systems, I am told, sports and physical culture are considered of great importance as a part of one's

368

education. The player is there to win against all odds, not merely for the love of the game. He tries not to think of the possibility of defeat. A friendly match is truly a field of battle. If defeated, the player's sense of honor bitterly accuses him. Should he lose the game, he may cry like a child.

During the sports, music was furnished by a bagpipe band. The members were attired in scarlet caps and jackets, black slacks.

Regaining the blocked throughfare outside the arena, I was just in time to observe the street for blocks suddenly cleared by the police. No one lingered. A long black limousine rolled by, a small national flag above the windshield. Within, a man in black hat and dark business suit glanced about, partly arose. Seated beside him were two young men, probably in their teens. And this was the King of Afghanistan and his two sons. His Majesty, King Almutawakal Allallah Mohammed Zahir Shah, to be exact, the first two names having this signifigance:

"He who puts his trust in God."

And on this same evening I attended a movie featuring Soraya, Indian movie star, but nevertheless the "sweetheart of Afghanistan." All day long recordings of her songs had emanated from radio loudspeakers along the main streets; Indian songs, Indian accompaniement, plaintive sweet refrains, beautifully melodious, that to this day remain in my memory. And here she was in this Indian film; a girl of delicately exquisite beauty, in a lovely sari, with a beautiful voice, and alluringly lovely was her dancing. But in addition to these attainments what other qualities endeared her to the Afghan people? Simply these: her attributes of simplicity, sincerity, modesty, of being unsophisticated, unaffected.

* * *

Again I was impressed with a feeling of out-of-placeness as concerned my own attire. But how could one transport a good suit with him to the capital city, when traveling under the circumstances just experienced by me? Now we had arrived at Paghman, eighteen miles northwesterly from Kabul across the Chardeh (four villages) Plain, and some 7,200 feet in elevation, well up on the southern slopes of the lofty Hindu Kush. In suntans, there I was. (It's true I wore a karakul cap—quite in style.) But my companions each were immaculate in brown and blue tailored suits, oxfords, white shirts, and new karakul caps to match.

We walked along a winding trail toward the King's Gardens. Paghman, a small town meticuously clean, is a summer resort — a haven for those in need of rest. All about on the hillsides are picturesque adobe and stone bungalows with exquisite terraces of shrubbery and colorful flowers, and winding walks and lanes.

Noor Mohammed is an instructor in the English college at Kabul (with some 4,000 students, he says). He teaches the Persian language. Seeing what looked to be the largest English walnut tree I had ever observed — fully 100 feet high and seven feet in diameter — I had both the young men pose in its shade for a picture.

And now we entered the King's Gardens, a wonderful terraced area overlooking Chardeh Plains. In beds alongside spacious lawns, roses, cannas, verbenas grew in profusion, and there were many varieties of shrubs. In the light breeze and clear sunshine, the swaying poplars were enveloped in a changing haze of silvery brilliance. The towering mountains to the north, with but one visible patch of snow, appeared green but not heavily covered with vegetation. Ten to fifteen miles away reared a peak to 15,400 feet elevation. Others far away to the northeast brushed the sky at 17,980 and 19,900 feet, on ranges bordering the Panshir (five lions) River watershed, tributary to the Kabul River.

On this afternoon there appeared less than a half-dozen visitors. A gardener entering the area with a large lawnmower on the back of a burro informed us the King had just arrived. Cautiously parting some shrubs at the top of a declivity, Noor Mohammed motioned me to peer down on the scene below.

There, on a broad terrace surrounded by smooth lawns of flawless freshness, with gorgeous flowers in sunken gardens and a scattering of shade trees, stood a modest dwelling, one-storied with low sweeping lines and a wide veranda and patios covered by pergolas. White, trimmed in yellow, were the colors of this attractive bungalow. That much I grasped in a fleeting moment, for a soldier patrolling nearby minutes before had cautioned us, "Don't look down over there!"

"The king's summer home?" I murmured.

"Ba-lee," nodded Noor.

Turning to leave we were soon confronted along the narrow trail by a lad of twelve to fourteen, his little sister and his mother, presumably, only loosely veiled. They were walking in the very direction toward which we but moments before had been so circumspectly gazing downward.

"What is the boy saying, Sayed?" I inquired, for the little fellow had just bowed to me ever so politely.

"He is saying, 'We want you to visit our home'."

"Sayed, his gesture is so simple and sincere. Tell him, tell his mother and little sister, from the bottom of my heart I thank them." And with misty eyes, I smiled and waved them goodbye.

The ozone-laden air at Paghman was so delightfully pure, dry, cool and invigorating; the mountain solitude; the azure sky with but a scattering of fleecy clouds — all caused a longing to remain here on an extended Afghan holiday, to become acquainted with the fastnesses of these mighty Hindu Kush — even to explore the passes and look down over the other side upon the valley of the Oxus River and the plains of Russia, perhaps, less than 100 miles away.

*   *   *

AFGHANISTAN VENTURE

At Alam's suggestion the tonga driver had disregarded a policeman's warning and turned into a street crowded to full width with pedestrians. At the next intersection another policeman demanded an explanation, forcing the vehicle to the curb to await investigation by higher authority. The driver posed undisturbed. Alam appeared worried, and argued vociferously with the law. Surprisingly soon a ranking officer appeared, talked in low tones to the policeman, who after all was only doing his duty, smiled and waved us on.

For many blocks on a broad, paved, well-lighted street, the horse jogged along, then suddenly turned into a pitch-black alley, zigzagged for a kilometer, and halted.

Alam walked fast. Once I lost him and turned down a blind passageway. "Mr. Paul — Polijens!" sounded a voice in the dark distance, seemingly from a wrong direction.

And we both chuckled in glee, as Alam fumbled for matches with which to find our way up to a second story and an apartment well lighted with both candles and electricity.

Would I meet Alam's famliy, his wife and baby of whom Alam had spoken quite proudly? We would see.

Soon I was comfortably seated on a rug with bolster to lean upon. A young boy and girl entered then. Brother and sister? No, cousins, said Alam; Mullalah was the girl's name, and she was in third grade at school. And a young man who then entered served tea. He was a brother-in-law, Abdullah. Did I speak German? No, I'd had only two years of it in high school. He was a college student — studied physics, chemistry, geography, languages — was planning to become a mechanical engineer.

Then Alam invited me into the next room. Here's where I meet the wife, and the rest of the family, thought I. But no, nor all evening. It's just not done in Afghanistan; that's for sure.

And then we gathered about on rugs to a bounteous repast. "Now you must eat plenty or we will all be unhappy," said Alam.

And there were *pelau,* chicken, mutton, potatoes, fried cucumbers, bread, nuts and candy — most delicious.

After that we retired to the living room and visited with a friend who had just returned from Iran. He'd been there eighteen years. His name was Abdul Kim, and he knew something about oil field development.

"Your government is selecting twenty M-K-A mechanics for sending to Saudi Arabia. They will work in the oil fields and learn to drill wells. Excellent idea. Possibly there is oil in the Seistan Basin and the lower Helmand Valley?" I suggested.

Said Abdul Kim: "Well, we think the big field is around Herat. That is, along the Hari River near Tirpul within fifteen miles of the Iran frontier."

"Sometime ago you Americans offered to develop this field," said Alam. "But the British and the Russians lodged objections against this with our government. So we dropped the idea temporarily."

"Julaladin tells me of oil indications he observed while with an American geologist in the Oxus River country," I ventured. "You fear to develop it because of the Russians?"

"Well, no, not anymore. We'll go ahead with it soon," countered Kim.

"There are fields available in the Province of Mazar-i-Sharif, also near Maimana. This is only about twenty-five miles from our border with the Soviets, in the northwest Province of Maimana," said Alam. "What we need most are good roads, along with the development of our mineral resources. Minerologists, Afghan and foreign, have explored our mountains, and have found coal, iron, chrome, lead, gold — even rubies."

"Rubies? Well, everywhere I've gone, I keep looking

in the gravels of your stream beds — out on the open desert — for signs of minerals," I said. "M-K-A located a mountain of chrome deposits. My friend, Walt Flannery of New York City, had charge of diamond drill operations all over the company's Afghan projects. He investigated this mountain near Kabul, which was exceedingly rich in chrome, he told me."

"Yes, that's right. It's of tremendous value! We have found rubies at Arghandeh Pass, twelve miles out of Kabul. You came through there. And also at Jagdalak, fifty miles east. And there's a hill of iron ore, eighteen miles of it, near Paghman, where you were today, Paul," explained Alam. "There's lead in six different localities."

"Say, Alam, do you know that the brigands at Haji Alam tie lead with wire to the end of their clubs, to hold up caravans and kill the drivers? Ask Shir Ahmad; he knows. We had a run-in with them on last 4th of July. Do you suppose they mine lead near Haji Alam? And there's gold at Paj Pass, I'm told — under the road on the north approach," I said.

"Well, our government is alive to the nation's potential mineral resources and wants to develop metallurgical and chemical industries — is keen to exploit them," said Abdul Kim. "But this requires capital, which we don't possess."

"Is it true, Alam, that in the harbor at Karachi several shiploads of Afghan ore have been anchored for at least two years? The Pakistani won't give them clearance? Or what is the trouble?" I asked.

And so on went the conversation throughout this delightful evening spent in the home of my friend, Alam Teraki.

"Now, Paul," said Alam, "it's ten o'clock. You have a long journey ahead of you tomorrow. So whenever you are ready, Abdullah will see that you get back to Hotel de Kabul."

This was an evening long to be treasured in my memory. And perchance should Alam Teraki read these notes, please may he bear with me for my inability to quote the picturesque wording that my Afghan friends used (their manner of expression in English slightly different from that of an American) and my own crude attempts to talk in their language.

*   *   *

Up before daylight at Hotel de Kabul, packed, paid hotel bill — 400 afghanis ($12.00) for five night's lodging and thirteen meals — tipped night clerk five *afghanis,* waiter ten *afghanis,* porter two *afghanis,* took tonga to bus depot.

Here were Hosain, laboratory technician at hospital, an X-ray specialist en route to visit his mechanic brother at Chah-i-anjir. Also Sayed and Ghulam Sakhai. Ghulam shouted, "Come out here. Shir and Hamina are coming!"

Sure enough. Snappily down the middle of the wide street walked the pair, she in a black purdah (not so far along as Shir had supposed, thought I). Without ado Shir turned off to the bus station, passing a leather case to her. She continued straight ahead with never a gesture or sideward or backward glance.

In rolled the Afghan Mail, white and clean-looking, with aisle the length of the vehicle, high straight-back chairs. It was the acme of comfort; we would ride in luxury to Kandahar. But, no, this goes north over the Hindu Kush to Mazar-i-Sharif. Ghulam Sakhai climbs aboard; off to his wedding, then back to the Boghra Project. Our bus pulls up, identical to one we came on from Kandahar except it has an aisle halfway through. Shir cajoled the driver into selling him a ticket for 150 afghanis even though the bus was full; he would sit to left of driver on the steps. Regular tickets like mine cost ninety-five *afghanis.*

This journey over the same road as before was uneventful. We left Kabul at 9:30 a.m. and at Saiydabad near noon the coach stopped to let everyone out for a break. We ate watermelons, and Shir and I got pictures of a splendid looking rice field ready for harvest. The water had been drained off. At this place also we transferred the water jug from its position as a stumbling block in the aisle — and a ready source of water supply for many of the passengers — to outside on the roof within the ring of a spare tire, and with the other baggage. A few jolts over the bumpy road as our journey continued, and water began running down, spraying the travelers next the open windows. They exchanged glances of questioning amusement, apparently in the belief passengers rode above on the open deck; hastily closed the windows, watched the water trickle over the dusty glass until after an hour the thing was empty and the windows dry and streaked.

My seatmate, Reza, wanted to carry on a long conversation. He appeared to be chewing on a black waxy substance he would take from a pouch, also on green powder from a small flat tin; opium, and dried leaves of the hemp, *charss* (marijuana)? I would doze off to sleep, only to be awakened by being elbowed with a coarse demand in English, "You asleep?" And this was beginning to attract amused attention from other passengers. So then I would pretend to be very much asleep, very difficult in fact to awaken, and with each pitch of the bus I would sway violently, crushing my seatmate against the window. Soon getting the purport of this defensive treatment on my part, even though dazed, Reza subsided into a deep slumber accompanied by irregular snorts. He was still a center of entertainment, especially from two army officers up front.

Near Moqor (Mookoor) all left the bus. There was only an old adobe ruin here, and twenty Moslems facing Mecca lined up for evening devotions. A strange scene this; a one-third moon shone from a clear sky to our left, the sun lowered behind the mountains, nomad camps lay scattered about; camels, goats, children.

And here was a spring beside the road, the outlet of a *kareese*. Three women filled goat skins with water. An army officer holding thumbs and forefingers in front of his eyes said "Aks-Aks," and suggested I get a picture of them. But I looked at the light conditions over the nearby mountains, then at the women (whose faces it's true were very brown, almost black) and said, "Too dark, too dark!" And why that caused such an outburst of mirth, I don't know yet.

At Kalat-i-Ghilzai, the driver walked along the main street in the darkness shouting, "Post-vala-ah, post-vala!" searching for the postmaster. The mail from Kabul was due in the Kandahar post office before eight a.m., or the driver would forfeit fifty *afganis*.

At Shahr-i-Safa I joined "Shorty" Becan and Shir Ahmad in eating three eggs apiece fried in ghee, and a slab of bread. Shir had procured onions and tomatoes, fixed what he termed a "sal-laad," which was very good. Here we waited three hours, out of petrol, tried to sleep on an adobe platform away from a chilling north wind. Finally the driver collected five *afghanis* from each passenger for purchase of fuel and we were on our way.

Near Azam Kala at dawn we stopped to wash and clean up. Here we drew water from a well with a windlass, and had morning devotions.

Near Manzel Bagh, "Shorty" bound for Kajakai Dam, and Shir and I debarked. Lastly, I ascended to the baggage deck; descended with a thermos jug in one hand and with the other grasped rounds of the steel ladder. Missing the bottom round, I went sprawling headlong, and the jinx rolled defiantly down a decline.

Seven-thirty a.m. at M-K-A hospital:

Mrs. Oleson, nurse applying bandage: "That fist struck a hard blow."

AFGHANISTAN VENTURE

Doctor Black: "When did this happen?"

PSJ: "This morning at dawn." As nurse and doctor exchanged puzzled glances, I strode out to my waiting car bound for Arghandab Dam.

> "The important criterion is not the rate of progress
> of a people, but the standard of life its leaders
> espouse and to which they aspire."
>
> Justice William O. Douglas

XVIII
Moslem Holiday

Abraham & Isaac
Easter?
Picturesque Scene
Religion — State — Military — in One
Id Prayers
Anywhere — Five Times Daily
A Lone Foreigner
Moslem Benediction
Salute to the Colors!
In a Mosque — Memorial Service

CHAPTER XVIII

Moslem Holiday

THIS WAS Id (eed) Day all over Afghanistan; this late day in August. A festival occasion based upon the biblical story of Abraham declared to have been tempted to offer up his only son, Isaac, as a burnt offering to the Lord, but at the last moment sacrificed a sheep instead. So that's why today flocks of sheep were being driven through the streets of Kandahar and sold off singly to families for feasting, much as we would use turkeys on Christmas. In fact our friends would try to explain in English to us Americans, "This is Christmas." I for one, however, failed to understand the comparison. It was more like Easter. People put on their finest attire. Leaving through the north gate of this ancient walled city, they assembled in the early morning on the desert in a large space surrounded by a low wall. Along the westerly side of this was a small, white-domed mosque. Here were a scattering of hoary tamarisk trees, gnarled and smoky gray.

AFGHANISTAN VENTURE

The area was marked off with lime in long strips six feet wide. Men and boys wore their best turbans of sky blue and clean white. Young girls were picturesque in filmy floating coverings of white, green, crimson, golden, blue, pink; with fancy waists, pantaloons and sandals, earrings, and shiny metallic discs in bands about the head or over one nostril.

I saw no other foreigners. I had no idea how people might react to my taking color pictures of this scenic occasion so I tried to remain inconspicuous. Once I was politely invited by a lieutenant to move back toward the east wall so as not to walk between the people and the mosque, and finally climbed on top of the wall.

Preceded by a brass band and interspersed with the national colors of black, green and red and drum and bugle corps, the local military forces paraded from the presidio. They filled a place reserved for them immediately in front of the mosque in long faded green lines. The people arose as the Governor-General and his staff entered last and took places in the open mosque facing a little southwesterly toward Mecca.

Then, led by the Governor-General, there began the offering of congregational Id prayers during which in unison and perfect solemnity 10,000 Moslems executed three series of attitudes in humble petition to Allah. This was no different than when I had seen hundreds of men serenely pray five times a day out on the construction jobs mid loud clatter of machinery; in the wheat fields at harvest time during the intense heat of mid-afternoon, in the cool of the evening far out on the desert at camps of the nomads. With shoes removed they first stood up straight with thumbs to ears, open palms to the front facing Mecca, appearing to listen; then with hands folded at belt line, head bowed in reverence; next with knees and back straight, hands on knees, they meditated; then they went down on knees and elbows with hands and forehead to the ground in deep humility; next sat upright on heels, knees to the ground, head erect, hands to the front at chest level with palms up, and prayed for several minutes; then stood up straight again. This procedure repeated twice more. This all had tremendous meaning to them.

Then the military reformed in such a way as to leave an aisle up to the mosque. Prominent personages, I assumed, passed forward and then returned to the rear, having been given some special benediction. To satisfy my curiosity about this particular point, I casually strolled forward myself, to get a near view. Several men with well trimmed black beards and mustaches, pure white turbans and flowing or loose garments, seized my right hand in both of theirs and bowed slightly, placing one hand to breast. What they said I could not understand, but they smiled in a friendly manner. In addition one pushed back my karakul cap, then drew his open palm down over my forehead and face.

To close the services and dismiss the people the Governor-General took his post in front of the troops and in loud staccato tones commanded:

Hazer_____bash! (Attention!)
Peesh_____fang! (Present_____arms!)

Bugles sounded a salute to the colors, cannons outside the walls boomed a ten-gun salute, the band played the national anthem.

Az selah taht! (Order_____arms!)
Rehat_____bash! (Stand at_____ease!

Soon the troops were marching briskly away with colors floating in the gentle breeze, and to the flare of trumpets and beating drums. The crowd dispersed.

* * *

"Follow me. Do as I do," said Shir Ahmad.

It was in Kandahar. With shoes removed I was entering a mosque for the first time. We settled ourselves cross-legged on mats. The floor was entirely covered with coarse woven reeds, fresh and clean. This 75-foot by 100-foot assembly place through high open windows was flooded with sunshine and the walls and ceiling were a brilliant white. The high ceiling was of half cylinders.

To my right sat Sayet Wuhdut Shah Khan, director general, technical branch, of the Royal Afghan Commission for M-K-A projects; a Cornell graduate, a civil engineer.

These services, at which many friends had gathered, were in memory of a young man, a quiet thoughtful fellow, it was said, who the day before had been overtaken by a fatal accident. He had been hit by a company truck at Manzel Bagh and was buried before sundown. The victim's family lived in Kabul. So Mr. Shah had taken over as if the twenty-two-year-old lad were his own son.

The mullah, a handsome man of about thirty-five, was seated cross-legged at the end of a long rug. He swayed forward and back as he read from the Koran. I could clearly see from our side view the large clear-cut black script in Arabic on the yellow pages of a long and narrow book. This holy man intoned in Arabic slowly and distinctly.

During the reading I listened and watched intently; held both hands palms up and open across knees.

Then the mullah would close the book, and in the same tone continue in prayer, at the end of which I followed the others by raising both hands to forehead and slowly down over face.

This service was repeated three times, the reading of the Koran and prayer, and in my own mind and own way I offered to Allah what I thought suitable.

As we left the mosque, a well dressed man in the yard

hurried to grasp my hand in sincerity and apparent appreciation.

Shir Ahmad said in answer to my questions, "Well, I'll explain, please. It was just that the mullah read appropriate verses from the Koran and offered prayers to God that He would forgive, or make allowances for any shortcomings of the young man; do the best he could for him in heaven."

"Well, Shir, that tallies exactly with what I had in mind," said I.

And then Shir explained about Koosh Del, driver of the truck. As in any accident of this kind, the Government assumes the driver is wholly responsible. So Koosh had fled to a mosque to avoid arrest, and would remain there sustained on food provided by his friends until he could leave unnoticed for another part of the country.

> "Turn, therefore, thy face towards the holy
> temple of Mecca; and wherever ye be, turn
> your faces towards that place."
>
> The Koran.

XIX
Comes the Dawn --
A New Era

CHAPTER XIX

Comes the Dawn -- A New Era

IT WAS AT our canal construction camp on the desert,
late evening in the mess hall. In progress was a "bull
session" over coffee, tea, or Pabst Blue Ribbon and sandwiches before retiring. Here events of the job were discussed. Here men made comparisons as to the number of
days left until they would embark for home; what countries,
what cities they proposed to visit along the way. Mr. H. A.
Berry, Chief Administrative Assistant and from the faculty
of a California university, with his gracious wife, had joined
us. Said he, "Jones, I trust you are making ample notes on
our life and experiences in Afghanistan. I have read some
of your reports in office at Kandahar and they make good
reading; contain much first-hand information."

And John Lindquist, Camp Manager, had added, "Yes, I
always read Paul's accounts when I go to Kandahar; he's got
interesting facts we wouldn't know about otherwise," and
poured another glass of beer.

And from Engineer Joe Smith of Seattle, somewhat of a philosopher, "People in the States are interested in this little-known kingdom. There should be a record made of what we see. After all we're just a few foreigners who, because of the M-K project, are privileged to be in the country. Otherwise never."

Said I, pouring another cup of tea, "Well, I do conscientiously keep a diary and make frequent written reports to the General Manager at Kandahar. I keep my friends and home folks interested (I hope) through letters. In the out country I do meet some dangerous people. Just the other day Ted expressed concern about my safety. "Jones, you're apt to get shot right through the heart!"

"But you don't dare show timidity," I said. "Just go prepared and you'll be safe. And Ted, should your prediction ever materialize, use diesel fuel and fire on the open desert before sundown. Just forward the ashes home by plane from Karachi! It would be that simple."

And as Abdul's helpers cleared away the table, "We'll be looking for your write-up on Afghanistan; O.K. Paul?" And then all adjourned to a sound sleep in the cool of the desert night.

Here was autumn with its glorious days of sunshine and frostless nights. Flocking in from the colder north came many wildfowl to settle on the rivers, canals and desert swamp lands. But *mirabs* (ditchtenders), many of them, were suffering from malaria, a deadly disease. Our Medical Department had fought it with aralen and paludrine, the efficacy of which was emphasized:

"The aralen does not prevent malarial infection but suppresses the symptons and cures the disease without one's knowing he has had malaria. The paludrine prevents the infection or infestation of the red blood cells by the malarial parasite and thus prevents the illness from occurring.

"For persons who have never had malaria, paludrine

390

is preferred for its prevention. The recommended dosage in the Kandahar area is one tablet per week. For personnel in all other areas, two tablets a week at three to four day intervals is recommended. This same instruction also applies to anyone who has had malaria in the past and has been completely cured before now.

"Aralen is to be used by all personnel who have had malaria recently or exposed to it so recently as to likely have it in the incubation phase, which lasts about two weeks. Such persons may shift from aralen to paludrine by taking both simultaneously for a period of two or three weeks and then dropping the aralen. The prophylactic dosage for aralen is two tablets a week for such regions as Manzel Bagh, and four per week in areas more heavily infested with mosquitos. The dose is two tablets every six hours for three doses, then two tablets daily for a minimum of nine days more."

This was the manner of using the ammunition prescribed by the M-K-A Medical Department in its battle against the scourge of the ages, malaria, in so much as it affected the workers in Afghanistan on this modern construction job.

Being no respecter of persons, this malady had felled one of the greatest generals of all time. Thrusting through Afghanistan, he had extended his empire for 3,000 miles from Greece to the Indus River in 324 B.C., and had turned back across the deserts to Susa (in modern Iran). There at the age of thirty-three, Alexander the Great succumbed to malaria.

Our Medical Director, Doctor W. A. Black, likewise had ideas about combatting the debilitating effects of extreme heat conditions:

"During the hot summer months it is advisable to take extra salt to make up for that lost in perspiration, and thus prevent heat cramps developing in the muscles.

"At meal times it is suggested that one-quarter more

391

salt be used than normally. In mid-morning and mid-afternoon, for personnel working outdoors or in hot indoor places, one or two salt tablets should be taken with a glass or two of water. The number of tablets to be taken depends upon how profusely a person is perspiring. A rough check on this is that when salt is left behind on clothing after the perspiration dries, ample salt has been taken. The salt tablets are coated with a substance which prevents their being dissolved in the stomach or in the water. This prevents nausea from developing. The salt tablets then pass into the intestines where they are dissolved and absorbed. Contraindications to the taking of additional salt tablets is any unusual swelling in the tissues anywhere in the body, particularly in the legs, hands and face."

And so it was that dispensaries were placed at convenient places about the mess halls where men could help themselves to the proper amount of salt to maintain normal energy during the heat of the summer.

Not only that, vitamin capsules were made readily available in the mess hall at Manzel Bagh.

*   *   *

Thanksgiving Day, *November 27, 1952*

Note from diary: 'Splendid dinner in camp — turkey, etc., etc., twenty-two at one long table, Americans, Italians, Filipinos. Many men have come down from Kajakai Dam since the completion of the earth fill there ten days ago.'

And so engineering plans on a large scale were being consummated on this tremendous Afghan irrigation project.

On both of the dam construction jobs men had been surplused to go home, or to leave for M-K projects in other countries, as the major phases of this spectacular undertaking were completed. Storage of water was underway at

392

Arghandab, 350,000 acre-feet; at Kajakai this would begin in the spring — 3,000,000 to 4,000,000 acre-feet of it.

At Arghandab reservoir, the Commission had arbitrarily ordered cessation, or curtailment of water releases at one juncture. This had interfered with the supplying of irrigation water we had definitely promised to owners of new grape plantings, also to new crop acreages already planted and dependent upon this new and additional source of moisture hitherto unavailable on so large a scale in the late summer and fall. Because of the Arghandab reservoir, irrigated acreage in the valley was being increased from 90,000 to 120,000 or more; that is, provided storage and distribution of water would be efficiently managed.

But in addition, this artificial water shortage was leaving dry the city of Kandahar with its 60,000 people. This lasted for some twelve days, during which the city's only source of supply in quantity, the Patow Canal, was but a series of small, shallow, stagnant pools.

And the reason for this rugged procedure on the part of the Royal Afghan Commission? To exert pressure upon the people for the payment of water taxes.

On the Boghra Project, the forty-two-mile long Shamalon Canal paralleling the Helmand River was just about finished. Come spring, eight existing valley canals, hitherto high and dry in late summer and fall, would be amply supplied every month of the year and 55,000 acres would yield abundantly. A new era of prosperity was opening for the Helmand River valley between Girishk and Shamalon.

The main Boghra Canal was complete, except for the construction of several concrete checks. However, a certain difficulty had developed. Underlying strata of "gutch," or gypsum, had been encountered in canal excavation. This mineral, hydrous calcium sulphate, readily absorbs water and is dissolved by it. Hence seepage from the canal followed the resulting cavities and channels, and on a down grade traveled long distances where the gypsum was continuous. The presence of this condition was indicated by coffee brown or black alkaline deposit upon the ground surface, rendering the soil unfit for plant growth.

Where small areas of gutch were causing canal leakage, it appeared that a remedy to the situation was ample excavation of these outcroppings followed by replacement with compacted impervious materials readily available nearby. Also, that on any future canal construction through such gutch-impregnated areas, the wetted perimeter of the waterway shold be lined with compacted impervious materials of such thickness as would prevent escape of the water. Also no material containing gutch should be allowed in the canal banks. It was noted that apart from portions of the canal affected by gutch, seepage was surprisingly lacking elsewhere.

Under the Boghra Canal, the Ft. Nad-i-ali lateral systems were completed. Some 16,000 acres were thus open to settlement. Here could settle down some 3,500 nomadic people, who would live at the villages in the adobe dwellings recently completed by Jan Mohammed. These lands were being offered for assignment to families of such people on the following basis:

The first year the Government provides seed, oxen, plows, water and all sustenance.

During the second year the settler is on his own.

The third year and thereafter the settler pays taxes — a percentage of the crop returns.

After a period of time as of yet undisclosed, he would own the land.

And now with the advent of colder weather, tribesmen and farmers from distant places were moving into these villages; preparing to cultivate, irrigate and seed the land assigned them by the Agricultural Exploitation Department at Nad-i-ali, of which Aslam Khan was in charge.

However, conditions were different on the East Marja, although the area is traversed by the completed sixty-two mile long main canal which can run an ample supply of water. But funds for the construction and completion of the laterals had not materialized. Sandy, silty, smooth, of good slope and deep fertile soil, this East Marja with its sparse covering of low sagebrush reminds one of parts of Idaho, eastern Oregon and Washington which once looked just like this, but which now are among the most productive agricultural regions of the United States. Here during the summer and fall had come tribesmen on camel trains from as far away as Ghazni, Baluchistan and Chakhansur to occupy these lands. The Government had given them permission to do this on a temporary basis while awaiting assignment to lands under completed lateral systems, to divert water from the Boghra in ditches of their own making for the raising of food for man and animals. And in this they were doing surprisingly well.

In October, Abdur Rahim, an assistant of Aslam Khan, had been assigned to work with me, to accompany me on my rounds every day. He had received a college education at Kabul, had specialized in agriculture and worked for Frank Youngs, director of the Nad-i-ali agricultural experiment station. He had a home with his wife and children at Nad-i-ali. But, although I had eaten several meals in Abdur's home, by Afghan custom I was never to meet the missus.

Every day Abdur and I would contact Ibrahim, who had supervision over forty *mirabs*. He was from Ghazni where lived his three wives. A picturesque figure was Ibrahim. Rather oldish, but keen of mind, alert and physically active, and with a mustache that added individuality, he rode erect and dignified on a well groomed horse. He dwelt with his two sons, *mirabs*, in an adobe hut erected by the company along the canal. He was said to be an ex-army colonel, and I well believed it.

One morning we three went to the camp of the Baluch in East Marja; we had heard their chief, Jamai, was sick and dying. We had known Jamai for months. The tribespeople grouped about us. We followed a son, Daulet, to the quarters of the old man. On the bare ground he lay covered by sheepskins and fleeces. The top of his abode, black strips of coarse woven wool, had been lifted from the tamarisk latticework supports. This arrangement still protected from the winds and in addition allowed the warm sunshine to pour in.

The chief's wife lay on the ground near him with less covering. Were Jamai one hundred and twenty years old as he claimed, the wife could well have been over one hundred. Her black eyes searched my face inquiringly. In return, by look and expression of countenance, I attempted to convey to this venerable centenarian my great respect and well wishes for herself, Jamai, and all their tribespeople.

Jamai mumbled incoherently.

"What does he say?" we asked Daulet.

"Just that he does not know what is to become of his people; where can they obtain land and water?" interpreted Abdur Rahim.

"Tell the chief that Aslam Khan and all of us are exerting every effort to get his people happily settled on the irrigated lands," I explained to Abdur, who in turn told Daulet.

Jamai I had last seen astride a rapidly moving camel. He was then on his way to inspect fields in which his tribesmen were working; their irrigation ditches, their growing melons, beans, corn, carrots, sorghum, quinjet. (This quinjet has possibilities. It looks like a thrifty rag weed and has large pods within which are an abundance of edible, flat oily seeds like flax.)

Now, as Daulet repeated to him our message, the chief opened his eyes and his countenance flashed a look of understanding and peace. He moved slightly, then relaxed, motionless. The spirit of this courageous, unselfish Baluch leader, patriarch of the tribe, had gone to Allah. Daulet lay the fleece gently over his father's shoulders and face.

We respectfully saluted the elderly woman, now so alone. Soon, any hour, she too would depart. In silence we left the Baluch camp and its saddened people.

So, each day our activities took us afar over the Boghra and Arghandab Valley projects. Returning to camp one late afternoon, I was surrounded immediately by Kharoti tribesmen and their chief, a husky, tall, colorful-looking fellow with large revolver in his belt and a well-filled black ammunition bandolier over his right shoulder. Tall, brown, with closely-trimmed black beard and whiskers, and of patrician features, he presented a striking appearance. He shook my hand and was saying something in Pakhtu earnestly, the full meaning of which I did not grasp. I glanced about for a *tageman* to interpret and at that moment the door to the barracks nearby opened and out walked Ali, driver of a "Point Four" car that had just arrived from Kabul, followed by a familiar looking American.

"Ali, what is the chief saying, please?" I said.

"That he is deeply joyed and grateful that you have made it possible for his people to receive plenty of water with which to grow their crops. Says he likes you, that you are a 'brother' to all of his tribe," interpreted Ali.

Turning, I faced — of all men; the world isn't so big after all — Stanley Elcock, fellow civil engineer and former co-worker with the U. S. Bureau of Reclamation at Stockton, California — a friend indeed from home! He stood there smiling and explained that about two years' work under our State Department in this land of the Afghans confronted him, an engineering assignment under the American technical aid program.

*   *   *

397

AFGHANISTAN VENTURE

The situation along the Shamalon Canal was then demanding much attention. Abdur and I, often accompanied by Ibrahim, made frequent trips down the valley over a road atop the canal bank in places almost impassable because of a six-inch layer of fine dust. Construction was nearing completion and this important carrier of water to a thirsty, fertile valley was about to pass into the operating stage. In anticipation of this, much "spade work" preparation remained to be done.

Between times, Abdur Rahim was giving me a portrayal of some things of which hitherto I had been unaware. Passing the provincial prison grounds in the outskirts of Kandahar one late afternoon, he said. "Oh, there are ninety-one Russian mens in there. They are from Kabul."

Said I, "Why are they under arrest?"

"Oh, they gets news!" replied Abdur. "There are twenty-nine Pakistani in there, too. They gets news!"

"Well, Abdur, this is enlightening," I rejoined. "You mean spies?"

"Oh, yes — spies. Have no passports maybe. Political prisoners, foreign or Afghan, are dealt with severely; cast into dark cells for three years," said Abdur. "An Afghan is afraid to cross into Pakistan without a passport. Pakistani are cruel to prisoners; may even gouge out their eyes by hand."

*　　　*　　　*

January 9, 1953

We were entering Rubah (fox) village. Men dashed from dwellings excitedly brandishing stout clubs. Hovering over the far end of the street was a low cloud of dust. Reluctantly withdrawing from the village to the open desert was a large pack of gray wolves; big, lean, hungry-looking

398

rascals. An Afghan winter was setting in. Shepherds would now be doubly on guard.

Later we passed a lone herder with his flock far out on the desert. With unexpected suddenness — out of nowhere seemingly — a huge husky at high speed hit the left front wheel of the Ford a bounding blow and deflected our course. Had it been a wolf or man instead of a rubber tire, the target would have suffered broken legs, been knocked senseless, or even killed. Surprised by the wheel's unsuspected resistance, partly run over and bruised, the animal limped slowly back toward his master, who I felt certain had signaled the dog to attack. To Abdul I remarked:

"In animal-like ignorance that fellow blames me. We'll be on guard! Most likely the dog will die from the blow."

And sure enough, days later as we returned from the West Marja in another vicinity, this same shepherd hailed us and wanted a ride to Ft. Nad-i-ali. Here were some 300 sheep; no dog, no other shepherd. This fellow would leave his sheep unguarded and ride with us to Ft. Nad-i-ali!

"He's up to something, Abdur," I said, but nevertheless pulled up near him. Abdur, beside me, and Baran, in the rear seat, sat fixed and dumb. Then as the man moved to get aboard he exposed a short stout club with gnarled and knotted end which he until then had kept concealed under his long shepherd cloak. I stepped on the gas throttle. With a roar the Ford picked up speed. We circled around and around the surprised and frustrated fellow and made an occasional spurt directly at him. Following this gesture of retaliation we continued our way across this Dasht-i- Margo.

"You were angry with him, Pol-i-jens," said Abdur. "But these people don't know you and are suspicious of foreigners. They can't understand what you say. Besides they want our valuables, and would kill us as they would a wolf even for our clothing, thinking nothing of it."

One afternoon on foot we followed through on a water

399

situation to a group of huts on the fringe of the Shamalon project. "Here live *bekhans,* merchants from India," said Abdur. A man lay beside a wall. He raised his shirt, pointed to his ribs and said he hadn't eaten for three days, but to me he didn't appear emaciated. Just then some women leaned over a broken adobe fence and laughed merrily. Stripped to the waist myself, I couldn't decide whether I was the object of their frivolity, or was it our apparent gullibility at showing sympathy for this victim of some "cruel circumstance."

"Oh," said another man hurrying over, "he tells everyone that. He's so angry he won't eat; he has a family of girls!"

At this a heated argument developed between Abdur and the two men. "This is none of our business! Let's get out of here, Abdur!" I shouted.

At another time with Ghulam Sakhai, I was hailed by a young woman beside the road holding up a pumpkin. She motioned for a ride. This was most unusual. I hadn't seen it done in Afghanistan before. She wore no veil.

"It's OK to let her aboard, Ghulam?" I ventured.

"Ba-le — oh, yes!" my friend agreed with alacrity.

Had I heard correctly! My observations heretofore indicated that to menfolks, women appeared non-existent. But for several miles and until we came to one of the new farm villages where she wanted off, this unabashed young woman chatted incessantly. Bidding me goodbye, she added in Persian, "I will pray for you!"

"Say, Ghulam, this reminds me. Driving along through the outskirts of Kandahar I've been pleasantly surprised on several occasions. At such times no men were in evidence. And no women other than the one approaching in black purdah heavily veiled. What happened? Just this. Noting through the narrow slit before one eye that she was being observed by a curious American, what did she do? With one pass she flung off all covering about her head and shoulders and with dignity and poise smiled reservedly and continued on her way. Did you know some of your women do that? And Ghulam, if such few as I've seen are fair samples, I must say your country is to be congratulated on the beauty and attractiveness of its women . . . their patrician bearing and modest dignity!"

To these comments, made with enthusiasm, Ghulam looked somewhat puzzled. He smiled, remained silent.

* * *

It was at the engineering headquarters in Manzel Bagh. Heavy frost covered the lawns and sunken gardens, but the clear sky and bright morning sun promised a clear warm day. Already the company gardeners were bringing out the numerous potted plants they had removed to protective cover the previous evening. Geraniums, asters, chrysanthemums — now in their flowering glory — enlivened the grounds with cheer and color.

Before going-to-work time, Sardiq casually seated himself in my office to await his truck transportation to the Tarnak Valley. There he was engaged in making tests of water percolation through various types of soils. A new man on the job, he was anxious to get acquainted.

Sardiq belonged to a class of technical men not long out of college — young men aware of the need for the more rapid advancement of their country along modern lines. They wanted the general standard of living raised, and had already received about the best scientific training the country afforded. A graduate of the agricultural college at Kabul, specializing in soils, Sardiq was being employed on this extensive M-K-A project. He appeared most happy for this opportunity to acquire practical knowledge and experience about land and its management under irrigation. In addition, this ambitious, intelligent young fellow had a desire to attend the University of California on its Davis campus,

401

to study irrigation. Possibly I had suggested this for his consideration. Sardiq said he was building a library of his own on agricultural subjects, and had made a payment of 800 *afs.* to get it started.

So before other personnel arrived, Sardiq and I talked about a number of things.

In Sardiq's estimation, Kabul leads the country in educational facilities. Boys and girls there are compelled to attend school through the eight grades; elsewhere the children's education is of little concern to their parents. The parents would rather the boys attend sheep than attend school. And as for Kandahar people, they are lazy, don't want to work, waste their time, are still living like Adam!

Said Sardiq, "Our government each year sends a few men to study in American universities. Next spring twenty mechanics are to be sent to Saudi Arabia to gain experience in oil production. And right now a group is being selected to attend your University of Wyoming, where they'll study irrigation," he continued, an element of longing in his voice.

"What's all of this I hear about Pakhtunistan?" I suggested.

Springing to his feet, Sardiq grabbed a pointed stick and stood before a wall map depicting Afghanistan and neighboring nations. He delineated this course: Kandahar — Chaman — Quetta — Kalat — Surab — Mashkai River — Hingol River — Kanrach — coastline of the Arabian Sea. Said he: "We need to develop this outlet to the ocean. This is the route we propose to follow from Kandahar!"

Hastily, I took from my desk two *National Geographic* maps:

April 1946 ——— "India and Burma."

June 1952 ——— "Southwest Asia, India, Pakistan and Northeast Africa."

"From Chaman on the Afghan border to the coast, Sardiq, that route measures 440 miles down through Baluchistan, a big undertaking for the government but well worth to Afghanistan all it may cost. You need to be independent of Pakistan economically and commercially in order to progress as a nation and to gain closer contact with other nations. Now you are land-locked, cut off from the sea."

"*Ba-le* — yes — but please, this route also we must improve." And Sardiq promptly pointed out another caravan route extending northeasterly from Quetta 450 miles through northern Baluchistan and the North West Frontier Province to Peshawar, thence up the Kabul River through the Khyber Pass to Jalalabad and Kabul in Afghanistan, and from that a route northerly up the Kunar River to Mastuj in Chitral bordering the southerly slopes of the Hindu Kush in Afghanistan, where peaks tower skyward above glaciers to 24,000 feet, 10,000 feet higher than Mt. Shasta.

"And this is the land of the Paktuns — Paktunistan," added Sardiq with enthusiasm and utmost sincerity, "extending from these lofty Hindu Kush in Chitral to the Arabian Sea coast of Baluchistan, from the Khyber Pass to the Bolan Pass to the Indus River." (See map within cover.)

"Sardiq, that's as long as the State of California, as long as Texas is wide. and you say its population is 8,000,000."

Said Sardiq, "The history of Paktunistan forms part of the history of Afghanistan from long ago. Historians say that the original inhabitants of Aryana or ancient Afghanistan, cradle of the Aryan race, being more powerful and warlike, moved eastward and succeeded in conquering and inhabiting the fertile Indus River Valley as far east as the river itself. They withstood Cyrus of Persia in the 5th century B.C., and Cyrus himself was killed in action in Afghanistan, and waged prolonged and determined resistance to Alexander as he attempted to proceed into India. Pakhtun and Afghan clansmen fought side by side; held strategically important regions, mountain fastnesses, mountain passes against all foreign aggressors. They were unconquerable. They successfully attacked exposed enemy positions on the plains of India and for 100 years fiercely fought off the English and Sikh armies of the British Empire." Sardiq's voice rang with fervor. His face beamed with confidence as in fluent English he recalled the prowess of his ancestry, and visualized the future of his country.

A horn sounded outside. Grabbing his lunch, Sardiq was off to his work for the day. This young Afghan, and many others like him, was getting wondrous training and experience under the indomitable ('Chuck') Swett, graduate agriculturist, and recently with his lovely wife and small son from Missouri. Chuck had charge of soil surveys and studies over all the M-K-A projects.

* * *

Also branching out into the realms of future development of the project on a grand scale was Civil Engineer F. R. Charles with his motley crew of surveymen. They were laying out a triangulation system covering the Helmand River wilderness clear to the Iran-Afghanistan boundary. Upon this would be based the aerial surveys soon to be undertaken. Charles' job entailed much moving of camp, a nomadic existence. But the outfit was well provided with the very latest from the States in the way of trailer cabins containing office, dining and mess equipment, food refrigeration, water, and sleeping quarters; was self-sustaining and pulled by a Caterpillar tractor. We were all much impressed with this latest equipment from which to launch desert surveys. "Operation Nomad" this activity was dubbed.

* * *

Seating himself opposite me at camp breakfast had been a man of white hair, firm step, large frame, and a tan acquired only by years of life in the open. His alert bright

404

eyes reflected friendliness, inherent power and readiness for action. About him was an unassuming air of purpose, quiet dignity and modesty.

Far out on the Dasht-i-Margo, such had been my impression on this Afghan winter morning of a most eminent American, a man whose present attention was being focused on the closing stages of construction at Kajakai Dam. For John Lucien ("Jack") Savage had been Chief Designing Engineer for more big dams than any other man in the chronicles of time! Upwards of sixty he had to his credit: Boulder, Grand Coulee, Shasta, and of late another which would dwarf all others into insignifigance!

For it was in 1945, within a few miles of the Japanese lines at the Gorge of the Yangtze River, that Dr. Savage had visualized a dam project overshadowing the classic exploits of all mankind. Here would rise a structure of concrete that would impound the waters of a lake 250 miles long; make navigable the Yangtze River 1,000 miles inland to Chungking; control hitherto merciless floods; provide irrigation for millions of acres of ancient farm lands; place in the middle of China the equivalent of a dozen TVA's; benefit directly a population of 140,000,000 at a cost of one billion dollars, or about $7.15 per capita. In short would industrialize China.

And then at Denver under a contract between the United States and Chinese governments, Jack Savage had supervised the design of this tremendous project. With him had worked upwards of thirty Chinese engineers. Involved had been the expenditure of $500,000.

So impressed had been the Chinese government with these designs and plans for advancement that Chiang Kai-Shek had requested of the U.S. Government the services of Mr. Savage for superintending the development of all China's natural resources.

Where Dr. Savage had gone on his many engineering

assignments, so often had followed men of the Morrison-Knudsen Company, Inc., Contractors and Engineers of Boise, Idaho, or the Associated Corporations. "We are prepared to undertake the engineering and construction of projects of any magnitude anywhere," they say.

And that's why to such effective purpose M-K-A, Inc., had become engaged on this Afghan project in the first place. And for the same reason they had entered the Yangtze Gorge from Ichang with core drilling teams, had become the targets for Japanese bullets and had been driven out. But with dogged determination they had returned in 1947 with Bob Selby as boss of the drilling outfits and acquired additional information about foundation conditions. Then again they had to withdraw before advance of other enemies, the oncoming communist hordes swarming like locusts from out of Manchuria.

But even as today Afghanistan shines brightly in the Middle East as the "Star of Asia," a free nation, just so one day will loom forth this currently dark star from out the depths of communist blackness, this Yangtze Gorge Project, in brilliance and reality as the guiding light of China, a free nation in a free world.

"The day we equip Chiang Kai-Shek to make a landing on the China coast and *hold it,* a vital blow will have been struck at communist aims of world conquest," writes Geraldine Fitch in her book, *Formosa Beachhead.* And with emphasis it could be added that despite current intrigues and manipulations of the 'pacifist-fellow traveler' combination within our own gates, that day will come. And with it will follow release from servitude of 600,000,000 people all the way from Formosa to beyond Sinkiang — from *Mengtsz* to beyond Manchuria!

* * *

January, 1953, was fleeting. On February 2nd my two year contract with the Company would be completed.

406

It was at camp breakfast on the 8th that our genial indefatigable General Manager, his face wreathed in smiles, confided to me that his own contract was up on that day. In a matter of hours he would be in Washington, D.C., in San Francisco within a few days. But he would come back to Afghanistan, I knew.

"Have you made your reservations, Jones? Which way are you returning to the States?" Ted inquired.

"To reach San Francisco, I'm taking my own time. En route I shall travel and visit 'Down Under,'" I rejoined. "Your M-K man in Karachi, that big Irishman, Ray Dillon, is getting it all arranged with the American Express Agency there; a travel tour home! I'm all set!"

"Why you can't do that!" Johnston's tone had assumed a manner of mock disapproval. Just beyond him sat a stranger who had been listening with interest. A scholarly, dignified, substantial appearing gentlemen; possibly of the old school, slightly oldish, distinguished looking with a gray goatee, he had walked into the mess hall with a springy step and air of general alertness. Such an American would attract favorable attention anywhere.

And then, "Oh, say Paul, meet Mr. Ward," Ted said without formality.

"Yes, yes, I've heard a lot about Paul Jones," said our United States Ambassador to Afghanistan warmly but with characteristic diplomacy.

*　　　*　　　*

The sky was gray, the wind cold on this January afternoon. At Ft. Nad-i-ali hundreds of tribesmen, many heavily armed in friendly gesture were assembling to greet a high official of the Government. As Abdur Rahim and I drove up to a standstill, several chiefs came forward. They wore bright warm shawls about shoulders and neck. Today they would press for an understanding with the Government about assignment of irrigated lands to their people for settlement and purchase, they explained. Two claimed to have received already certain assurances from the Prime Minister at Kabul concerning these matters.

As for me, I had come mostly to put in a good word for the apointment of Abdur to be among several young Afghans soon to be sent by their government to the University of Wyoming for study of agriculture under irrigation. To me it had seemed evident that climatic conditions in Arizona are more comparable to those of Afghanistan, and that in Arizona these men could better receive instruction in irrigation suitable to their purpose. But about this I had nothing to say.

Soon we were on a large sun porch and I was bidding farewell to Aslam Khan, Acting Director of the Agricultural Exploitation Department; Rafig Khan, District Governor of Girishk; Murid Khan, President of the Royal Afghan Commission for M-K-A, Inc. These men all during my stay in Afghanistan had displayed an active and helpful interest in the work with which I had been connected. For this I thanked them. Then turning to a business-like appearing man of perhaps fifty-five, Rafiq conversed in Persian. This stranger to me, grasped my hand in warmth and sincerity and in a few words, which his secretary translated, I was saying both "hello" and "goodbye" to Abdullah Khan, President of the Helmand River Valley Authority whom the King had recently promoted from his portfolio as Governor-General of the Province of Herat.

*   *   *

And now I could not close this narrative without paying humble tribute to the character of the Afghan people, as personally observed by me as a foreigner among them for two years. In all sincerity, I claim certain attributes are outstanding among a vast majority of these people.

They are remarkably hardy and athletic, as from the the very nature of the country they are exposed to heat and cold; have to climb mountains; make long journeys on foot; swim broad and torrential rivers.

They are bony and muscular; have handsome features, high noses, beautiful complexions. Their hair and beard are usually black, though sometimes brown.

Their countenances bear an air of manliness, of deliberation, of simplicity without weakness.

Their manners are frank and open. They are free from any affectation of military pride or ferocity.

Their religion is innate.

Should a stranger enter an Afghan's home, his tent or house, the master will protect him as long as he stays there, even though he be a fugitive from justice, even though he be the master's bitterest enemy.

Nothing exceeds the civility of the country people.

They may be poor, but they are also honest.

Despite a mixture of races and tongues, the Afghans form one nation, and are united to die or live in defense of country. Love of country, love of freedom form a bond of union among the people. And with these traditional qualities is combined an intense love of nature — flowers, hills, mountains, valleys.

Their sense of honor is keen, their loyalty to King and country intense.

> "There is a certain blend of courage, integrity,
> character and principle which has no satisfactory
> dictionary name but has been called different
> things at different times in different countries.
> Our American name for it is *'guts.'* "
>
> Louis Adamic (1899-1951)

XX
Around This Way

Back Tracking
New Delhi
Down the Ganges
Calcutta
Over Burma
Bangkok
Malay Peninsula
Singapore
Crossing the Equator
Sumatra
Java — and Wondrous Islands
Ahoy, Australia!
Darwin — Northern Frontier
Queensland
New South Wales
Victoria
South Australia
New Zealand
Fiji — Hawaii — Home!

CHAPTER XX

Around This Way

A ND FOLKS, NEITHER CAN I close this account without brief mention of my journey from Afghanistan half way around the planet back to California via "down under." To enter into the many details concerning strange lands visited would in itself compose a small volume. Such must wait, for primarily this narrative is of an *Afghanistan venture*.

From Kandahar to Spinbaldak and Chaman on the Afghan-Pakistan border was over the well paved M.K.A. road. From there the route led across rugged terrain of desert valleys and snow-capped mountains to Quetta; trading center, resort town, military outpost commanding a far-flung frontier. And then twenty-four hours by train across Baluchistan, land of rugged mountains and deserts, and down the irrigated Indus River Valley to Karachi, teeming metropolis and port of entry. Here a week was spent in securing visas and perfecting travel arrangements.

413

AFGHANISTAN VENTURE

And then there was New Delhi, capital city of India, impressive for its magnificent government buildings artfully arranged along a broad and lengthy mall beautifully landscaped. On the extensive grounds of the great Hindu Temple "Birla Mandir," holiday crowds were gathered; nicely dressed people. Especially so were the women in gaily colored sarees, a long wide piece of cloth silk was wrapped around the waist to cover the legs, draped full in front, and then wound over the bosom, the left shoulder, and head when desired. Over the left nostril some wore a metal disc ornament. Many wore anklets, even rings on their toes. From the temple emanated sounds like the continuous clanging of gongs, bells, and a weird musical rushing of winds.

Streets radiating from circular parks were flanked by rows of wide spreading trees. Bungalow homes stood mid spacious lawns and flower gardens. Project housing apartments were surrounded also by wide lawns with nearby children's playgrounds. Such were the residential sections that I saw in New Delhi.

From my notes written on plane: So this is Northern India out about 125 miles from New Delhi en route by Bharat Airways. Below is the sprawling Ganges River in four channels, each sandy and very winding, perhaps two miles apart. The irrigation canals are full of water but there is little in the river. The people all live in small towns several miles apart, in mud-thatched huts with compounds. The landscape spreads out in a patchwork of green wheat fields and sugar cane, with a few orchards. On the roads are heavy carts pulled by bullocks. That was Patna back there where we landed, a place of gorgeous shrubbery and flowers; dahlias, sweet peas, snapdragon, red poppies, salvia, bougainvilla, coconut palms, bananas, and Hindu women in sarees of colors to match the flowers.

Calcutta. Folks, you wouldn't enjoy the sight of millions

414

of half starved people living in quarters unfit even for animals, nor the sight of Brahma cows and bulls looking as if they owned the place, complacently chewing their cuds in the downtown financial district. Nor the millions of dollars in gold, silver and precious gems used for ornamentation in the Hindu temples, nor a view of the many congested square miles — here for Moslems only — there for Hindus only — this a Chinatown, and in this area a mixture of everyone. How would you like living here in such a city of 5,000,000 unhappy people?

Then came the afternoon journey over mountainous jungles of Burma; no towns, no evidence of human habitation, even beyond the boundary into Thailand, until suddenly there were clearings and groups of houses and at 7 p.m. the plane alighted on the Bangkok airfield.

During the forenoon was a trip by boat to the back country, or beyond the suburbs to the floating markets which extended along a large slough with many branches into the jungles. Here people live just above the water in small houses on stilts; some have little businesses, or engage in production of bananas and coconuts. At 8 a.m. it seemed every man, woman and child was bathing in the stream, or had just had a bath, so meticulously clean did they appear. The homes were open to the full view of people cooking or eating their breakfasts. They smiled in greeting and the children waved. Long narrow canoes almost filled the channel. Mostly young women did the rowing with just one long oar in the bow. Their movements were skillful and graceful. Each boat was loaded with coconuts, bananas, small melons, sugar cane, pomelos, bamboo, etc., from the out country. And along shore much rice in sacks awaited shipment. High tide was almost up to the level of the land. Along shore were boatworks, teakwood being used.

Of all the people I had thus far seen in the Middle and

415

Far East, these Siamese of Bangkok seemed at once the most intelligent, progressive and happy.

Our guide said education is compulsory through the lower grades, voluntary for high school and university. Students crowded the streets afoot, in buses, on pedicars. The girls wore white waists, black ties and short skirts; the boys white shirts and knee length blue or suntan slacks. In stores and business establishments, the younger intelligent generation has taken over; so courteous, well mannered and business-like, with hair-do's and western clothing exactly as would be seen in San Francisco.

And then there was the visit to the King's Palace where in spite of the terrific heat one was required to don coat and tie. Here for a square mile the oriental splendor concentrated on these grounds is inconceivable. However, this can be more aptly described by the 35 mm. snapshots I secured.

But to continue as condensed from my notes written aboard the plane: "We are over the Gulf of Siam en route from Bangkok to Singapore via KLM. The passengers seem mostly Dutch, bound for Indonesia. To the west is the Malay Peninsula. Back at the airfield the jetliner *Comet* was undergoing some repairs before taking off. The sun rose a deep blood red in color. In its upper left quarter for no visible reason, a large bite of it had been taken out, which after an hour or so was gradually replaced. Elevation 13,500 the captain announces. Now we are moving directly over the peninsula. Can't see a road, clearings or any sign of human occupancy. Only a winding river or slough, reflecting the early morning sunlight, gives variation to a dark green vegetation completely covering the land. It must be an impenetrable jungle. But this is where much of the world's rubber supply is located, also where the British are fighting communist guerillas. And then several hundred miles more without change of scenery, the densest of jungle-

416

lands. No imagination is required to visualize crocodiles, huge reptiles, tigers and elephants 13,000 feet below us."

And as written at Singapore, "The city is eighty per cent Chinese and a three-day New Year celebration is on. Fire-crackers, people in holiday mood and dress, men in the whitest of shirts and the best looking slacks; daughters, wives, lady friends in the fanciest of colorful kimona-like garments with designs of flowers, trees, plants. In the sub-urbs are the nicest homes, from plain ones to the more ex-pensive and elaborate set in among coconut and banana trees. One could look right into the houses which are open all around and set high off the ground, and all about were wide lawns and flowers. Every home seemed to be holding open house with friends going and coming. You could see many homes having family gatherings; grandparents, sons and daughters and children, all Chinese. In the middle of the city St. Andrews Cathedral occupied a large green park, a magnificent edifice. It was thrilling to see again this evi-dence of Christian civilization."

"Here we go again! Below are many islands set in a sea of glistening sunlight, the Riouw and Lingge Archipelagos. We are now crossing the Equator! Beside me sits a young Dutchman returning to Djakarta after six weeks in Su-matra; buying rubber, I think. I said, 'Do you Dutch get pushed around much by the Indonesians?' As he did not understand this expression, I repeated, 'Do the Dutch get any consideration from the Indonesians since the war?'

"He said, 'We pass as British or Americans often, as regis-tered in New York or London.'

" 'How are conditions in Sumatra?' I casually inquired.

" 'People are peaceful, bring raw rubber down to river boat landings. From there we get it out to the coast. I travel-ed five days in a jeep and continuously through rubber plan-tations. Crossing of streams is perilous. There are crocodiles. Tigers lunge out of the bush at passing jeeps. One day fifty

417

wild elephants headed for our camp. We fired rifles. The noise confused them. They turned in another direction. You are missing something not to visit Java. But the countryside is much disturbed now. Also there is a strike every time a ship comes in to be unloaded. These Indonesians pretend not to understand English — want you to talk Malayan, concluded Mr. Van Don Yssel, as I studied the jungles of southern Sumatra about a mile below."

Leaving Djakarta and its red tiled roofs of homes scattered among the coconut palms and clumps of banana trees, we were off on our 1,750-mile flight to Darwin, Australia. The Island of Java is about 500 miles long. We traveled about twenty-five miles inland from the north coast at 15,-000 feet altitude. One could plainly see that the land is intensively cultivated, continuous patchwork of green fields separated along property lines by what appeared to be double rows of coconut palms. The roads led far distances to plantations. Villages were almost hidden among the trees. There were intermittent strips of densely forested areas.

And from my notes aboard the plane; "Surabaja is plainly visible, a well laid out sizeable city of good streets and homes with red tile roofs. Just across a narrow straight is the Isle of Madura with rice fields right down to the seashore. Below us now is an islet barely submerged; looks like an emerald set in a field of deep blue. And just to its north is one with deep green vegetation. The narrow sandy shore or beach reflects a golden glow. The shadow submerged part of the beach is emerald, farther out the breakers form a white band. All of this is set in the inky blue of the surrounding sea, and above is a scattering of fleecy misty white clouds; indeed a beautiful sight.

"And from Djakarta eastward there have been no vistas so beautiful as these thus far on my journey from Afghanistan.

"Now we're over Bali, famed by Nevil Shute in his

novel, *Round the Bend,* about like Java in appearance. And suddenly we are above a dazzling snow-like expanse of clouds with white masses projecting upward like mountains. The plane goes between them as through snowy canyons, until as suddenly the Isle of Lombok breaks into full view. Its landscape is like that of Bali and Java. And then we are over the Island of Sumbawa, beautiful beyond description; the indigo of the sea, the white breakers, the emerald green of the shallower water, the golden shore line, the deep green vegetation of the island itself.

"Then Flores to the north, Sumba to the south, over the west end of Timor; all much the same as others, and this was all a part of beautiful Indonesia.

"We are now over the calm Timor Sea and after two hours there appears on the horizon the far-flung coast line of Australia."

The thrill upon landing at Darwin, the stay there of a few days at this small northern outpost of Australia and a civilization dear to us all — this will linger forever in my memory.

First I proceeded to look up the American Express office and in doing so stepped into Lloyd's of London, an insurance office. These Australians speak softly with entirely different expressions and pronunciations from ours.

"Have ya lauked in the faun bouk?" said the young lady coming over to the counter and apologizing for the telephone book being so small. "Ah, here iteez. In the Baink of New South Wailes. Ya just follow thait paith. The graiss is a bit tall. How do ya like the hait? Kinda staimy todai, isn't it?" she continued.

"How's that? I mean I don't quite understand?" I said embarrassed-like.

"Haut aind staimy," she repeated.

"Oh, now I understand," I voiced apology. "But say this

is God's country, this is really heaven after where I've been for two years."

"Ya've not been in Austrailya long?" she countered innocently.

"Oh no. You, you mean you can't tell? I've just come from Afghanistan."

Darwin with its wide well graded streets, is scattered out among brilliant flowers, blooming shrubbery and trees; the fern-like poinciana with bright red flowers, the mango, and grass as high as one's shoulders. The Navy, Airforce and Army have bases here. Extensive commerce is not evident. Darwin seemingly is just a frontier outpost much as was San Francisco before the gold rush days of '49.

Aborigines are scattered about but may live on reservations if they desire. Some live in town and do menial work for the white folks, and are quartered in compounds by themselves. As a race they just seem incapable of advancement, I'm told, although provision is made for their education and training to follow trades or agriculture. However these blacks are treated kindly by the white people.

"These Chinese one sees here, how about that? I thought you didn't allow Orientals to settle in Australia?" I asked a man.

"We don't. The few you see here are descendants of pearl fishermen," he said.

But to continue from my notes: "The air is cool and refreshing, brilliantly clear is the blue sky, warm is the tropical sunshine, a beautiful late August morning were this in the States, but now in Australia the last of February and late summer. Here is a wilderness for 640 miles of eucalyptus trees and grass as high as a horse. It is the rainy season with frequent showers and everywhere is green vegetation. One can see that creeks have flowed high because the tall grass is lying down. About every fifty miles this bus, Bond's Australian Greyhound Lines, halts at a general store, cafe, and

420

bore (well). There are no habitations between such stops. The bus fare includes meals and lodging — quite reasonable in price. We are in Northern Territory at the north end of the vast *outback* country of Australia.

"Our first stop is Adelaide River; every one has tea and biscuits. Here is brilliant bougainvilla. And fifty miles further is Hayes Creek. Here in the store behind the counter a young pet wallaby is demanding much attention. The store people don't think he'll run away. He hops out to the lawn and stands for a long time with the top of his head on the ground between his paws.

"Further along our stop is at a bore on a cattle *station*. Here an extremely large windmill pumps water into a reservoir for the stock. These stations, explained a cattleman, are as large as a county in Texas — have bores about fifteen miles apart. Cattle are driven hundreds of miles easterly into the State of Queensland to the railheads for marketing. En route are *stock channels* (trails) with bores at frequent intervals. These are provided for the stockmen by the State or Commonwealth (federal) Governments. From the railheads the cattle travel hundreds of miles further to fattening areas along the coast of Queensland. From there to the packing plant, to be put aboard refrigeration ships, overseas to England — thence to European markets.

"It seems big companies operate these stations, fattening corrals, packing plants, shipping and distribution facilities. An immense amount of capital is involved. The bores alone constitute a tremendous investment on the stations, as well as the fencing, if any. These bores provide water during nine months of the dry season when the grass dries up. But the grass is feed for the cattle anyway. And at such times, said the cattleman, fires may break out. He had lost 3,500 breeders last year during a prolonged drought.

"And more about these bores was told me by another stockman. They do not provide enough water during

421

droughts and stock en route to the railroad may perish from thirst. Also on some stations bores are not close enough together. Cattle will feed out a day's travel from a bore. Then it's a choice of traveling further than this radius of eight to ten miles for feed and perishing for lack of water, or staying within the ten-mile radius and perishing for lack of feed. So it goes when a drought like that of last year hits Australia.

"Lunch at Pine Creek the first day; a few scattering houses in an open meadow built of corrugated iron and made to look attractive and comfortable.

"And in the early afternoon there is Katherine, a trading center with banks, a few stores, bakeries, various businesses, and an agricultural experiment station. Here is a black land of deep fertile soil, whereas all the way to the north was disintegrated granite. One sign along the road reads, 'Banana plantation thirteen and one-half miles.'

"At 6 p.m. we pulled into Larimer for the night. Here are nice sleeping accomodations. Huge mosquito nets are over each bed. This place is near the end of the narrow gauge railway we followed all day. The track is almost hidden by the grass. All day I had seen but one small freight train.

"A marked characteristic of these people in Northern Territory is their friendliness and fewness of words.

"Second day out from Darwin: Rolling south through an unbroken wilderness of eucalyptus and grass. Around one turn a dingo dog is unavoidably run down.

"A wallaby sitting in the road upon the sound of the horn takes off through the trees like a deer, clearing the tall grass with each hop. It seems these animals are smaller and more daring than are the kangaroos.

" 'Where are the kangaroos?' I asked of the driver.

" 'Oh, they come out in the cool of the evening or early morning to feed; they sleep during the day. Also they have an instinct to follow the rain storms; to eat the green young shoots, go in droves. When the wet season is over they scatter out and you see them then,' was the reply. 'Very few Australians have ever been in the Northern Territory like you are now,' he added.

"Well, as we get further south the eucalyptus trees become scrubbier, the grass shorter, but still green and more succulent. Also the country is getting rougher with areas of higher tablelands. Along the streams are immense stretches of open meadow.

"We pull into what is apparently the headquarters of a cattle sation. Here are a number of red buildings; living quarters, implement sheds, store houses, etc. Three nicely dressed little girls, say ten to fifteen, watch from a distance. The young lad on the bus does his best to attract their attention, but his failure is 100 per cent. The boy is going on to Alice Springs, another day's journey to the center of Australia, a sort of jewel set down in the great desert, they say.

"The bus driver asks the cattleman: 'Well, how's she going, Fred?'

"The reply: 'Plainty rain. So now ya town blokes'll get some beef.'

"The name of this ranch is 'Banka Banka.' A big old colored mammy (these aborigines surely look like negroes but it's claimed there's no connection) is irrigating a newly made garden surrounded by a corral fence. Beyond is sweet corn and a watermelon patch; other black people are working about the premises.

"The ranchman comes up to the coach and talks kindly to some fifteen black children that have gotten on at Daly Waters; they are about six to eight years old and are going to some church mission school at Alice Springs. At noon they all had sat at one table in the dining room and eaten their lunch with perfect manners.

"During the afternoon we cross many creeks of running

423

water following the rains.

"Well, we get to Tennant Creek about 6 p.m. I shall stay over here Saturday, February 21st, to make connections with the motor coach going easterly to Queensland at 6 a. m. Sunday.

"This is a small mining town. At my table in the dining room are a couple of mining engineers, a geologist, and a metallurgist, I judge from their conversation. As I join them unobtrusively, something like the following conversation takes place:

"M. E. to Geologist: 'Have you ever worked in America?'

"G. — Oh, yes, I spent a number of years there. Got to know the damn-Yanks quite well.'

"M. E. 'Well, I worked there five years myself — a grait country thait. Those gawd-damn-Yanks have a grait country!'

"And all the time the four of them keep straight faces and not even once glance in my direction.

"I have talked to several prospectors around also. This seems to be a prospector's paradise. Anything he finds worthwhile the Government helps him to finance in setting up mining operations.

"Here at Tennant Creek are several gold mines, fabulously rich. Some 1,000,000 Australian pounds worth of gold have been mined already in several small workings. The Government provides the *battery* which is a diesel electric power plant to crush the ore and run the mining equipment.

"Also prospectors are getting out wolfrom ore the same way it seems, or tungsten.

"In one newspaper casual mention is made of how gold shows up in some areas following rains.

"Miners under contract make six to eight pounds ($13.00 to $17.00 U.S.) per day as laborers, I am told.

"The Government is about to start an uranium survey

424

of the Northern Territory using geiger counters, jeeps and planes, it seems.

"I must tell you folks about the anthills of Northern Territory. In places there are as many as there are trees. You see them projecting upward through the grass, pillars of dried mud anywhere from a foot to twelve feet high. These big black ants encase the loose material, sand, etc. they excavate in compartments, the outer walls of which is an impervious adobe coating. They build these pillars to keep out of the wet. They extract sugar from the sap of trees and store it like bees; carry it on their backs in a ball like a bee carries pollen. It is said the aborigines in their wild state eat honey, ants and all for sustenance."

*   *   *

February 23, 1953 Monday

(Same as August, 23)

On board train "Inlander," Queensland R. R.

This finds me in central Queensland; the fourth day of travel southerly and southeasterly from Darwin in the outback country of Northern Territory and Queensland. These two areas are equal in size to one-third of the United States, or about sixteen of our average states. Australia is almost identically the size of the United States, also shaped something like it. So the route I am taking to Sydney would be about like going from Duluth to Omaha to Boston to Savannah.

All afternoon the train has been wending its way through a vast expanse of green grasslands, an unlimited prairie meeting the horizon on all sides. Something like the prairies of the Middle West in the days of the buffalo. The creeks are subsiding from recent heavy rainfall.

425

AFGHANISTAN VENTURE

I have seen no cattle for several hours in this wilderness of grass. There is scarcely a fence, even along the railroad right of way. Now I do see a herd about a mile to the north. A little further and another about one-half mile north; about 125 head each — a mixture of Hereford and Shorthorn.

The setting sun makes this vast prairie take on a silvery glimmer. The train proceeds very cautiously in the wet areas. The embankment is only slightly above the general ground level. Railroad ties are universally of eucalyptus.

All forenoon from Mt. Isa to Cloncurry there were low hills and valleys and running water, grass and eucalyptus trees. We have just passed a railroad siding — Maxwellton — just a store and a few houses and corrals and railroad maintenance quarters. This train runs between Mt. Isa and Townsville on the east coast.

People boarding the train "ah" and "oh" at its wonders. It is the first of such to be put into operation in Australia, and only within the last month. A beautiful train — a diesel locomotive — coaches of sky blue and cream color. I haven't been on a modern train for ages, and never one as fine as this. It appears to me this train has everything, even down to shower baths. The dining car service is operated by a steward and a number of young women; the last word in service for everybody on the train. Meals are included in your fare.

I stayed at Mt. Isa last night. This is the scene of tremendously large mining activities, the largest in the southern hemisphere for lead, zinc, copper and silver, they say. It is operated by American engineers. The ore is fabulously rich. It is operated continuously on a twenty-four-hour basis. And they have started a duplicate of this plant on another site nearby. A large mountain was lighted as bright as day. It appears there are no labor troubles. The miners share in some of the profits. All are housed under the best of liv-

426

ing conditions. This country seems to be a miner's paradise.

8 p.m. and we have just pulled out of Richmond. Several hundred people were out to see friends off and to view the new train. Everybody seems dressed up and to own an automobile. Fine looking boys and girls.

Yesterday I came from Tennant Creek to Mt. Isa by Royal Mail stage called the *Queenslander*. This took from 6 a.m. to 6 p.m. over a smooth improved one-lane road. Scrubby eucalyptus trees and grass almost played out in places, almost a desert. A sign at one place read "Water 103 miles." Crossed into Queensland near Camooweal. Until late afternoon we met no one on the road. At one place windmills were generating electricity for the telephone line which crosses this vast region.

Everywhere at stops the flies were bent on biting, and people wore nets for protection. We met a truck and trailer upon which was loaded a new R. D. No. 7 caterpillar tractor. The road bed was soft and both truck and trailer were down to their axles in breaking through the light paving into the soft moist ground below.

*   *   *

4:30 a.m. February (Aug.) 24, 1953

Yesterday afternoon not far from the train I saw a pair of emus, very much like ostriches. They say these birds can go right through a No. 10 gage wire fence, can kick like a horse. The ranchers consider them more than a nuisance.

Daylight and Charters Towers — quite a town — once a mining center.

The countryside is no longer prairie but semi-mountainous. It's the coastal divide. To the east water flows into the Pacific Ocean. To the west inland toward the center of the continent and the Darling River, or northerly to the Gulf of Carpentaria.

A kangaroo takes off into the bush, then stops to watch the train go by. He looks to have had a wet night of it as much rain has fallen.

Down into the flat coastal plain there is water everywhere right up to the tracks; muddy water and grass and eucalyptus covered low rolling lands, thirteen miles from Townsville and the coast of the Coral Sea. It's too wet here for people to build habitations.

*　　　*　　　*

February 25 (Aug.) 1953

To resume:　Now aboard the "Blaxland" of the Trans-Australia Airlines (T.A.A.) (tai-ai-ai) en route from Townsville to Brisbane. Left at 8 a.m. Route skirts the coast line; part of time over sea, then overland. Great Coral Reef Barrier to the left. Just passed the Whitsunday Islands. An indigo sea surrounds the deep green of these tropical islands.

Yesterday it was mercilessly tropical at Townsville. I decided not to journey to the country to the north around Cairns, said to be the most beautiful tropic lands in all Australia. Better to go into such a country in the winter time.

The coastal plain is interlaced with winding waterways; rivers, small streams and estuaries swollen by the rain. The rolling land between is covered with fields of sugar cane and pineapple. However, the undeveloped area is vast; may be ninety per cent.

To the west the foothills rise to the continental divide. These mountains are only 1200 to 1500 feet in elevation. There seem to be a few cultivated areas, but for the most part these rolling green, grass-covered foothills are an undeveloped empire.

The whole landscape below is the most beautiful of any seen thus far on my journey.

At 11:30 a.m. we are leaving Rockhampton, a large town somewhat inland on high ground, but still on the coastal plain, along a large river or estuary. The houses are built about ten feet off the ground on wooden posts or concrete columns, with air space all around for coolness. This is the custom throughout the tropics I've observed, from Singapore to Brisbane. Also the whole house is open to the outside without closed windows or doors or screen. People sleep under mosquito bars when necessary. It rains every day or so and this must make the heat bearable. A man at Townsville told me it had rained five feet there since January 1st.

"When does it cool off?"

"When winter comes — about June 1st," he said.

There is a great irrigation and flood control project underway for this area. West of the mountains there is a marked decrease in rainfall; hence the Burdekin River Project, involving some 50,000 square miles along the route of and to the west of this flight, over the highlands to the west.

Since leaving Rockhampton we are above the clouds. Now and again large openings reveal the same splendour on the land below. We have just crossed the Tropic of Capricorn and are entering the South Temperate Zone.

The city of Bandaberg appears to our left on the southerly shore of a wide muddy river and just back from the coast.

A long coast line is now visible with wide sandy beach and many large rivers and streams emptying into the Pacific Ocean.

AFGHANISTAN VENTURE

One can look out over Hervey Bay to what appears to be the large sandy Frazer Island.

Here is a long sandy beach backed by a sizable town. Now Brisbane is in sight; a large city and the plane circles for a landing. And that was the State of Queensland as I had seen it from Camooweal in the northwest to Brisbane in the southeast; spacious, undeveloped, a wondrous land.

*   *   *

Five marvelous weeks were spent in Australia among people so like us in the Western and Southwestern United States; a friendly, independent, rugged type — bound with Americans in a common character, sentiment, and culture.

There is not space in this writing to recount details of the wonderful journey overland from Brisbane to Sydney to Canberra; down the Murray River Valley, frontiersmen's paradise, (reminder of the Lower Rio Grande Valley in Texas) to Adelaide, through the States of New South Wales, Victoria and South Australia, and back along the south coast to Melbourne. All a wildly beautiful land of wide open spaces whose resources are boundless and scarcely touched as yet.

Nor is there space to write of the flight across the lonely Tasman Sea to New Zealand and the two weeks among its friendly people; its mountains, lakes and streams, its beautiful countryside, national parks, towns and cities.

There followed a brief visit to the Island of Viti Levu, Fiji Islands. Here were trips through this countryside of coconut, pineapple and sugar cane plantations, and hikes into the back country and contacts with these friendly dark people. They remembered encampments in their land of New Zealand and American servicemen. Grateful to these brave men for this protection from an oncoming ruthless enemy, were these Fijians.

430

A brief stop at dawn on Canton Island and then only hours to Hawaii — my own land. I was practically home.

And at the San Francisco Municipal Airport to greet me was son Bruce of the U. S. Naval Air Force. This was a joyous reunion.

And that's all, folks.

"There is no Security
On this earth —
Only Opportunity."

General Douglas MacArthur

PAKHTUNISTAN

Addendum: Pakhtunistan

By Dr. Aurang Shah, M.D., Sacramento,
California*

* At the suggestion of the author.

Dr. AURANG SHAH, M.D., is a Pakhtun,
born and raised on the Afghan border near
the historic Khyber Pass. He is a direct
descendant of Khushal Khan Khatak, — famous poet, warrior, leader of the Phaktun
people who fought against the aggression of
the Moguel Empire in the 17th century.

The first Pakhtun student to come to the
United States for education, Dr. Shah attended Stanford University, Washington
University at Seattle and Tufts University
School of Medicine. From the latter he grad-
uated with an M.D. degree. Under a fellowship of The Rockefeller Foundation in
New York City, he also obtained the degree
of Master of Public Health.

To acquaint the people of the United
States with those of Pakhtunistan, the Azad
(free) Pakhtunistan Asociation of America
was founded by Dr. Shah in 1916. Of this
he is now the president. With the development work being accomplished by American
engineers and contractors in Afghanistan,
Dr. Shah is quite familiar.

In conformity with the traditions of his
family, Dr. Shah is vitally concerned in the
continued self-determination and freedom
of the Pakhtun and Afghan people.

Pakhtunistan

EASTWARD from Afghanistan, extending to the Indus River and the Arabian Sea, is the land of the Pakhtuns. Westerners may know them better as the "Pathan tribesmen" who fought British soldiers in the Khyber Pass country, or North-West Frontier Territory. Stories of these encounters, written by Englishmen, naturally described these tribesmen as ruthless enemies. But the Pakhtuns viewed their struggle as a fight for independence. The English spelling, "Pathan," comes from the Indian pronunication of Pakhtun.

Pakhtunistan, which means "The Land of the Pakhtuns," is bounded by Persia and Afghanistan to the west. To the east, its neighbor was British India, but is now the Moslem state of Pakistan. Pakistan comes frequently into any discussion of modern Pakhtunistan because its armies have been fighting the Pakhtuns over their refusal to be annexed.

Pakhtuns have resisted Pakistan for the same reason they resisted the British for 100 years. They fought the advancing armies of Alexander the Great, and gave other Asian empire-builders a bad time. Also, they have a passion for freedom, and geography is on their side.

A brief history of the Pakhtuns and of their neighbors may help to explain the continuing struggle.

Pakhtuns are essentially the same people as the Afghans, having been part of Afghanistan until late in the 19th century. Both Pakhtuns and Afghans are of the Aryan race and speak Paktho (also spelled Pukhto, Pushtu and Pashto). It is an Aryan language closely related to Sanskrit, from which most of our western languages stem.

The ancient Greek historian, Herodotus, described these people as the inhabitants of Paktya, "one of the most mountainous regions of central Asia." Some of the ancient Pakhtuns moved in a westerly direction to Europe; others remained in their mountains, and others established themselve on the fertile bank of the Indus river. The Pakhto word for river is "Sindh," from which comes "Hindu" and "India."

The extended their political influence over all of India from the 10th through 14th centuries, A. D. Their administration, which modern historians generally describe as "The Afghan Empire," eventually crumbled before the onslaughts of the Moghuls and the British.

Pakhtun provinces adjacent to British India were separated from Afghanistan during the 19th century, at a time when Afghans were weakened by civil war, threatened by Russia, and over-run by Sikhs in the northern part of the Indus River Valley.

In 1894 a British commission led by Sir Mortimer Durand and backed by a British military expedition, forced upon the ruler of Afghanistan a line of demarcation which later became known as the Durand Line. This line was resented bitterly by all the tribes because they were not consulted. It detached from Afghanistan the important Pakhtun territories of Khyber, Mohman, Kurram and Waziristan.

By similar methods in 1878 British officials had carved away the southernmost Afghan province, Baluchistan, which

436

included the port of Karachi on the Arabian Sea. With the loss of the coastal province, Afghanistan was landlocked; but her people continued to use the Khyber and other passes to the outside world for transportation of their principal exports and imports. After the British withdrawal, when Pakistan occupied this province and blockaded this trade route, Afghanistan found itself in a desperate position, as will be described later.

Though these treaties severed the land of the Pakhtuns from Afghanistan (on the map), the majority of Pakhtuns never accepted British rule. Pakhtun tribes were still fighting the British when they withdrew from India in 1947.

During these years of resistance, every mountain home and cave became a fortress. When a man left his lookout post near his home, his wife took over his gun. If he could possibly afford it, he provided a rifle for every member of his family from the age of seven upward. He bought Springfields from America, for they were considered the best. Men who could not afford guns were handy with knives, and captured rifles and ammunition from the British. Small children carried food to their fathers. Signals from neighbors told if friend or foe was near. Dogs were trained to bring food, water, and ammunition to the outposts and return home with the rifles of the dead or mortally wounded — to lunge directly at the throats of the enemy.

Military expeditions into these mountains became so costly of life and materials that the British generally contented themselves with a situation resembling an armed truce. They paid Pakhtun officials for the use of toll roads through their century (including the important route over the Khyber Pass to Afghanistan), and were not allowed to stray more than fifty feet on either side from the edge of the road.

When the British prepared to withdrew from India in 1947, the Pakhtuns rejoiced. They believed that they, as well as the Indians, would be free and at peace with the world. But events took an unexpected turn.

Before withdrawing, British officials offered Indians a chance to vote *Hindu* or *Moslem*. Accordingly Moslem leaders made plans to establish the religious state of Pakistan, which would be governed by the law of the Koran. Pakhtuns in the British-occupied area of their country were also given this same chance to vote. However, the majority did not vote. Although Pakhtuns are Moslem, they did not wish to join a religious state. Pakhtun leaders tried to arrange with the British a more inclusive plebiscite, which would offer the people (1) a chance to vote on whether they wanted independence, or (2) the chance to rejoin Afghanistan, or (3) a religious state.

British officials refused to arrange anything more than the Moslem-Hindu plebiscite, so the vote cast in the Occupied Area went in favor of the Moslems. Only five per cent of the population in the Occupied Area was Hindu. The majority of voters in the Occupied Area, including members of the major political party, had boycotted the referendum, as their political leaders had suggested. The referendum had not been offered at all in Free Pakhtunistan.

Of the eight million Pakhtuns, two-thirds live in the free area and one-third in the occupied area. Yet Pakistan claimed all the land of the Pakhtuns, both occupied and free.

Pakhtun leaders offered several reasons why they did not wish to join Pakistan:

Pakistan would be an Indian state, and the Pakhtuns were not Indians. They were Aryans who looked different, spoke a different language, had different customs and different ideas about government. They had nothing in common except the Moslem religion.

They had Moslem neighbors to both east and west. Their Afghan neighbors had much in common with them. In ad-

438

dition to being Moslem, these Afghans spoke the same language and were the same people. If Pakhtuns couldn't have their independence, why shouldn't they be offered a plebiscite on whether they wanted to join with Pakistan or Afghanistan?

The Pakhtun political leaders in occupied Pakhtunistan who voiced these sentiments to Pakistan officials were thrown into Pakistan prisons without trial. There they still remain. Pakhtunistan was one of the few areas in that part of the world which did not suffer from the miseries of overpopulation, and Pakistan, which was crowded, wanted this land. Pakistan's army took possession of the Occupied Area as the British withdrew and tried to enter Free Pakhtunistan. But they got no farther than the British.

Immediately after the partition of India, bloody fighting broke out between Pakistanis and Hindus. More than a thousand Hindus who had been living in the Occupied Area fled into Free Pakhtunistan, where they were safe. Most of these Hindus established small businesses and have continued to remain in Free Pakhtunistan, at peace with their Moslem neighbors.

Pakhtuns were puzzled when they learned that the United States, traditionally on the side of freedom of religion and self-determination of peoples, had armed Pakistan. At the suggestion of Great Britain, the United States had provided the new state of Pakistan with bombing planes and modern weapons, hopeful that an all-Moslem state would be a bulwark against the spread of Communism. Great Britain was interested in checking Communism, and also wanted to see British investments in Pakistan protected.

Serious trouble developed when Pakistan sent its new planes to bomb and strafe Pakhtun villages. The Pakhtuns moved into caves and sought help from their Afghan kinsmen. The Afghans long had been in the habit of crossing the border to help their kinsmen fight the British, and some

439

of them now helped in the fight against Pakistan.

Though the Durand Line had been drawn on maps, it was ignored by the native people. They were accustomed to cross it any time they chose. Their summer and winter sheep ranges straddled the border, and many families lived part of the year in Afghanistan and part of the year in the Pakhtun land which the British had tried to claim, but could not occupy. On both sides of the line, the natives continued to regard themselves as *one people*.

Pakistan realized that it would have to control the Pakhtuns through Afghanistan, and that it could effectively blockade the Afghans. So the government of Pakistan, which had taken over the port of Karachi along with the rest of the Occupied Area, now placed an embargo on freight destined for Afghanistan. As explained earlier, this Arabian Sea coastline, which includes Karachi, had belonged to Afghanistan until the British took political control in 1878, and the Afghans had continued to rely on this trade route. The Khyber Pass — Karachi route was the principal link between Afghanistan and the outside world. The only other feasible trade route was through Soviet Russia.

The blockade interrupted, among other things, the supply of materials which Afghanistan had bought from the United States to modernize its agriculture. Huge dams and irrigation projects being constructed by contractors from the United States, and paid for by the government of Afghanistan, could not be completed. Soviet Russia offered to help Afghanistan, but the Afghans had liked doing business with American contractors and wanted to so continue.

The government of Afghanistan began to feel that war with Pakistan was the only solution, and called home its representatives from Karachi. But as war threatened, Pakistan lifted the blockade provisionally. Afghanistan had suffered from the long months of blockade and her leaders had seen that the country's future lay with a free Pakhtunistan rather than with Pakistan as a neighbor.

Arming of Pakistan did not work out as the free world had hoped. The blockade had made Afghans and Pakhtuns economically dependent on their Communist neighbor, Russia, which joined them in enmity against Pakistan. Since these indignant neighbors would not trade with Pakistan, and relations between Pakistan and India were strained, Pakistan's leaders began to look to the Communist countries for trade.

Pakhtun leaders welcome American correspondents into Free Pakhtunistan, for in this way they have faith that truth will win out. An American reporter returning from a trip into the Khyber Pass area relates that he found the natives highly organized — have skill, determination and geography on their side. He suggests that the Pakhtuns will continue to fight until their independence is recognized, even if this means another 100 years. Not only will they defend their mountain homes, but they will raid the lowlands until these also are free. Of the eight million Pakhtuns, two-thirds now live in Free Pakhtunistan.

So until all Pakhtuns are free and independent, history indicates that every Pakhtun over seven years of age will continue to keep his rifle handy, — that the smaller children will carry food to their sharp-shooting fathers. These people, and their Afghan brothers, are the greatest champions of the democratic way of life. They have fought for these principles down through their history — they will die fighting for them.

Index

*O — Orientation

443

445

446

447